Ceremony and symbolism
in the Japanese home

日本 研究 Japanese Studies

Michael Jeremy

M. E. Robinson

Photographs by Urata Hoichi

Ceremony and symbolism

in the Japanese home

University Of Hawaii Press

HONOLULU • HAWAII

Published in North America by
University of Hawaii Press
2840 Kolowalu Street
Honolulu, Hawaii 96822

First published in the United Kingdom by
Manchester University Press
Oxford Road
Manchester, M13 9PL
England

Library of Congress Cataloging-in-Publication Data
Jeremy, Michael, 1957–
   Ceremony and symbolism in the Japanese home/by Michael Jeremy
   and M. E. Robinson.
      p.   cm.
   Bibliography: p. 186
   Includes index.
   ISBN 0-8248-1226-3 (alk. paper): $35.00
      1. Family—Japan—Tōno-shi.   2. Rites and ceremonies—Japan—Tōno-shi.
3. Tōno-shi (Japan)—Social conditions.   4. Tōno-shi (Japan)—Religious life and
customs.   I. Robinson, M. E. (Michael Ernest), 1940–   .   II. Title.
HQ682.15.T66J47 1989
392′.0952—dc19

Printed in England on long-life paper

Contents

Tables

Figures

Plates

Endpapers:
front – The Shirahatas
rear – Horses are a local passion

This book is for our families

DMHJ and MER

1988

Preface

In Western eyes Japan remains enigmatic, an incongruous mixture of the impenetrable and the unavoidable. Her economic successes have transformed the material condition of the nation, elevated its status in the international community, and promoted a flood of interest in Japanese styles of management and business organisation. The basic question is usually the same: to what extent, if any, is Japan's peculiar success a function of Japan's peculiar society? Some conclude comfortably that the two are separate and that it is in consequence of the adaptation of essentially Western modes of production and management, allied perhaps to the extreme loyalty of Japanese consumers and the relative openness of foreign markets that industry has forged so forcefully on. Others see things differently. They emphasise societal characteristics and behavioural qualities which, they believe, have played a major part in Japan's distinctive progress. To most people in the West, though, these 'qualities' remain obscure. In so far as they are contemplated at all, it is usually assumed that economic transformation necessitates a transformation in society which shifts Japan inevitably closer to the ideals, values, and ways of the West. In due course, the homogenising spread of Western culture will absorb the remnants of an Eastern tradition. In the course of this book, though, we find much evidence to suggest that the distinctiveness of the Japanese outlook on life still persists and that, in the minds of ordinary folk, things have changed less radically than crude social and material manifestations might suggest.

Michael Jeremy and his wife Julie first went to Japan in 1981. Within a short time he had developed a fascination with the Japanese *ie* (pronounced 'ee-eh'). It is a concept that has no direct equivalent in Western experience. Amongst other things, *ie* embraces the structure of relationships that we might call an 'extended household'. In addition, it accommodates the emotional and physical attachments to people and place that we sometimes signify in the notion of 'home'. It also includes the dimensions of responsibility and connectivity that 'family' implies, and it incorporates, too, an idea of 'lineage' that for most westerners is only dim and tenuous. To the Japanese, *ie* is all these things and more besides.

In modern Japan the outward expression of *ie* has declined. Migration and the pressures of modernity have seen a rapid shift to family organisation on a Western, nuclear, model. Yet the *ie* never functioned solely as a unit for family groupings. It also served as a vehicle which simultaneously nurtured conceptions of appropriate socialised behaviour and which drew its resilience from adherence to them. Thus the traits of character which the Japanese still display, arguably developed under the influence of the *ie* and out of its particular needs: the attraction of communality; the recognition of mutual interdependence; the willing acceptance of hierarchy; the veneration of ancestors; and so on. In turn, and despite the physical changes in family organisation, these traits have contributed to the survival of *ie* as a concept with which ordinary people readily identify. Moreover, they have also been fed into the expanding world of Japanese social and economic life. The processes of modernisation, which have effected such marked material change, have had much less impact on other aspects of existence. Interpersonal relationships, public and private behaviour, senses of propriety, status, and the like, remain distinctively Japanese. The ideas and influences of *ie*, in other words, may have weakened in the context of the family whilst retaining their symbolic significance for society as a whole. Indeed it could be argued, in some respects at least, that the lineations of public and corporate life in Japan mirror the essential qualities of value which were embodied in the *ie*.

To effect a translation of the concept and its significance for the Japanese demands at least some idea of motives and aspirations which are generated in a particular context of social and cultural accountability and concurrence. But in describing the meaning of the *ie* it is all too easy to impose Western preconceptions on the process and, in doing so, to obscure differences in beliefs and values, experiences and expectations. Its significance, though, also finds expression in more immediate and pragmatic ways. It can be seen in the things that people do and in the ways of doing them. This much at least is open to any observer given only that the conditions for observation are appropriate. Michael Jeremy sought those conditions by becoming immersed in the life of a single Japanese family in a remote and conservative area of north-eastern Honshu. By submitting to the unstructured experiences of daily and annual routine and opportunity, he tried to absorb something of the meaning of being Japanese. This book is an attempt to give context, shape and expression to that meaning. In so far as it has a theme, this is best summarised in the Japanese character *ma* (間) which conveys the general idea of relationship and relativity in the social realm and in the realms of space-time. Notably it suggests that the objects and events which appear to structure reality are only temporary aspects of an interlinked and changing whole. At any point in time, *ma* implies, these objects and events are perceived in consequence of their relationships with each other. In this light, *ie* finds its social identity, its spatial locus, and its temporal continuity as relative expressions in wider realms.

The study took place in the north-east of Honshu, in the mountainous region of Tohoku. It is a difficult area, heavily wooded, hilly, and relatively inaccessible. But it is also an area rich in history, proud in tradition, and conservative in outlook. Like the rest of Japan, it has shared in postwar progress, but it remains essentially agrarian and within the framework of modernity it preserves many of the remnants of traditional folk-belief and practice. Tōno is a small town in Iwate prefecture in the Kitakami hills. It has a population of about thirty thousand and serves as a market centre for the hamlets and farms of the surrounding lowland. Michael and Julie Jeremy lived there, with the Tada family, for a period of eighteen months. The choice of Tōno was influenced by a number of factors. It seemed large enough to offer the hope of finding families willing to share their home with two strangers for an extended period. At the same time it seemed small enough to promise eventual familiarity. But most important was Tōno's reputation for the preservation of tradition. It has a strong association with the rich legacy of north-eastern folk legends through the work of Yanagita Kunio (1875–1962), Japan's most revered folklorist. It is also the focus of a rural community with a vernacular architecture peculiar to the region and which, though threatened and in decline, has not yet been totally erased. Cut off from the immediate influences of the West and of academia, and speaking only Japanese except between themselves, the Jeremys sought an infusion of a new and different culture.

The stream of experience, though, seldom lends itself to easy recording. It is often chaotic and always disjointed, layered and faulted, and sometimes so splintered as to be beyond reconstruction. Looking for the consistency and character in disparate occurrences demands that they be shuffled and recombined if they are to be understood. In the process, each of them loses something: detail is sloughed off; peripheral associations are lost; novelty, surprise and the inquisitive spirit are neglected. By imposing order we move further from reality, paying an inevitable and unavoidable price in the sacrifice of immediacy. Recognising this, we have still tried to place personal experience in a broader context, seeking points of connection and clues to interpretation, but relying in the main on description and intuitive response. We begin in a more or less formal way in the Introduction by considering some views on the Japanese people as a whole. We focus attention on those characteristics that seem to bear most strongly on the idea of *ie*, on interpersonal and intra-familial behaviour, and on the spiritual context of family life. Our sources for this are mainly secondary ones and we owe a large debt to those writers on whom we have relied.

In the first chapter we relax our approach in describing Tōno and its adjacent areas. We rely more on recall and impression than on the copious statistics produced by the town council. Our purpose is to convey something of Tōno as a place to live, rather than to dissemble its social or physical or economic morphology. It is certainly a place that seems to inspire real affection, and Tada *san*, with whom the Jeremys stayed, believes that it captures some of 'the soul of the Japanese people'. It has, he said, 'the appearance of being a hidden valley set in the heart of Japan's northern mountains'.

In the chapters that follow we begin our exploration of the *ie*. First, we consider its general significance in family life, discussing the over-arching *ie* concept, its realisation in modes of address within the family, the responsibilities that attach to the roles of family members, and the humdrum routine of everyday life against which these roles are articulated. In Chapter 3 we turn to the seemingly more exotic expressions of *ie* location in a spiritual world defined in the ceremonial activities which centre on the household. We describe the Buddhist altar, the daily devotions that centre on it, and the powerful summer festival of *obon* when the spirits of the dead return to their *ie*. We describe, too, the *kamidana*, or god-shelf, which is the focus of Shinto belief and the object of special attention in the celebration of the New Year. We then turn our attention to other folk practices and ceremonies that survive in the Tōno area, concentrating especially on the lunar New Year, called *koshōgatsu*. These very old observances seem to be in rapid decline, but they still find precarious expression in some *ie* and in some small hamlets. We conclude our account of ceremonial life by describing some of the more obscure, or less dramatic, or more modern, activities which the Jeremys witnessed, and we suggest that these events, which may seem exceptional in Western eyes, have a curiously immanent quality in the life of the Japanese *ie*.

Chapters 4 and 5 complete our record. They deal with two events which, in different ways, serve periodically to redefine the *ie* and to re-affirm its essential character. The first is the marriage of the eldest son in the Tada household. Marriage is an act of great importance wherever it occurs. In Japan, this importance attaches largely to the anticipation of the birth of children, especially a first male child, through which the continuation of the *ie* can be projected for another generation. The second manner of redefinition is discussed in Chapter 5. An integral part of the *ie* concept resides in the physical structure which it occupies. Building a new house, or replacing an old one, is therefore a matter of profound significance for those families which still identify with *ie*. It is attended by a variety of ceremonials. We begin by describing the employment of geomancy in 'liberating' the space of the house within the spirit world. We also describe the variety of ceremonies that accompany different stages in the completion of the structure. We record the features of traditional vernacular farmhouses in the region and show how the influence of their form finds echoes in the modern buildings that are rapidly replacing them.

In Chapter 6 we return again to the theme of experience as we have tried to express it. We reflect on the most basic impressions created by the time spent in Tōno and on their significance for the Japanese concept of *ie*. We are keenly aware that our words still fall far short of a complete record and it is for this reason that we have included a variety of photographs taken by our friend Urata Hoichi of Tōno. They portray something of the visual dimension of experience which is beyond the capacity of language. Their purpose, therefore, is not to serve as decoration but to stand as independent testimony of reality in this small part of Japan.

In 1984 Michael Jeremy wrote a preliminary account of his experiences in Tōno (Jeremy, 1984). He then returned to live in Japan and to work in the hectic world of international finance. His commitments meant that little time was available to prepare a manuscript for publication and so, out of a long-standing familiarity with the project, the task fell to me. Given the nature of the book, which resides in experiences I have shared only vicariously, it was a daunting one. I have tried to retain the integrity of the original and to give his observations on family life and ceremony a general context within my limited knowledge of Japanese culture. I have also tried to respect the sensitivities of the people whose life the book considers. Thus, although it is built around this life, it does not, I hope, constitute an 'invasion' of it. Quite possibly I have fallen between a number of stools and I take full responsibility for any errors, omissions, or indiscretions. I am convinced, though, that the perspective that Michael Jeremy employed is an important and under-represented one and to the extent that any of this has survived my treatment of it, the credit belongs entirely to him. The photographs, by Urata Hoichi, speak for themselves.

The co-operative nature of the venture is very obvious, and out of that grow many debts of gratitude. The most immediate is to the family of Tada Rioki *san*. In the Tada *ie* the Jeremys found not merely a base and a focus for inquiry, but a real affection which has persisted and which has been renewed since their return to Japan. In Tōno, too, they were helped and guided in many particulars by the staff of the Local Council, the Education Committee, and particularly Tamonoki *sensei*. Of their many friends there, I know that they would like to extend special thanks to Urata *san*, Horiuchi *san*, Tada Hitoe, and to the people in the Silver Sand Ravine. Elsewhere in Japan, they were befriended and advised by numerous people in the Department of Anthropology at Hitotsubashi University in Tokyo, and at Osaka University of Foreign Studies. I know that they would wish me to extend special thanks to Professor Nagashima and to Professor Sugiura. The period of their stay was only made possible by the generosity of a Monbusho scholarship from the Japanese Ministry of Education.

Debts were accumulated in England too. Financial assistance came from the Social Science Research Council, as it was then called, and also from the Royal

Geographical Society. Academic assistance came from many directions, but especially from the Centre of Japanese Studies at Sheffield University, from John Sargent at the School of Oriental and African Studies, and from Joy Hendry at Oxford Polytechnic.

In preparing the manuscript for publication, I have relied on many people. Nick Scarle drew Fig. 1, and Graham Bowden and Anne Lowcock helped him to standardise some of the other figures which Michael Jeremy had prepared. Jean Mellor has typed and re-typed from my untidy longhand with enormous patience and skill. I have received encouragement and support from several of my colleagues in the Department of Geography at Manchester University, and our editor, John Banks of Manchester University Press, has been unfailingly enthusiastic and helpful. I must also mention Penny Dale and Sue Harrand, who have helped me with a number of tedious but necessary chores. Outside all this, though, there is a kind of support which is as vital as it is unwitting, and so I want to thank Miriam, Joe and John Henry, Anne, Miriam, Olly and Dave. I also want to thank Shimmy, Marian, George, Pat, Regan, Georgie Mac, and Danny the Fiddler. Thanks, too, to Tommy Binns, Dave the Butcher, Roger, Alan, Charlie, Barry, Vinnie, Pete, and all the members of the 'life-boat'.

Mike Robinson

Department of Geography
Manchester University

February 1988

Introduction

This book deals mostly with personal experiences. They unfolded in a cultural context which was strange at first but which slowly grew to be familiar. Inevitably the context helped to shape the experience: distinctive events and differences in behaviour forced themselves on our attention and continue to colour our reflections. Equally, though, our experiences helped to define the context, shaping our view of it and gradually narrowing the gap between the unusual and the commonplace, connecting but not uniting two different cultures.

The idea of 'culture' is a nebulous one, difficult to define but almost impossible to manage without. It is basically concerned with the way people live: the things that they do; the values and beliefs that they hold; the kinds of organisations and institutions within which their collective lives are located; and the way in which living is reflected in symbolic forms. For the native no less than the newcomer all this requires learning in some degree. For ourselves, some things were readily absorbed because they were not very different from the things that we were used to in Britain. But other distinctions persisted and still persist. We will never know the extent to which we understand them, though in the course of this book we attempt to describe some of them as they appeared to us.

To a greater extent than most countries, perhaps, Japan has been pressured into, or has sought, rapid sociocultural change. Some writers have suggested that the extent of these changes has been sufficient to render Japanese society accessible to understanding and interpretation in familiar Western terms. Twenty years ago, for example, Bennett (1967) wrote of the need 'to consider Japan in the context of Western, rather than Asian or perhaps "feudal" society'. The consumer revolution, he argued, had seen the emergence of a new middle class and 'a picture of social stratification resembling the West in considerable detail'. In this view the remnants of Japanese social tradition were 'lag phenomena' that might be expected to disappear with continuing adaptation to Western ways and values.

Other writers, however, believe that aspects of Western culture have been absorbed by the Japanese without penetrating the deeper recesses of a more enduring order and without displacing the conservatism that governs Japanese social relations. Indeed, some people would argue that it is precisely in the old pattern of traditional values that part of the explanation for Japan's recent progress can be found. Thus, Vogel (1967) attributes much of the smoothness of the transition to modernity to the resilience and adaptability of the Japanese kinship system. The suggestion is not that Japanese culture is in any sense static or immutable, or that it has remained untouched by contact with the West: on the contrary, their capacity for 'cultural borrowing' is well documented. Rather, the implication is that such 'borrowings' have invariably become 'Japanised to some degree', such that the directions of social change have been constrained and guided by a traditional system of social relativism that is deeply imprinted on the national character (Lebra, 1976).

From our Western viewpoint, of course, recognising these constraints is a necessary condition of locating this culture as 'Japanese'. Most of our narrative dwells upon the distinctive or the different. Nevertheless, although we lean strongly to the view that Japan remains distinctive, it is worth pointing out that differences alone are not sufficient to describe a culture, and we have no wish to imply that everything Japanese people do is somehow unique or strange. Least of all do we wish to convey the impression, in the pages that follow, that the observance of tradition is in any way theatrically self-conscious. Indeed, our abiding impression is of families who treat all aspects of their life as ordinary, distinguishing little between the old and the new, the material and the metaphysical, the mundane and the sublime (Plate III). In this sense, to begin to dissemble Japanese culture, to consign this, or that, or the other characteristic to a particular pigeonhole, threatens its complementary wholeness and shifts it out of the realm of our lived experience. This point is important because, by breaking down some situations and events, by relating them in places to the more analytical statements of specialists in Japanese culture, we can create a framework for our description. But the framework itself is irrelevant to the things it allows us to describe. It facilitates our project only at the cost of removing it in some degree from the circumstances it depicts. It is, in other words, imposed from the outside rather than given from the inside.

Bearing this abstract but still significant qualification in mind, we turn now to make some general observations on Japanese culture. These are very eclectic and necessarily selective. We focus particularly on those things which seem to have the strongest bearing on the rest of the text. Thus, we say little about economic activity, which seems to dominate so much comment on the country, or about the governmental and institutional structures which facilitate the public face of Japanese living. Instead we concentrate on those influences which penetrate most deeply the private world of intra-familial behaviour and social relationships.

Socialisation

The process of socialisation involves learning to live within the bounds and according to the constraints of a society. The absorption of beliefs, values, and cultural norms then serves to mediate patterns of behaviour which are socially acceptable. Socialisation begins at birth and continues in the development of family and personal relationships, in the experiences of formal and informal 'schooling', and in the widening sphere of life-cycle changes, employment, marriage, parenthood, old age, and so on. The childhood phase of this process is especially important because it occurs in conjunction with the development of intellect and personality, and because it is then that the idea that social relationships are reciprocal is first absorbed.

Cross-cultural studies suggest that the socialisation of the Japanese child differs from its Western counterpart, fostering attitudes towards the self and others that are quite distinctive (Stevenson *et al.*, 1986). Moreover, these differences begin immediately with the birth of a child. Most commentators seem to agree that they stem from the particular character of mother–child relationships. In this sense they embody something of the special quality of intra-familial status within the traditional Japanese family. Thus, the father is emphatically its head, responsible for its economic wellbeing and for its position in the public sphere. The mother, in a sense, 'serves' him by her control and management of the domestic sphere. The two roles are parallel rather than intertwined and since caring for children falls clearly within the domestic sphere, it falls to the mother. For female children this alignment of mother–daughter persists throughout the life-cycle. For the eldest male child it is modified with approaching adulthood as he is led by the father into the responsibilities of the *kōkei-sha*, the future family head. Nevertheless, the strength of early mother–child relationships seems to persist amongst the Japanese in the form of a sentimentalised mother-fixation (Lebra, 1976).

The particular character of mother–child relationships in Japan has been the object of extensive study. Some authors seem to emphasise the aims and objectives of child-rearing in an abstract, conceptual sense, while others stress the behavioural connections between the mother and the young child. In general, though, there is little disagreement or inconsistency in the various characterisations of the relationship. One of the most influential studies was conducted by the psychoanalyst Doi (1973). He

3

focuses on a single concept, *amae*, which describes a kind of emotional dependency into which the Japanese child is led by the indulgent nature of his mother's behaviour. The extent of this dependency far exceeds its Western equivalent and, in Doi's view, forms a persistent trait in the Japanese personality. Its purpose reflects the over-riding objective of maternal care which is to foster the bonding of mother and child and to create a sense of 'oneness' (*ittai-ka*) between them. The Japanese child, therefore, is viewed as an extension of the mother rather than as a 'separate and autonomous being' (Miyaki *et al.*, 1986).

Amae is expressed in a variety of ways, some passive and some active. Amongst the passive expressions is the willingness of the Japanese mother to avoid verbal and physical correction wherever possible, preferring instead to resort to appeasement or persuasion in order to gain compliance. As Hendry (1986) says, this reflects the belief that the young child is 'still to some extent within the sphere of the divine world' from whence it came and therefore possesses 'neither sin nor pollution'. This means that non-compliance is usually interpreted as a failure on the mother's part, but even then it is not regarded with great seriousness since 'obedience itself is not considered a desired goal' (Miyaki *et al.*, 1986).

Amae is also fostered more actively. In general Japanese mothers tend to shelter their young children from contacts outside the family and to minimise their exposure to unusual or uncertain situations (Vogel and Vogel, 1961). This is achieved by ensuring the mothers' own constant presence as a source of comfort and protection, and especially by a very high degree of actual physical contact. The outcome, as Lebra (1976) says, is that the child comes to identify its own security with the presence of the mother. In her absence the young Japanese child may appear fearful, shy and inhibited (Miyaki *et al.*, 1986).

Many writers have commented on the extent of actual physical contact between mother and child, especially in infancy. This is apparent, for example, in bathing practices which usually involve mother and child sharing a bath with the baby held tightly to the mother's body. It is apparent, too, in the widespread practice of breast feeding which may persist for up to three years and breast play which may last even longer (Lebra, 1976). It is facilitated because it is normal for the youngest child in a Japanese family to sleep with the mother. Single-sleeping, which is a valued norm for the child in a Western family, is not a desirable goal: the mother who is intent on fostering interdependence has no interest in promoting separateness in this most intimate phase of daily routine. As a result, Hendry (1986) found, bedtimes tend to be flexible and it is common for the child to be allowed to stay up until the mother is ready to go to bed herself. It is also very unusual for Japanese parents to employ babysitters to care for a child in the evening (Vogel and Vogel, 1961). This means that any social contacts which they enjoy must include the child, though as Hendry (1986) points out, a shared social life for husband and wife is not regarded as a priority once a child is born.

Befu (1986) argues that the outcome of powerful maternal bonding in the Japanese family has an important effect on the 'emotional alignment of family members'. In the typical Western model it is usually assumed that the most powerful coalition within the household will be the one between husband and wife. In the Japanese equivalent, however, it is the coalition between mother and children from which the father is emotionally excluded. This has a number of consequences. Through the mother, the child learns to accept the 'unchallenged authority' which resides in the remote and detached figure of the father. He becomes, as it were, a benign but potentially threatening force who may sometimes serve to represent the ultimate sanction for misbehaving children. In the modern nuclear family, the remoteness of the father is physical as well as emotional. He spends little time with his children and is away from home for long hours fulfilling work and social obligations. As Hendry (1986) notes, it is quite common for him to leave the house before the children are awake and not to return until after they have gone to bed. These absences serve to strengthen the mother–child relationship, to emphasise the isolation of the father, and to restrict the opportunities for his involvement in the child-rearing process. During those limited periods when the father is present he is treated with 'deference and respect' and with a degree of cautious circumspection (Befu, 1986).

In many Japanese families, however, the modern nuclear ideal has failed to displace the more traditional family organisation where grandparents share the house with parents and children. Befu (1986) reports a 1980 survey which found that 37 per cent of Japanese families with parents still living shared one of these three-generation households. In these circumstances, Befu observes, a 'transgenerational coalition' may develop with grandparents and grandchildren forming an alliance against parents. Though it is exercised usually only in small matters, the nature of the coalition remains an essentially indulgent one directed principally to the 'emotional gratification' of the child. The role of the grandparents may, however, assume greater importance for those families in which the wife is a secondary breadwinner. The acceptance of working mothers in Japan is still far from complete since it is inconsistent with the deeply-held belief that a woman's principal duty lies in the rearing of children and the care of the home. The pressure on middle-class women to supplement family incomes has resulted, in Befu's (1986) view, in 'massive numbers of Japanese mothers ... working while feeling guilty in various degrees for transgression of the societal norm that urges them to stay at home and be full-time mothers'. In the event that grandparents are able to serve as a surrogate, the extent of disapproval is somewhat lessend (Plate II). Moreover, Hendry (1986) reports that in some families at least differences between mother and grandmother on matters of child-rearing are usually resolved by the mother deferring to the experience of the older woman.

The domestic environment of the Japanese family, therefore, is child-centred to a degree that distinguishes it from its Western equivalent. This is not to imply a different order of affection from the mother, but rather a different outlook on the socialisation of the child, different aims in early upbringing, and different consequences for the child's own emerging view of himself and his relations with others and with society in general. The closeness of mother–child relations allows the mother to appeal to empathy as a motivation for compliant behaviour. She tries to create a domestic atmosphere which is pleasant and congenial, flexible in the face of childish wilfulness, consoling in the presence of frustration, and offering in her own behaviour an exemplar of the kind of conduct into which the child is to be encouraged.

In itself, the kind of everyday behaviour which is valued by the Japanese mother is neither unusual nor remarkable. Lebra (1976), for example, says that 'there seems to be no outstanding difference between Japanese and American children in basic training' which relates to things like toilet habits, eating habits, locomotive, graphic, and verbal abilities. She notes a greater emphasis on orderliness and tidiness in Japan and on etiquette especially in modes of greeting. But the important distinctions appear to lie in matters of social relativity, in inter-personal harmony and in the promotion of self-restraint. In describing the 'good child', Hendry (1986) resorts to the Japanese word *sunao* which may be interpreted as 'compliant', 'obedient' and 'co-operative'. She distinguishes, however, between 'compliance' in the Japanese child and 'obedience' in the Western child. Referring to the work of Lanham (1966), she emphasises the importance of *willing* compliance as opposed to 'mere obedience'. Indeed, White and Levine (1986) caution specifically against the misconstruction of 'good behaviour' in the Japanese child as 'obedience' and 'submission'. They describe a *sunao* child as one who has

> not yielded his or her personal autonomy for the sake of co-operation; co-operation does not suggest giving up the self, as it may in the West; it implies that working with others is the appropriate way of expressing and enhancing the self. Engagement and harmony with others is, then, a positively valued goal and the bridge – to open-hearted co-operation, as in *sunao* – is through sensitivity, reiterated by the mothers' example and encouragement

Lebra (1976) believes that the mother–child relationship and the dependency it produces develops from four general elements. The first is the fact that the mother exercises power over the child because she represents the source of the child's 'security, protection, and survival'. Her role in these vital areas is enhanced by the traditional separation of responsibilities within the Japanese family. The same separation of responsibilities also enhances her role in the second element of dependency-development. This involves the physical activities of caretaking: 'feeding, toilet control, clothing, and health'. Once again, it is exclusively to the mother that these duties fall. The third element is the mutual appeal of dependency from the child and indulgence from the mother which can be expressed 'in the most intimate manner, without much inhibition'. Finally, Lebra (1976) believes, because of the degree of her devotion to the child's welfare, the mother comes to symbolise 'the ultimate in empathy and sacrifice, on which the helpless child depends'.

The theme of dependency which develops first and most emphatically between mother and child is repeated in a variety of social contexts as the child matures. The empathy which leads to the willing compliance of *sunao* behaviour finds later expression in the Japanese propensity to forego individual satisfaction and individual expressions of selfhood in favour of what Befu (1986) calls 'interpersonalism'. Just as the child's identity is defined in its relationship to the mother, so 'it is the interconnectedness of persons and the quality of that interconnectedness that determines who one is' (Befu, 1986). Individuality in a Western sense is therefore neither sought nor admired very much. In so far as it finds expression at all, this tends to be in the private world of introspection and self-reflection (Lebra, 1976). This means that many social relationships are able to assume the character of 'symbolic filiation', based on empathetic and dependent expectations that are almost obligatory in terms of their sanctions. Lebra (1976) notes these relationships in 'occupational, economic, and political groups, as well as gangsters', but whatever name is given to them 'the parent–child relationship tends to be the model'.

To the extent that Japanese social relations continue to conform to the values that are inculcated during childhood, they encourage a strong commitment to a series of 'roles' which the individual might be expected to fulfil (DeVos, 1973). Once again, motherhood is the critical model. It ranks highest amongst the duties of a Japanese woman and its neglect is 'inexcusable under any circumstances' (Befu, 1986). As an ideal, the values which are implied by this kind of dedicated role commitment soon become apparent in the child and persist in the adult. It is well known, for example, that Japanese schoolchildren display a general level of dedication and compliance that exceeds their North American counterparts (Hess *et al.*, 1986). Part of the reason for this is precisely because they *are* Japanese and they *are* schoolchildren. They are therefore more devoted to perfecting the schoolchildren's role in accordance with adult expectations.

Later in life, the same trait helps to determine the attitude of the employer or the employee to the role which he occupies (Abbeglen and Stalk, 1985). This applies no less to a road sweeper than to a company president and at least goes some way towards explaining the Japanese 'work ethic'. Allied as it is to the values of interpersonalism, it also allows the satisfaction of personal role commitment to be identified with success at the level of the company or the work group. Within the context of the family, and especially the more traditional families, this same ability to subsume selfhood in the pursuit of an idealised role model – grandparent, father, mother, older son, daughter, and so on – is a powerful stabilising influence. It localises authority within the group and amongst family members, it moderates the exercise of that authority, and it justifies its acceptance. We will see examples of it in the chapters which follow. Moreover, the acceptance of a role, either within the family or in the wider spheres of social and economic life, also involves accepting the status which attaches to that role and behaving accordingly (Lebra, 1976). But since any individual may be called upon to play a variety of different roles, sometimes with a senior status and sometimes with a junior one, considerable public adaptability is necessary. Some idea of the extent of role commitment in Japan can be gathered from Lebra's (1976) description of the way in which role failure, once publicly exposed, is a major motive for suicide. It is also quite obviously a powerful influence on Japanese views of public propriety and etiquette.

In all of this we should make it quite clear that we are discussing ideals and values, and that like all ideals and values these are often honoured as much in the breach as in the observance. Yet the degree of consensus which seems to exist amongst scholars of Japanese behaviour, and which seems to have persisted with little change, suggests a conservatism and a consistency which is deeply rooted in the national character. It also suggests that beneath the material similarities in Japanese and Western life, and beneath the similarities in commercial and economic life, there remain fundamental culture differences. These differences stem, as we have tried to indicate, from values which have their origins in the powerful influence of family ideals on virtually all aspects of public behaviour. That they often fail, that Japan has its share of crime and deliquency, that the later generations of children may be less tractable and less compliant than their parents, is all true. But in our own experience the traditional models not only continue to survive; they continue to be valued and they continue to work as a basis for the organisation of Japanese society.

Religion

It is probably impossible for most Westerners to enter into the nature of those Japanese experiences which we might label 'religious'. They exist in a view of man's relationship to a universe of gods and spirits which is radically different from the general Western outlook. Yet, as many of the following pages will show, ceremonial and symbolic activity within the family is often conducted in the context of religiously-inspired propitiation, thanksgiving, and the like. Moreover, it is often conducted by family members rather than by ecclesiastics and is a distinctive and integral part of the daily and annual round. Some overview of Japanese religion, therefore, helps to provide a context for these activities. It does not, and cannot, adequately explain them or account for the mode of their conduct.

The major institutionalised religions of Japan are Shinto and Buddhism. Shinto is the oldest and is generally regarded as the indigenous Japanese religion. But Buddhism, which came into the country from China in the sixth century, is so deeply ingrained and familiar that it has 'lost its foreign flavor and become "naturalized"' (Befu, 1971). In the main, Shinto and Buddhism co-exist without tension because neither makes exclusive demands of adherents. That is to say that it is possible in general to observe the rituals of both without offending either. Needless to say, this is a very different view of religious devotion from the one which is common in the West. It is complicated, too, by the fact that the openness of both religions encourages not only syncretism between them, but also with a diffuse body of folk beliefs which have ancient origins and a lingering appeal, especially to the rural Japanese.

The institutional separation of the two great religions allows some orderly description of them, but it creates a distinction that, in our own experience as well as in the views of others, is singularly unimportant in the lives of ordinary Japanese people (Blacker, 1975). The demarcation that exists seems principally to be a matter of appropriate emphasis and pragmatism rather than doctrine. Shinto, for example, tends to serve as the focus of family aspirations for wellbeing, good fortune, and purity. Buddhism, on the other hand, is more associated with caring for and placating the dead. It should be stressed, though, that these are only tendencies and there are many occasions when the ritual of a ceremony may take on either a Buddhist or Shinto complexion without altering its purpose in any significant way.

The success and the persistence of both Shinto and Buddhism probably owes most to their ability to accommodate deeply rooted folk beliefs. Shinto, in fact, originated out of folk religion. It has 'no founder, no inspired scriptures, no moral code', yet it has an especial value for the

Japanese since it embodies something of their 'deep feelings for nature and their strong love of country' (Scott Morton, 1974). Buddhism, though it was originally established in opposition to folk beliefs, has progressively adapted to or accommodated them: indeed, in Hori's (1968) view, this has 'really been the weak point of institutionalized religion' in Japan. The outcome for ordinary people, though, has been a system of religious observance, ritual, and ceremony that is very much geared to their own perceived needs, that is relatively untrammelled by formal theology, and that neither demands nor receives much ecclesiastical ascription.

Under these circumstances it becomes artificial to disentangle Shinto and Buddhism in addressing the Japanese view of the spiritual world. Because neither is exclusive and because neither recognises a unique universal God, each is able to contribute separately, or both together, in conceptions of religious fulfilment. Moreover, they demand no consensual agreement as to the nature and origins of particular beliefs, or even the meanings of particular rituals. In consequence, it is especially difficult to summarise a Japanese outlook on the 'other world'. In the version offered by Yanagita (1970) there were four 'conspicuously Japanese elements'. First, he believed that the souls of the dead remained in their own country, rather than leaving for some far place. Second, because the relationship between life and death is essentially one of continuity rather than severance, he believed that there were frequent comings and goings between the two worlds which he called 'the clear and the dark'. Third, he believed that the unfulfilled wishes of the living were still capable of realisation after death, and that finally rebirth could complete the cycle of continuity. 'These', he wrote, 'are not empty dreams started by only a few people in a certain time':

> We believe in the divine protection of our ancestors, we entrust ourselves to their favour, and we think there is no need to demand or worry or suffer concerning their assistance, and thus our festivals become occasions for returning thanks and pouring out our complete joys; and this is due to our knowledge learned from past generations; that is, we know through long experience that our ancestors have the power and pleasure to help us under any circumstances.

Yanagita's observations are not offered as a summary of a generally accepted, consensual view. Probably no such consensus exists. Hori and Ooms (1970), for example, specifically assert that the belief in reincarnation was never really accepted by the Japanese, except sometimes with respect to the souls of very young children and occasionally grandfathers whose soul might be reincarnated in a grandchild. In these cases, they believe, the idea of rebirth reflects 'an ideology centered around the continuation of the household'. Despite this, Yanagita's own description of a set of beliefs that were clearly personally and deeply held serves peculiarly

well to convey something of the atmosphere of experiences that defy summary systematisation. It also draws attention to the exceptional importance of ancestral veneration in Japanese religious practice (Smith, 1974). It is a veneration that probably falls short of the Western concept of 'worship' since it involves a greater assumption of reciprocity between the living and the dead. For their part, the living recognise a duty to the dead which, being fulfilled, ensures a degree of divine protection for the individual and the family. In turn, the souls of the dead afford this protection in return for the care and solicitation which only the living can provide.

Two things seem apparent which allow us to return, momentarily, to the general alignment of particular religious observations with Shinto and with Buddhism. The first is that wellbeing for the living is wholly consistent with the belief in ancestral influence. The second is that this influence is more likely to be benevolent if proper attention is paid to the dead. Shinto practices, since they tend towards praise and thanksgiving at least as much as they do towards placation and mollification, are aligned in popular devotion with the care afforded by the spirit world for the world of the living. It is, as Scott Morton (1974) says, 'on the whole a sunny rather than a somber religion'. The other side of this coin concerns the attention paid by the living to the dead, and it is in this area that Buddhism found its appeal for the Japanese. Even here, of course, we must acknowledge the common divisibility of these alignments, and the general sense of ecclesiastical indifference which ordinary people bring to religious observance.

The Japanese believe that everyone becomes a deity sooner or later (Befu, 1971). Inevitably, the most likely source of immediate family protection is from lineal ancestors and it is towards these ancestors that many devotions are performed. These include not only the recently dead, venerated by the individual household, but also the distantly dead. Not surprisingly, therefore, different branches of the same family and even entire villages may recognise some common ancestral origin which resides in a particular deity. There is considerable uncertainty and many different views with regard to these *uji-gami* (Smith, 1974). Yanagita (1970) certainly believed that the process of modernisation in Japan was masking the individual ancestral shrines in an essentially political search for a more sharply focused national religion. This occurred in the indiscriminate combination of shrines which were then nominally devoted to the gods, (*kami*), of one of the nationally-recognised founders of religious sects, such as Hachiman sama or Tenjin sama. Thereafter, he argued, either through accident or neglect the identification of the shrine with *uji-gami* was diluted and sometimes lost. The outcome has been a tendency, which we identify with considerably uncertainty, to restrict religious observance into two phases. The first is the continued veneration of the souls of the recently dead and remembered ancestors. This occurs in the essential privacy of a single household or a small group of closely related ones. The second is the public veneration accorded to the great *kami*, like Hachiman, who enjoy national recognition. Identification with the more distantly dead 'clan' ancestors of the *uji-gami* type seems, on the surface at least, to be rare. On the other hand, as Smith (1974) says, it is equally likely that the collectivity of ancestors 'no longer remembered as persons' continue to be asked for 'guidance and assistance' and to be welcomed back into the home at the midsummer Festival of the Dead.

It is also a feature of religious belief that, despite the emphasis on ancestral spirits and historical figures whose existence was real enough and whose deification followed their demise, the Japanese also recognise mythological gods. The most important of these, perhaps, is the Sun-Goddess, Amaterasu-ō-mikami, from whom the imperial house claimed direct descent. It was this connection, of course, that conferred a deified status on living emperors 'who alone could approach the tutelary deity of the country' (Smith, 1974). Yet another is the god who guards the demon gate of the north-east. He is Ushitora-no-Konjin and, unlike the generally benevolent ancestral spirits, is 'a very dangerous deity, quick to take offence and to mete out punishment to those who incur his displeasure' (Smith, 1974). In the more remote rural areas, as we shall see, many people continue to consult diviners concerning the orientation of their houses lest they offend Konjin by locating impure rooms, like the lavatory, in an aspect which he would not approve. By cheerful contrast, though, Daikoku sama is a smiling god and a bringer of good fortune in whatever place and for whatever purpose he is venerated.

In this very brief, and very selective, account we have tended to emphasise Japanese *beliefs*. There is a sense, though, in which this may be less appropriate than it is in the context of Western religion. This is because our own experience indicated that the meaning of religion for ordinary people consisted much more in practice than in reflection. This is not to deny belief, or to suggest that it is, in any pejorative sense, shallow. On the contrary, the actions of ritual observance appeared to satisfy needs which were so integral that they rarely demanded articulation. They were not a source of real or even potential uncertainty and consequently they neither attracted nor received much social or philosophical debate. Ancestors were venerated as part of the everyday round in ways which were as unceremonious and unselfconscious as the habitual brewing of tea or boiling of rice. In their turn, the major festival observances acquired their propriety from the actions and manner of their celebration rather than from doctrinal or inspirational sources.

The principal characteristics of Japanese religion, therefore, lie in three things. First, in the recognition of a natural world which accommodates myriads of supernatural beings: *kami* are in some way 'above' mere mortals, but they are neither so distant nor so independent as the universal God of Judeo-Christian tradition. They find their abode in anything un- usual or extraordinary, natural or man-made, and their existence is manifest in the feelings which they inspire, the circumstances which they contrive, and the actions which they control. Some of them are 'small' *kami*, like the souls of most plants and animals. Others, including the souls of people and of certain animals like the fox, must be treated more seriously since they have the capacity to inspire danger and harm (Befu, 1971). Second, access to the spirits is afforded through rituals which may be associated more or less strongly with an institutionalised religion and with folk practices which probably have ancient and indigenous origins. In the minds of most ordinary people, though, the significance of ritual lies not in its ascription to Shinto or to Buddhism or to anything else, but in the appropriate nature of the actions it comprises as these are understood in tradition. Neglectful or inappropriate behaviour invites retribution in the form of earthly misfortune. Finally, a central focus of Japanese reli- gious practice is the veneration of ancestors. These may be real or im- agined, remembered or forgotten, immediate or distant. The inspiration stems from the family rather than from individual association with an institutionalised religion. It reaffirms the continuity of the family and the indissoluble ties between the living and the dead that are directed, through their reciprocity, to the perpetuation of well being for both.

Socialisation, religion and the family

We have made frequent reference to the Japanese family and we shall have cause to return to it on many occasions in the following pages. We will be concerned to identify the way in which family relations are conceptualised in a tradition that has no real Western equivalent. It resides in the idea of the *ie*. Although we will elaborate this idea at a later stage, the themes of socialisation and religious practice bear heavily upon it and are given added significance as a result. The relationships are reciprocal and mutual- ly supporting; the processes of socialisation, the beliefs of religion, and the ideology of the *ie*, come together to help confer a cultural distinctiveness on the Japanese people. Each of them, in some measure, may be breaking down under the pressures and the opportunities of postwar modernism. This is especially the case with the external or physical expression of *ie* living, as more and more Japanese families become nuclear and privatised (Morioka, 1986). On the other hand, or so it has seemed to us, people

13

have been able to accommodate and exploit changes in form without necessarily abandoning traditional values. The reasons seem to lie in a propensity to accept apparent contradiction, to foster seeming ambiguity, and to create a *modus vivendi* which is essentially pragmatic.

The Japanese have traditionally conceptualised the family as a frame through which living members are passing, through which ancestors have already passed, and towards which the unborn are heading. It is a frame which affords brief but transient illumination in an irresistible temporal continuum. The duties of the living lie in the preservation of the frame, in ensuring that it survives their own mortality to welcome future generations and to make certain that the dead are neither neglected nor forgotten. Dedication to this ideal imposes particular constraints on the living with regard to their relationships with each other and with the dead. To the extent that it is possible to separate the two, it might be claimed that the processes of socialisation evolved out of the former, whilst religious observance facilitated the latter.

The distinctiveness of the Japanese family, and certainly of the *ie* ideal lies in this concept of continuity from the unborn, the living, and the dead and in the acceptance of the peculiar responsibilities which this imposes. Necessarily they are responsibilities which fall most heavily on the mature. The very young and the very old are, in their different ways, close to the other world and therefore worthy of indulgence and respect. Relations between the mature, of both sexes, demand stability and conformity if the fragile thread of continuity is not to be broken. This is best achieved by the acceptance, but not the imposition, of hierarchical status amongst individuals, the willing assumption of differential duties and their no-less-willing surrender under appropriate circumstances and at a suitable time.

In those Japanese families where the *ie* ideal continues to exercise an important influence it is still possible to see the way in which dependency relationships serve these values, giving a physical expression to motives which are largely metaphysical. They are directed towards an ideal which transcends individualism in a Western sense and which emphasises a collectivity of mutual needs and contributions drawn from the past, absorbing the present, and extending into the future. It has been observed often enough that the familial base of these ideas has been thoroughly eroded in the recent past. In this short and descriptive record of some aspects of our own life with a Japanese family there were nevertheless powerful echoes of a system of beliefs that seems far from being abandoned.

I

Tōno

Tōno is in the mountainous region known as Tohoku in north-eastern Honshu. The railway from Tokyo follows a series of basins and river valleys which separate the uplands of Abukuma and Kitakami from the Central mountains. South of Morioka, near the small town of Hanamiki, a branch line swings east into the Kitakami hills to Tōno, and eventually to Kamaishi on the coast (Fig. 1). The route into the hills is steep and winding. Because of the precipitous slopes, and the many tunnels that riddle them, there is little to see, except for the occasional glimpse of a small village. For the rest, the view is of deeply ravined hills, forested mostly with conifers. In summer they are a uniform dark green, but in autumn they are relieved by the brilliance of an occasional maple, blazing red on the volcanic soils.

Tōno lies in a small basin in the heart of the Kitakami uplands. It is drained by the Saru ga Ishi, a major tributary of the Kitakami. The town is crammed between a bend in the river and the close southern hills. To the north, the vista is of bright green rice fields, occasional farms and hamlets, and orchards and fields of yellowing tobacco laid out in the luxuriant shadow of the lower hillslopes. This spring or summer scene gives an impression of order, prosperity and tranquility, broken only by the whine and roar of sawmills and by skeins of overhead cables and lights in the town. On every side, though, the horizon is serrated with lines of receding hills (Plate I) and the course to the sea is dominated by Mount Rokkōshi (1,294 metres), one of the three sacred 'sister-goddess' mountains of the area. On a clear winter's day the hills seem close and low, every line sharpened by the cold and etched by the winds sweeping down into the valley. They are less visible in summer's haze when the view is focussed on the patchwork of greens in the fields and the blue and red tin roofs of houses and hamlets. On the farms in summer it is a race to keep abreast of the flourishing tall grasses and the weeds that would clog the fields. The valleys teem with life and activity, with the noises of water flowing between paddies, with the throaty call of frogs, with ubiquitous snakes and birds of prey. But even in summer, the hills themselves are quiet

15

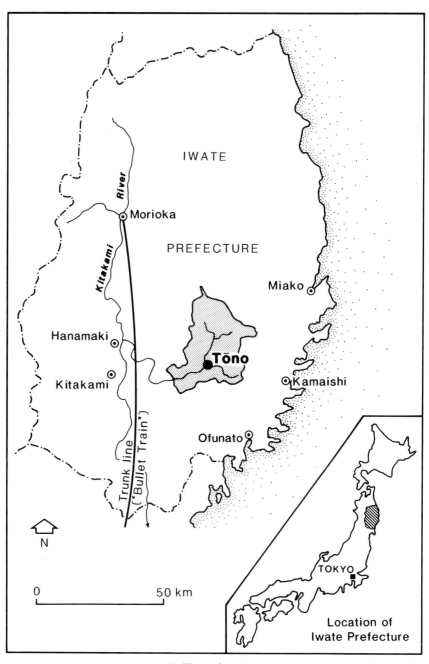

1 Tōno: location

except for the call of the bush warbler, and in winter only the wind and the occasional cry of a kite disturbs their silence.

It is not surprising that the Japanese are intensely pre-occupied with their natural world. As Sansom (1977) notes, it is a feeling readily shared by Western visitors from the earliest times. In this part of Honshu, it is enhanced by the distinctive character of the seasons, each with its problems but each with its special pleasures too. Like all agricultural communities, the people of Tōno have reason to observe the vagaries of weather and the change of seasons which have such an important influence on daily life. Like the English, their greetings are usually meteorological! 'Lovely day, isn't it?', they will say.

The winters in Tōno are long and severe, even considering its northerly location. Temperatures are very low with a mean below freezing from November through to March. In February they can fall to minus 18°C, and they are usually exacerbated by a cruel wind. But many of the days are clear and bright, described by the Japanese as *Nihon bare*, or 'fine-weather Japan'. The balance of sharp, sunny days and extreme nocturnal cold also brings some spectacular sights. Immense displays of icicles are formed. Every branch of every tree may be decked with thick feathers of hoar frost, and in the clear air the crystal visibility of the hills brings all sense of scale tumbling down. Apart from some logging, though, these winter conditions preclude farm work (Plate V) and play their part in encouraging seasonal labour away from home. For those left behind, winter is a time for the relaxation of forced inactivity, for long conversations with friends, for a little gambling or a solitary game of chess. But in between the snowfalls of the quiet season, which can be copious and very thick, the air is often desiccated. House timbers dry out quickly and the extensive use of paraffin stoves and wood burners produces its annual crop of devastating house fires. For a visitor, an unusual feature of the winter weather forecast is the 'dry air warning'.

In the uplands of the northeast, winter drifts into spring and spring into summer without the waves of uncomfortable humidity that the 'plum rains' bring further south. Indeed rainfall in the spring months is low and variable. It begins to rise sharply only in July, when humidity is relatively high, when mean temperatures are in excess of 20°C, and when maximum temperatures edge to 35°C. But even then the combination of latitude and elevation ensures compensation in evenings which are cool and quiet, ideal times for relaxation inspired by cold beer and barbecues of fresh squid. The farmers, of course, worry about the weather in summer and its consequences for the rice harvest in September. More generally, everyone worries about the threat of late-season typhoons which sweep up through northern Japan as the winter wind system re-establishes itself. The effects of Typhoon 'No. 15' which struck the coast near Ofunato in 1981 were still apparent when we left Tōno in 1983. Floodwater had removed a major road bridge, stripped concreted river banks, and caused devastation to many of the roads which threaded their way between the steep hillslopes and the numerous streams of the valley. We heard, too, that the same storm demolished houses, inundated rice fields with sand, and devastated tobacco crops.

One other feature of the environment impresses itself indelibly on the consciousness of a visitor from the stable geological region of northwestern Europe: this is an earthquake zone. In the year and a half which we spent there, small earth tremors occurred with a frequency too common to record. Sometimes they reached force four on the Richter scale. To the local people they are a part of the natural world and, like the seasons, a part of the natural perspective. But to unfamiliar and timid outsiders they cause repeated unease and consternation. Hearing a distant rumble at night, spreading from the hills until it sets house timbers ticking and rocking against each other, it becomes somehow easier to appreciate the power of the mountains in legend and in life.

The people who live here are proud and protective of their own place. They believe that it is widely known throughout Japan, when other evidence suggests that it is not. They refer often to its 'isolation', which is now historical, and to the fact that the region was once called the 'Tibet' of Japan. Many of them remember the lean post-War years when people still died of starvation, and they indulge in the affectionate hyperbole which is probably common to the residents of small rural communities the world over. Yet, no less than the rest of the country, Tōno has shared in the changes which the last thirty years have brought. For the time being, at least, some of these changes are captured in the physical differences and outward appearance of the generations. Many old women are bent double, permanently shaped by a regime of work in the fields which mechanisation is relieving for the younger folk (Plate IV). Old men still wear a white towel tied below the chin which enhances the already medieval impression of their gaitered trousers and short, quilted coats. By contrast, the young affect a Western version of hairstyles and dress, and seek their entertainment not in the traditional drinking houses, called *sakeya*, but in the neon glitter of modern 'bars'. Moreover, for them the allure of the city is just as real as it is in European society and the consequences have been equally marked.

The town is growing older. Its population has declined from some 38,000 in 1950 to a little over 31,000 in 1980, and the losses have been amongst the young. Today, there are perhaps 12,500 people in Tōno under the age of thirty years. Three decades ago there were more than

18

23,000. Of even greater significance, though, is the fact that, despite these absolute changes in numbers, there has been an expansion in the total of independent households, while household membership has decreased. The message is unavoidable: in structural terms at least the traditional extended Japanese family household is giving ground rapidly to fragmentation into nuclear units on a typically Western model. In some of the pages that follow, however, we will suggest that structural changes of this kind do not necessarily imply the abandonment of the values and inspiration of the Japanese *ie*.

There have been other structural changes in the life of the people of Tōno. Full-time farming, which once dominated the economy of the area and the lives of the inhabitants, has declined. In family terms, farming has become a part-time occupation for all but a handful. For the rest, younger sons and household heads now take second jobs in construction, retailing, manufacturing, service industries and the like. The responsibility and the care of the farm thus falls substantially on the shoulders of women, diminishing the attractiveness of a rural life for the 'modern' girl. The unenviable position of the farm wife, toiling in the fields while her husband works in the city, is not lost on the rural Japanese: *kāsan nōgyō* or 'mothers farming' epitomises the loads that she is expected to bear. Many of the men take on migrant work, called *dekasegi*. Older sons, fathers, and even grandfathers may be away from home for up to eleven months in every year, returning to see their families only for the major festivals of *Obon* and New Year, or at harvest and planting time. It seems likely that over a quarter of the farm population is affected in this way and the consequences of *dekasegi* for many rural families must be hard indeed.

The farm economy has changed too. It was once much less diverse, heavily dependent on rice culture, on sericulture as a cottage industry, and on the breeding of horses. Horses are a local passion. Arguably, they influenced the way in which people built their houses and prompted the emergence of the L-shaped *magariya* farmhouse where animals shared the family roof. They also entered the world of myth, providing a rich legacy of symbolism and legend that survives their elimination in the economy of modern, mechanised farming. A few households still continue the tradition of horse-breeding, but they do so these days out of love for the horse (Plate VI), out of respect for its strength which is tested at annual 'horse-pulling' competitions, out of a cultivated taste for its meat which is eaten raw, and also for the social worth and standing which now attaches to horse ownership.

Sericulture has gone from the farms of Tōno, and the primacy of rice is not nearly as emphatic as it once was. The area planted has been curtailed, partly in consequence of government policy and over-production in Japan generally, and partly because tobacco and hops have proved to be a useful agrarian investment. Yet to the outsider there is a strange irony in the new rural landscape, as the silver light thrown up from flooded rice fields is reflected in the polythene-covered rows of young tobacco plants. There is no doubt, either, that people do not feel the quasi-religious attachment to tobacco and hops that they have always entertained for the rice plant (Plate VII). In a similar way, a new tractor may be a means of publicly demonstrating a measure of affluence, but it still cannot compare with the special pride of owning the winning entry in the 'horse-pulling' contest.

Not many of the people in Tōno have ventured abroad. The few that we met seemed to agree that the things they missed most on their travels were the commonplace tastes of local food, perhaps soya-bean paste (*miso*), or the ubiquitous salted radish called *daikon*. The latter is a particular favourite in this part of Japan. It has a pungent smell and a crisp texture and it seems to be consumed in dangerous quantities. Mixed with dried mushrooms (*shiitake*), it brings a distinctive flavour to the popular local stews, subtle, woody, and almost melancholy. The taste for tradition- al food seems to have changed little despite the abundance and variety of pre-packed supermarket offerings. The real difference is that ordinary things, like salt-pickled vegetables, vitamin-rich pumpkin, eggs and river fish, can now be enjoyed for their inherent quality: it is not long ago that they were the only available supplements to the monotony of a rural diet of rice and soya-bean. The business of searching in damp-ravined birch coppices for edible fungi, or scouring the lower hillslopes for herbs or wild vegetables, has been transformed from a necessity to an occasional pleasure.

There is no doubt that a strong sense of tradition, or at least of conservatism, permeates the region, especially in the outer rural areas where forty per cent of the population still live. Fine new houses may be replacing older thatched ones but, as we shall show, the influence of traditional design often finds expression in modern counterparts. Farming may be in decline as household interests diversify, but it still remains the leading employment sector and, despite the outward show of prosperity in the town, the entire region still depends heavily on the outcome of the annual harvest. Moreover, despite a crop of new local government offices, civic centres, and a genuinely fine museum, Tōno still lacks piped sewerage facilities. In summer this is unavoidably obvious and at New Year it sometimes seems that every single household is having its cess tank emptied at the same time.

The commercial and manufacturing life of the town is confined to small, local needs. It has a few factories which make bean curd (*tōfu*) and it has three rice-wine distilleries. It also has a large brick and tile works

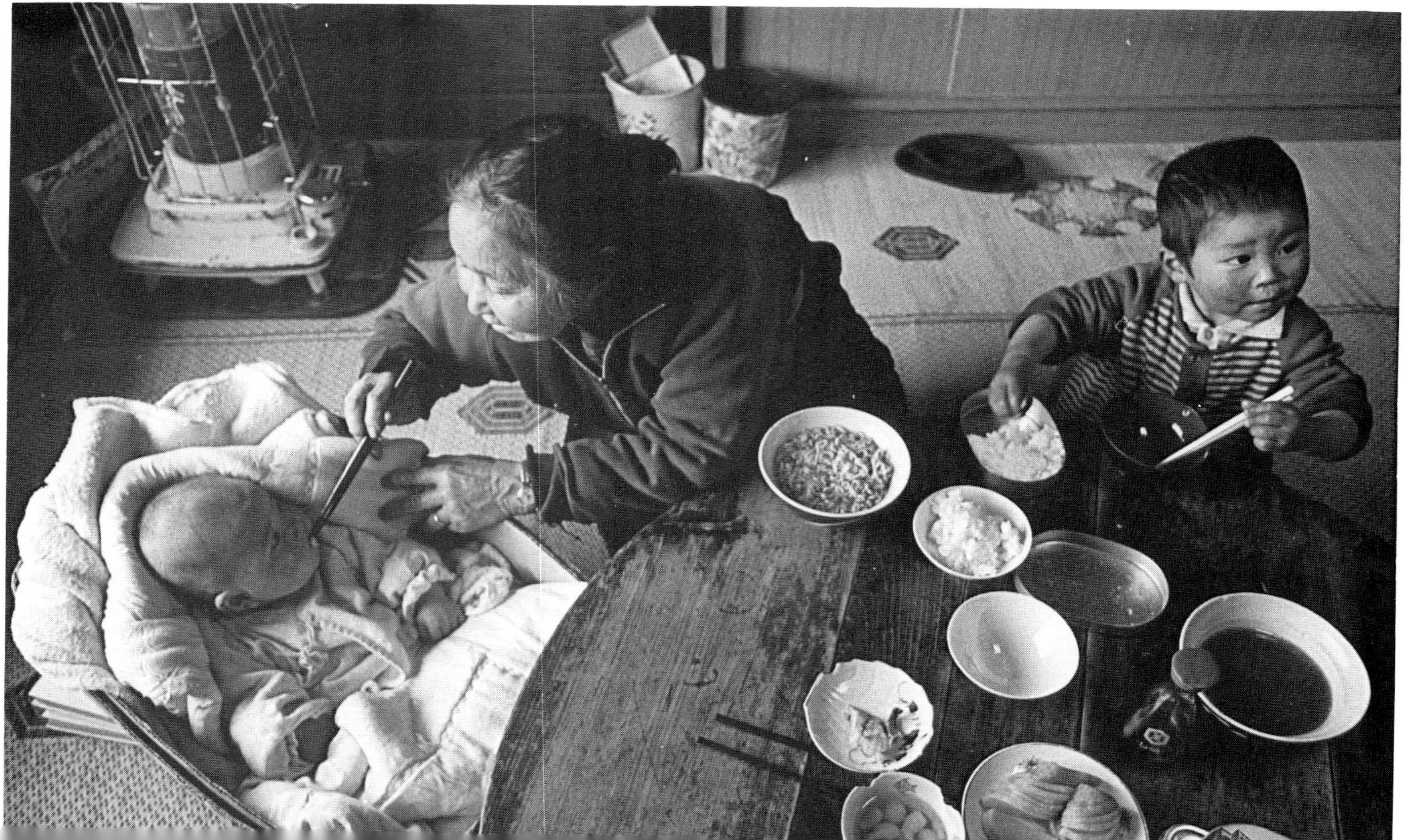

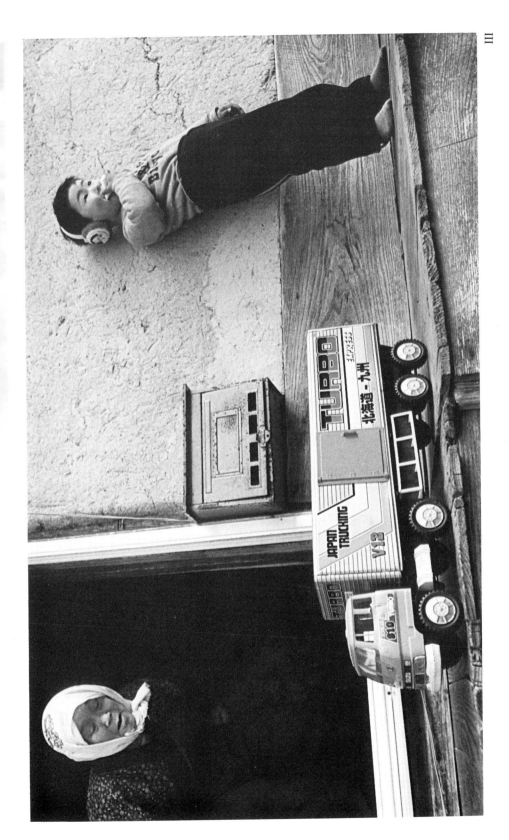

IV

VI

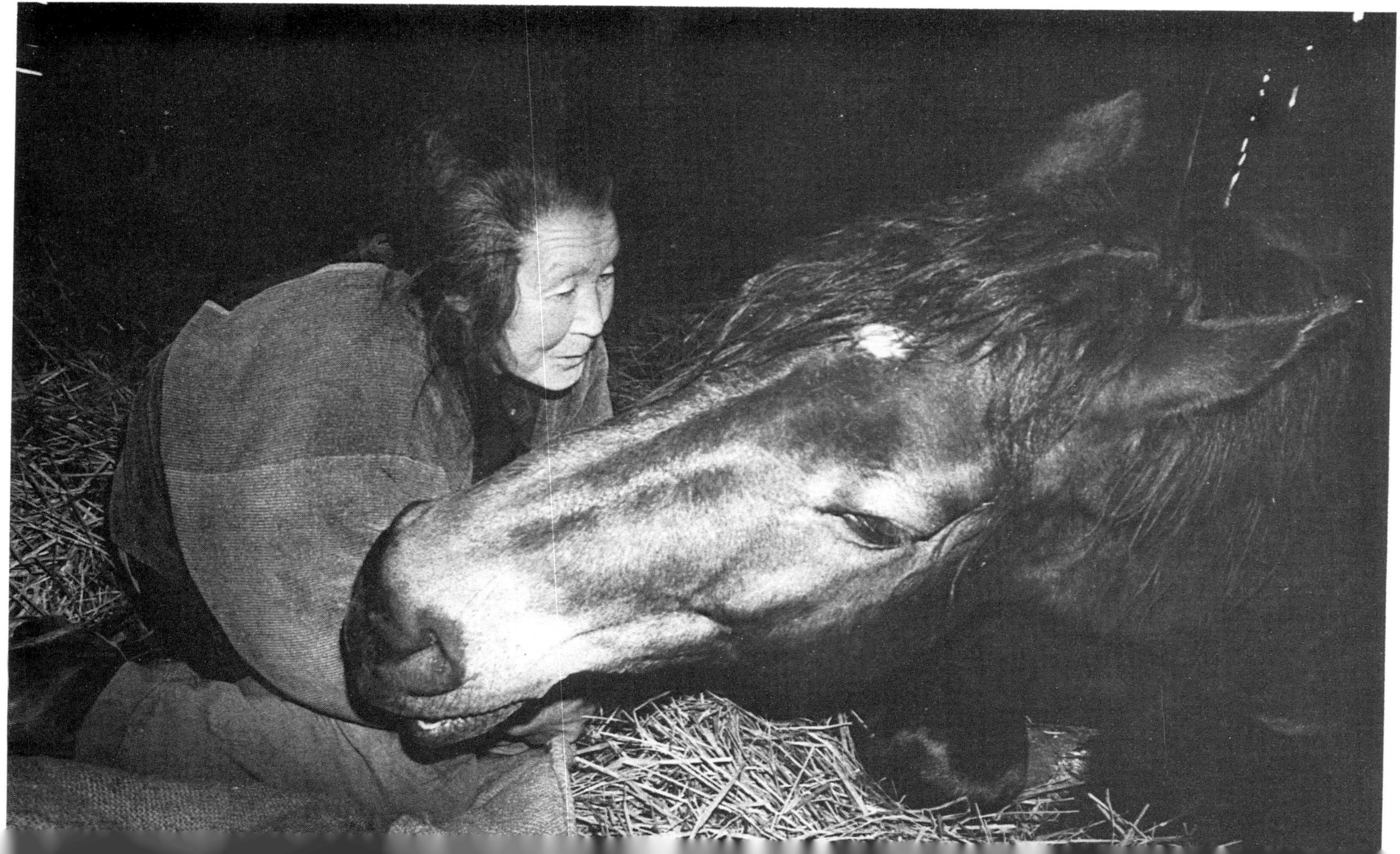

which occasionally undertakes specialist orders for temples outside Tōno. But, despite the profusion of saw-mills and carpenters' shops which ring the town, there are only a handful of places which offer employment to more than fifty people. The area remains tied to its rural base, bound by the lottery of summer weather and the influx of some of the immense wealth of the southern cities. This comes largely in the form of a quarter of a million people who visit Tōno as tourists every year. They are attracted by the vigorous promotion of its cultural heritage, its careful preservation of historic artefacts, and its reputation for tradition, folktale, and legend.

The older generations still speak in the dialect called Tōno-*ben*. Even for the Japanese, this can be difficult to understand, but to us its tones seemed rich and sweet, measured and slow, and somehow ideally suited to the simple, didactic way of telling stories. Like much that we saw in Tōno, the dialect is unlikely to survive for very much longer. Together with the old farmhouses it will probably disappear with the passing of the older generation. But there is a sense in which these homogenising changes are superficial: they lie like oil on deeper water, sometimes obscuring what goes on beneath, but having little real influence upon it. Our view of Tōno may be a romanticised one and certainly it is different from the world of local government statistics and the sharp analysis of urban and social morphology. Yet it is this view that experience bred and that memory inspires. It is this view too, perhaps, that makes a farmer (only slightly drunk) lie flat on the ground and stare up through the trees at the beauty of the maple in autumn.

preceding pages

I The horizon is serrated with lines of receding hills.

II In the event that grandparents are able to serve as a surrogate, the extent of disapproval is somewhat lessened.

III Families who distinguish little between the old and the new.

IV Many old women are bent double, permanently shaped by a regime of work in the fields.

V These winter conditions preclude farm work.

VI Those few households which continue the tradition of horse breeding do so out of love for the horse.

VII People do not feel the same attachment to tobacco that the rice plant engenders.

2

The *ie* and family life

There was a time when the humanity of foreigners was denied by the Japanese. They were called *anjin*, or 'non-person'. Today, an overseas visitor is *gaijin*, which is best translated as 'outsider'. It implies not merely a different nationality, but one who is unable to enter fully into the experience of the Japanese order of things. Even to approach this experience, as Scott Morton (1974) has said, it is necessary to submit to a 'soaking process' and in so doing to absorb both the physical expressions of Japanese life and the concepts around which it has evolved. This was our purpose in Tōno: to become absorbed in the life of ordinary Japanese families; to observe the ceremonies and symbols that punctuate or accompany routine; and to allow the integrity of personal intuition to accommodate a translation from a Western viewpoint to an Eastern one.

The immediate difficulties were practical. The most important factor, which was impossible to ensure in advance, was the element of good fortune which led us to people who were prepared to help. And it seems to be in the nature of rural Japanese society that it is open to this kind of observation, for it thrives on trust, and people respond warmly and wholeheartedly to a genuine willingness to share and to participate. Our immediate arrangements in Tōno were made by the local Education Committee. They envisaged trial periods of three months each, in four separate volunteer households. In the event, though, we were never to move. Our very first family accepted their foreign charges with an ease that allowed the three-month period to come and go virtually without comment, in true Japanese style. As plans were laid for the coming year it quickly became apparent that the *gaijin* had been accepted and might, if they wished, continue to live with their foster family.

In hindsight it is clear that our fortune could not have been better. Three or four months were required to allow everyone to get used to the initial intrusion; and frequent moves would have destroyed the continuity of experience which proved so valuable. Neighbours and friends were at first surprised by the growing trust which the family displayed for its foreign visitors, but this was to give way to curiosity and then to confidence, and so to a wider and more elaborate network of help and of information. The family name proved to be a passport into other parts of society in Tōno, reflecting the importance of having contacts and references in all aspects of Japanese life. From the first day we were encouraged to call the family by the names they used amongst themselves. Being senior in years to the son, I was thus able to call him by his first name and not the sibling term *oniisan* (older brother) which for example his sister used. Gradually it was explained to us that, just as we came under the protection of the household gods, so too we bore some responsibility to the good name and fortunes of our family.

The family spoke in Japanese at all times. They encouraged our learning of the standard language (*hyōjungo*) which we had pursued in England and subsequently in Tokyo. But in addition they also introduced us to much of the local dialect. Although this sometimes provoked amusement amongst other Japanese friends, it also made it much easier to understand and to be understood in the course of everyday conversation. For the same reason, too, the most fruitful work probably took place towards the end of our stay. Yet eighteen months in the same household gave an excellent opportunity to see the annual round of ceremonial activity unfold and to share in some of the less predictable experiences in the family life-cycle. Two of these were especially important. The first was the marriage of *oniisan* which allowed intimate observation of the associated ceremonies. The second was involvement in the construction of a new house. This came about as a consequence of meeting the man who had built our own family's home and who, because of his keen interest in cultural matters, was willing to become both a confidant and a good friend. Horiuchi *san* gave a unique insight into the meaning and significance of building practice and ceremonial symbolism, not only at the site of one of his new houses but also in the meticulous diagrams which he used to teach his ignorant pupil. He also provided a link between the host household and a wider local context since he came from a valley noted for its old farmhouses. More than most, indeed, he had played an active part in shaping the changing local scene.

Being an outsider in the small community of Tōno had other peculiar advantages. We were a focus of general curiosity. We became, in a minor way, 'media celebrities', and any local group who wanted to give their sports day, or soccer league, or cookery class, or festival, something of an 'international' flavour invariably invited our participation. In this way we were able to repay some of the immense kindness shown to us. This then is how the study progressed: designed, as it were, to be design-free, it developed as a communal effort built on the painstaking explanations of friends and the outcome of numerous social gatherings. Certainly it is difficult to envisage a different, or more enjoyable, way of approaching the Japanese experience of *ie*.

It is with this concept of the *ie* that this chapter is concerned. We begin by considering the nature of the concept and in this we rely on the work of both Eastern and Western scholars. We then turn to an account of family organisation and to a consideration of the terms of address that are used between family members since, in many ways, these forms of address seem to reveal something of the essential *ie* structure. Next, we say something of the general character of relations in the Japanese household and, finally, we describe some of the quite mundane, but none the less important, features of daily life within the home as we were able to observe them.

The *ie*

It is extremely difficult to render the Japanese concept of *ie* in succinct Western terms. Yet an understanding of it seems critical to an understanding of many aspects of family and social life and structure in Japan. As it is used at the present time it denotes the relationships which exist within, and to some extent between, Japanese families. Following Fukutaka (1972), therefore, Hendry (1981) suggests that its nearest equivalent in English is the concept of 'House' as it is used in 'House of Windsor'. The most obvious difference, however, is that in Japan the idea of *ie* does not denote a set of relationships of such exquisite exclusivity. It implies rather the basic organising principles around which Japanese family life has evolved. Moreover, despite the changes which modernisation is bringing to many aspects of traditional Japanese life, the structural patterns that are embodied in the *ie* continue to exercise great influence. This applies not only at the level of kinship relations but also, as Lebra (1976) has shown, at the scale of social organisation more generally.

The problems of adequately accommodating the translation of the *ie* concept are therefore considerable and, as Befu (1971) observes, the difficulties can generate confusion. Thus, although an important element in *ie* tradition is the continuity of residence in the same place and the communality of *ie* living, its essence cannot be accurately conveyed by resort to words like 'house' or 'home' or 'household'. These are embodied more clearly by the Japanese term *setai*. Nor can we turn to the word 'family' since, as Hall and Beardsley (1952) point out, the word *kazoku* was taken up by nineteenth-century Japanese scholars to translate 'family' *from* European languages. In a literal sense it means 'house-belongers' but in common usage it refers to 'a domestic unit composed of individuals related by blood or marriage' (Befu, 1971). Recognising these difficulties, Befu

31

(1971) offered the translation 'stem family', but since this is a notion which lacks appropriate correlates in everyday Western experience it remains tied to translation through description. In the main, therefore, after elaborating this description, we will refer directly to the *ie* and resort to other terms like 'household' and 'family' principally for the sake of variety.

We may begin to understand the *ie* by observing two basic principles of its structure. First, it embodies the notion of a genealogical line extending from the past, through the present, and into the future. Second, it observes the practice of primogeniture and patrilineal descent which, at least formally, subordinates the status of women in Japanese society (Fukutake, 1972; Befu, 1971; Kitano, 1962). Its most distinctive feature, however, is that the goal of the *ie* is to perpetuate itself 'as a unit independent of its constituent members' (Lebra, 1976). In this sense it has been likened to a corporation. Just as a corporation will find means to dispense with the services of the inept, the inefficient, or the recalcitrant in its own best interests, so too the *ie* finds means to ensure its all-important continuity, even to the extent of sacrificing biological kinship in the event of a failure in the bloodline. As Befu (1971) says, therefore, the relationship of genealogy and the *ie* is one of expediency: 'The two need not be conterminous, that is, blood-line may be continued even after the family name and occupation have been changed and, conversely, the family name and occupation may be continued not only by the eldest son but by someone else.' The rural *ie* was traditionally a corporate residential group rather than simply a house shared by generations of related family members. In the pre-modern period the economic activity of the group was of central importance (Befu, 1971). The kinship ties could be 'real or fictive' (Lebra, 1976) and this fictive element could be expressed in a number of different ways. The most immediate was the practice of incorporating non-kin, usually employees of one kind or another, into the *ie*. In Befu's (1971) view this 'blurring of the demarcation line between kin and non-kin' found wider expression in the early modern period in the 'efflorescence of ritual kinship' of the kind that Lebra (1976) calls 'simulated kinship'. At the same time, it also illustrates the willing subordination of kin interests to the interests and effectiveness of the *ie* as a whole since non-kin members were an important economic element in rural *ie* life. Even more unusual, in the Western view, is the practice of inviting an outsider to take over and carry forward the *ie* line in the absence of a male heir. The adoption of a 'foster-groom-son' or *muko yōshi* again illustrates the way in which continuity of the *ie* name transcends the kinship relations of its members. The difficulty, of course, is to find a *muko yōshi* who is willing to give deference to a group identity above his own (Befu, 1962). More unusual even than the marrying-in of a new son and heir is the practice reported by

Takeuchi (1959). Here, a complete stranger may be encouraged to take-up the family name of a line which has long since dwindled, in a process called *saiken* or 're-establishment'. A further variation, again unusual, is for an outsider to be persuaded to take on the family name of an *ie* on the verge of bankruptcy in return for assuming its debts. He becomes the 'buyer-adoptive-son' or *kaiyōshi* but, as Befu (1962) notes, he need not move into the family home.

There were other alternatives too for the preservation of *ie* continuity and, like the ones mentioned above, they centred usually on the acquisition of a male heir by one means or another. This is not to suggest that these practices were necessarily commonplace, and they are certainly rare today, but each of them reflects the overriding importance of the *ie* above that of its members and their kinship ties. In particular, as writers like Hendry (1981) have pointed out, the idea of succession is bound up with an active locating of the living family with respect to ancestors and to those not yet born. A constant reminder of this is the *butsudan* or Buddhist altar in which the memory of *ie* forebears is enshrined. Its presence affirms that, as Hendry (1981) says, the continuity of the *ie* is 'independent of those individuals who pass through'. It is thus preserved by ideas and principles, whether these are defined 'from the outside' (by the objective concept of primogeniture for instance), or defined simply in the things that people do.

The same theme of individual subordination emerges with regard to the traditional practice of arranged marriages. This is called *miai*, which means 'mutual viewing' and which stems from the custom of allowing the parties to the marriage to meet each other before the event through the services of a 'go-between' (Hendry, 1981). Western ideas of romantic marriage, called *ren'ai*, had no place in pre-War Japan and, despite post-war constitutional changes designed to allow unions of this kind, the older ways have proved remarkably resilient and resistant to change (Hendry, 1981; Fukutake, 1972). The reasons, again, seem to lie in the relationship of the act of marriage to the fortunes of the *ie* as a whole. Hendry (1981) identifies two general areas of concern which seem to influence Japanese practice. The first is the matter of the social standing of the *ie* and the need to preserve this standing 'by the choice of a suitable alliance'. The second, which was particularly important amongst poorer families, was the selection of an industrious partner to contribute to the economic wellbeing of the *ie*. At the same time, however, she notes the emphatic view that the 'main object of marriage was the perpetuation of the family line, not love, but the provision of an heir'. To the extent that these factors still obtain extensively in Japan the act of marriage is seen essentially as a linking of two *ie* rather than a union of lovers. Moreover, the contrast between the mutual sharing and personal discovery of the idealised Western relationship and the seemingly contractual arranged marriage of Japan under-scores once more the barrier of translation between 'household' and *ie*.

The influences which are embodied in the arrangement of marriages bring out something of the character of Japanese rural society in general, its conservatism, its pragmatism, and its concern with social respectability and hierarchy. And, just as these qualities are preserved in the internal relationships of the *ie*, they are also reflected in its external relationships. In northern Honshū the most important of these external relationships resided in the rural *dōzoku* system (Befu, 1971). In pre-modern times the *dōzoku* was a complex of kinship ties, social duties, and economic bonds between a senior household, called *honke*, and a number of subordinate branch households, called *bunke*. In some circumstances these branch households might simultaneously be the *honke* of others. As a system it has been well documented and its ideological origins have generated con-siderable debate (among others Befu, 1971, 1963; Brown, 1968, 1966; Nakane, 1967; Kitano, 1951; Ariga, 1943). But whether its evolution reflected the primacy of economic ties between rural families, or whether it reflected the primacy of descent patterns, it seems clear that, like the *ie*, its meaning was worked out in functional terms. Thus, although some of its rationale seems to be derived from principles of genealogy, non kin-related *ie* were frequently drawn into its structure where this improved the econo-mic opportunities of the group or contributed to its continuity (Befu, 1962). In modern Japan, however, the *dōzoku* system has become diluted and many of the functional connections between *honke* and *bunke* have been lost. Economic ties have largely disintegrated and the political sup-remacy of the main household is no longer significant. None the less the *dōzoku* survives in rural Japan, at least in the minds of many of the people there, and amongst some *ie* it still finds expression in the ritual remem-brance of ancestors and guardian deities (Befu, 1971).

There are, therefore, two overriding characteristics that attach to the concept of the *ie* and that are partly reflected in the relicts of *dōzoku*. The first is that the principles which appear to govern *ie* structure may be openly contradicted in their own interests. That is to say, for example, that genealogy, primogeniture, patrilineal descent and so forth are liable to subordination in the interests of *ie* continuity. Second, in those same interests there is a willing submission of individuality and a resigned acceptance of roles and status without which the *ie* could not survive. Yet it is apparent that these seeming inconsistencies have a functional purpose that is worked out with a profound pragmatism and that imposes a particularly Japanese view upon the idea of individuality and the concept of duty. Our presence in the Tada *ie* was an attempt to penetrate its experience rather than dissemble its structure.

34

Family organisation and naming

The changes which the demands of contemporary society are bringing to the life of the traditional rural *ie* have been noted by many observers (among others, Nakane, 1967; Fukutake, 1972; Vogel, 1967). Yet it seems clear that a number of general principles still govern its organisation, and that these principles have so far resisted dilution and redefinition. The primacy of men and the respect due to age are the most obvious ones, although Hall and Beardsley (1959) also point to the distinction between those who are born within the *ie* and those who enter it by virtue of an exogenous connection. The latter, clearly, touched upon our own status as 'outsiders' within the Tada *ie*. One way of explaining this status, and the changes which affected it as familiarity and intimacy grew, would be in terms of the dichotomies of *uchi–soto* (inside–outside) and *omote–ura* (public–private) which Lebra (1976) has elaborated in her discussion of social relativism in Japanese society. But, useful though such a character-isation might be, it cannot adequately reflect the subtlety of our private/public relations and responsibilities in the Tada *ie*. At first, for example, we were treated with the deference which is traditionally given to guests and which is necessarily imbued with a measure of formality. As the months passed, however, increasing familiarity caused our status to change. A developing bond of affection transcended our distinction as *gaijin* within the *ie*, yet our origins ensured the persistence of a public gaze and increased our awareness of responsibilities which extended beyond the nuclear support of our own mutual relationship. We also continued to be dependent upon others, largely through our linguistic incompetence. It was, perhaps, this feature of our life in Tōno which enabled the most substantial modification in our status as guests. Doi (1973) might char-acterise this dependence by resort to the term *amae* which implies a degree of presumption upon another's goodwill and which is often used to des-cribe a relationship between children and parents. It is interesting, in this regard, that towards the end of our stay the family concluded that it had been as though a daughter of theirs had married a *gaijin*. This feeling came out one mealtime, for example, when the father cautioned me to take care of my wife on a planned walking expedition. His remarks caused some hilarity because, it was agreed, he had appeared to address the husband of a daughter rather than an 'outsider'.

The nuances of status and interpersonal relationships within the *ie* are visible within the basic rules of naming. In 1962 Smith and Beardsley noted the resistance to change of the kinship terminology in Japanese households. This resistance is still apparent, particularly in front of chil-dren or outsiders when familiar terms must be complemented or replaced by those demanded by politeness or respect for elders (Hendry, 1981). In this way, for example, outsiders may be shown extreme deference either through the use of honorific terms of address, or by adopting a humble form of language when referring to one's own group. Moreover, the act of naming gives each member of the family a place within the structure of the *ie* and this finds expression in the roles and expectations which follow from *being* called 'father' or 'son'. But the *ie* structure is not a simple hierarchy culminating in the position of the 'head': it stretches out to an intangible past and future. Translated into intense feelings of duty and responsibility, it is one way in which the individual relates to the group. Thus children grow into a powerful sense of belonging which is expressed in the term *uchi* (in, inside) and which is the embodiment of the *ie*: indeed it is possible to write both words in the same way.

In characterising the organisation of the *ie* Hall and Beardsley (1959) emphasise the distinction between those who join and those who leave. The ones who join are the women who marry either a former head of the *ie*, an existing head of the *ie*, or a future head of the *ie*. In a household of three generations, they will be grandmother, mother and young wife respectively. Those who leave will be daughters and younger sons. *Ie* continuity, therefore, resides in the grandfather, the father, and the eldest son and in the continued presence of ancestral spirits. Hendry (1981) lays great emphasis on the facts of birth and death to emphasise the infinite quality of *ie* conception. Beyond the death line are ancestors from a seemingly limitless past. They are called *senzo*. The more recently deceased are identified as *hotoke*. At any given time the *ie* may be constituted along the lines described by Hall and Beardsley (1959). But by including also a 'birth line' Hendry (1981) is able to suggest the anticipation of descendants (*shison*) which, in the minds of *ie* members, provides temporal perspective on their own transient roles.

These structures are not merely abstractions. It was striking, for example, that everyone in the Tada *ie* had a clear picture of it which resembled Hendry's model. It was also worked out quite clearly in the matter of daily routine and expected behaviour. The elder son actually said to us that he saw himself as a link in a chain between his predecessors and children. His father, the incumbent head of the *ie*, showed evidence of the same sentiment in a different way. For some time he had been thinking about having the tombstone of his ancestors moved from an earlier site thirty kilometres away to a site nearer the present home. The stone recorded the memory of his parents and a sister who had died in infancy. During early 1982 it also became evident that his son wished to marry, and this major event occupied increasing attention as the year wore on. From our Western vantage the marriage seemed incomparably the most important of the two acts.

The father, however, insisted that they were of at least equal significance. By bringing the tombstone closer to home he wanted to encourage his son's interest in this part of the *ie*. The completion of the expensive and complicated business of moving the stone in time for the summer festival of *obon* caused a rare smile of satisfaction to cross his face.

The same principle of continuity is embodied in the household Buddhist altar, the *butsudan* which draws upon itself a variety of activities which may be called 'ritual' but which are certainly not doctrinaire. For the Japanese the experience of the *butsudan* resides in the practices which attach to it: it is not an object for reflection or debate. In this way departed ancestors continue to live as real members of the *ie*: in Befu's (1971) words, 'they provide moral guidance to the living', and are 'very much a part of the family, as they were before their death' (Plate VIII). This was apparent to us as we watched the grandmother sitting for long minutes on the ornate cushion in front of the *butsudan*, quietly conversing with her husband (some years deceased), asking advice, seeking consent, or simply offering the first fruits of a recent gift. The existence of the Buddhist altar and the significance of the tombstone underline the importance of having a *real* means of instilling the principles of the *ie*. And it is this process that is carried over into the act of naming.

In many *ie* three or four generations may live together. Terms of address and reference within and outside of the *ie* are shown in Table 1. It could be expected that as a result of the ageing process the transition which takes place as a father gives way as *ie* head to his son might be an important event. From the evidence available, however, it appears that the transition is usually gradual and effected without great disruption. Nakane (1967), for example, has emphasised the extent to which the *ie* as a corporate economic unit is able to respond to the changing capabilities of different contributors and also the way in which the succession rule 'amalgamates the statuses of father and (successor) son into one continuum'. Thus, despite its significance for the external relationships of the *ie* and the relations among *ie* members, it does not appear to be a source of strain or tension between father and son. This probably reflects the differential socialisation of the heir (Befu, 1971) and the mutuality of the father's role in the process. Though Nakane (1967) implies otherwise, our own experience suggested that the retired head continued to play an active role in decisions affecting the *ie*: increasing age bringing with it a status which was different but none the less real. It is likely that in this regard, as in the matter of inheritance and succession rules (Hendry, 1981), there is considerable variation between households.

With the arrival of children in the household the father becomes, for them, *jiichan* or, more politely, *ojiisan*. If the *san* suffix is replaced by

Table 1: Terms of address and terms of reference

Position	Familiar address (within the *ie*)	Polite address (outside the *ie*)	Humble reference (within the *ie*)
grandfather	*jiichan*	*ojiisan*	*sofu*
grandmother	*bāchan*	*obāsan*	*sobo*
father	*tōchan*	*otōsan*	*chichi*
mother	*kāchan*	*okāsan*	*haha*
eldest son	name	*chōnansan*	*chōnan*
elder brother	*niichan* name	*oniisan*	*ani*
second son	name	*jinansan*	*jinan*
younger brother	name	*otōtosan*	*otōto*
eldest sister	*nēchan* name	*onēsan*	*ane*
elder daughter	name	*chōjosan*	*chōjo*
younger daughter	name	*musumesan*	*jijo*
younger sister	name	*imōtosan*	*imōto*
children	name	*kodomosan*	(boy) *otoko-no-ko* (girl) *onna-no-ko*
grandchild	name	*magosan*	*mago*
young wife	name	*oyomesan*	*yome*
husband	name	*shujinsan* *dannasan*	*shujin* *danna*
ancestors		(*hotokesama*)	*senzo*

Descriptive terms (functional)

Role	Name	Status
ancestors	*senzo*	forebears
grandfather	*inkyo*	retired
father	*shujin*	*ie* head
elder son	*chōnan*	first son
younger son	*jinan*	second son
elder daughter	*chōjo*	first daughter
younger daughter	*jijo*	second daughter
mother	*kanai*	wife

sama, however, the implication is derogatory. *Sama* is the most polite form of *san*, and is used for example in 'king' (*ōsama*). In familiar circumstances such over-politeness implies mockery. Grandmothers are *obasān* and many women, including the mother of our household, look forward to the birth of a grandchild because of the feeling of establishment and success which the event confers on the *ie*. The words *obāsan* and *obāchan* are quite difficult for small children to pronounce: they are allowed to use the diminutive *baba*, though this is only rarely acceptable amongst adults because it can have connotations that are either humorous or insulting. Children are also allowed to elaborate the basic form of address in ways which reveal the depth of affection within the *ie*. One grandmother who would immediately recognise this reference is called *ume-bāchan* by her grandchildren. Her first name is *Umeko* and her face, especially after a little rice-wine, easily brings to mind the *ume*, a bright red plum.

The father in a Japanese household is called *otōsan*, and by children *tōchan*. Familiar speech thus eliminates the need for the honorific *o* prefix and *san* suffix. In the local dialect of our own area *otōsan* could also be rendered as *todo* and it is not unusual to hear the European corruption *papa* which slips easily into Japanese pronunciation. Although the dialect equivalent now seems to be acceptable in polite speech, the European version is still generally discouraged. The father may also be described as *setai nushi*, head of the home or dwelling; as *shujin*, 'head of the home'; or as *koshu*, 'head of the *ie*'. Hendry (1981) also points to the use of the word *taisho*, meaning 'chief' or 'boss', as an address sometimes used to men in the Japanese household. Each one of these terms reveals the status of the father as leader of the family. In discussing this status the father in our own family said that his role was that of a 'mediator' with the outside world and his symbolic role was revealed on one occasion when he was described as the *Daikoku sama* of the *ie*. *Daikoku sama*, of course, is the name given to the Shinto god of good-fortune, a guardian of the well-being and success of the *ie*. The spirit of *Daikoku sama* is also transferred to the physical form of the house by calling its 'central' supporting pillar the *daikoku bashira*. Just as the *daikoku bashira* symbolically holds up the house, so *otōsan* as *Daikoku sama* embodies within the family the good fortune on which the *ie* depends.

Again, practices may vary in this regard from place to place in Japan. It is interesting, for example, that Hendry (1981), working in the Kyūshū village of Kurotsuchi, records the use of the term *daikoku bashira* to 'emphasise the importance of the role of the younger man' in a situation of emerging succession. In both these different cases, however, the spiritual, spatial, and social aspects of the *ie* are blended together in a tripartite structure in which the name *Daikoku* is superimposed on each manifestation: the god, the man, and the dwelling.

If the father stands between the *ie* and the outside world, then the place of his wife is definitely indoors, at least so far as her public status is concerned. Many writers have documented the inferiority of the woman's position in the traditional Japanese *ie* (Fukutake, 1972) but, as Nakane (1967) has observed, much depends on the economic contribution made by the woman, on competing personal relationships within the household and, critically, on whether or not the woman holds the position of wife to the *ie* head. Moreover, a consideration of the naming of wives allows at least two interpretations. The first sees the role of the wife in a confined and strictly domestic role. It stems from the names *okusan*, which is used in polite speech to address another's wife, and *kanai*, which is used to express 'my wife' from the humble standpoint of *uchi* (the 'inside' of the house). Both words have the same meaning: the *oku* component of *okusan* implies the 'inner recess' of the house, and likewise *kanai* suggests 'inside the house', or 'home', or 'family'. It may be inferred from this that the wife is seen as inhabiting the heart of the *ie*, reflecting something of her real power over domestic matters and implying a degree of dependency on the part of the working husband. Certainly this situation fits more closely with our own intimate experience of life in one Japanese family. It also accords with Nakane's (1967) observation that, despite the 'sociological weakness' of the wife's position, her eventual role as 'mistress of the household' ensures that the 'power and influence of women' is 'discreetly maintained in Japanese society'. For the women of Kurotsuchi, Hendry (1981) points to their important economic role in the household and concludes that 'a household without women ... would be more at a loss than one without men'. It seems likely that behind the traditional inequalities of *otōsan* and *okāsan* there lies a levelling balance of mutual dependence which confirms something of the variety of circumstance summarised by Nakane (1967).

An amusing and not altogether irreverent or irrelevant light is thrown on to the Japanese view of women by the locally-used equivalent of *kanai*. The word is *kakā* and it comes from an oral tradition to which loan characters have subsequently been attached. In this written form it contains the two components 'woman' (*onna*) and 'nose' (hana). *Okāsan* offered two alternative translations of this peculiar word for 'wife'. The first, she said, referred to the proper area of interest for a woman, who should confine her attention to the house. Alternatively, we were told, *kakā* implies that a woman should not come too close to her husband when he returns from evening engagements, lest she guess at his escapades from the smell of perfume on his collar.

From their earliest years children are encouraged to appreciate the guiding principles of age and male superiority by which the *ie* is organised. Naming is an important way of instilling these ideas. The eldest son is shown proper deference by virtue of his role as *kōkeisha* or heir when he is addressed as *oniisan* (or *oniichan*) by his younger siblings. Older children are entitled to use the first names of those who are younger, but in their turn they may expect their own name to carry the suffix *niisan* as a mark of respect (Hendry, 1981). When children describe their position in the family they do this by enumerating themselves in relation to the established hierarchy. A third son, for example, would describe himself as *san-ban-me-no oniisan* or 'number-three-elder-brother'. Within the family younger sons may be called *onji*, which reflects the expectation that they will one day leave the house, and the youngest brother of all may have his status as last and least revealed in the name *mabokochan*. The youngest of all the family's children, whatever the sex, may be called *suekko*. Moreover this hierarchy of names established amongst siblings may persist indefinitely.

Once again, local dialect extends the naming options that are available in the Japanese family. In our own area, for example, *oniisan* may be replaced by '*anko*', and the eldest sister, or *onesan*, may be called '*aneko*'. These acceptable alternatives seem to be a reflection of the common practice of abbreviating a word to suit the *ko* suffix which is widely used in the *Tōno-ben* dialect. It should be said, though, that *aneko* also has the connotation of *jochūsan* or 'maidservant' and it is not always a welcome form of address.

The names used within the *ie* give children some of the ideas of ranking according to age status which are so important in later years and which extend hierarchical concepts beyond the limits of the *ie* itself. In Japan, people age in groups, since there is no attention paid to individual birthdays. On New Year's Day, therefore, everyone in the country ages by one year. This has a profound effect when it is coupled to the duties and responsibilities which age-status confers. In school, for example, it is difficult for a child to form close friendships with anyone who is not of his or her *dōkyūsei*, or same-age group. The persistence of school *dōkyūsei* was revealed to us in 1982 when *otōsan* was busy for some weeks organising a reunion of his old classmates.

An important corollary of this situation is that children are led quickly into the ideas of senior–junior relationships which penetrate all aspects of adult life. Lebra (1976) sees in these *sempai–kōhai* relationships a clear reflection of the family basis of Japanese social structure when she refers to them in terms of 'symbolic filiation'. Such is the sensitivity to rank in Japanese society that there seems to be no incongruity if a man of greater authority seeks the advice or help of a man of lesser authority who also happens to be his *sempai*. Similarly, it is difficult for a *sempai*, as a vicarious older brother, to refuse assistance to his *kōhai* in whatever walk of life these relationships apply. But the duality of responsibility and respect which is implied in *sempai–kōhai* dealings appears simultaneously to inhibit the formation of friendships which cross the barrier of age-status. Thus, although strong group affiliations may be developed with *dōkyūsei*, persistent limits are also created to the expression and meaning

41

of experiences like friendship. On one occasion, for example, a *kōhai* of *otōsan* explained that true friendship between Japanese may take decades to form. The distinguishing feature of this situation is that it is not just an abstraction from Japanese experience, but is an objective part of social relations in the home, in the school and in the wider world of work (Lebra, 1976; Watsuji, 1961).

Family life

The process of naming in the *ie* provides some objective evidence of the way the family sees itself. The relative status implied by fixed terms gives an idea of how people orientate themselves and behave with these in mind. The name *otōsan* thus implies responsibilities and elicits responses because it is one 'place' in a relative structure. The structure itself is not an abstract one, but a real pattern to which people refer, and one which must be upheld and reaffirmed. This is achieved, in part, through the predictable qualities of mundane daily activities. Even the important idea of the ancestral line must, it seems, be brought into real experience by involvement in familiar routine. Moreover, the consistency of that routine allows a sense of group identity to be projected into the future in the belief that things will always be the same. In this way, the basic experiences of living, which can only be described in terms of tastes, objects, or actions, are able to create a feeling of 'home'.

For us, the most remarkable feature of life in the Tada *ie* was the absence of family quarrels or dissent. There were occasional differences of opinion, but these were resolved by traditional reference to status rather than by the merit of argument, or by expediency or wilfulness. For example, the daughter returned home one day with a new hairstyle. Her mother immediately made it clear that the style was unacceptable, given the dignity of her father's role of head of the council's finance department. The girl was not pleased, but she washed out the new hairstyle without hesitation, accepting that her duty to the *ie* would not permit her to jeopardise her father's standing in the community.

Japanese commentators frequently refer to this awareness on the part of the individual of a wider responsibility to the *ie* as a whole. They turn to a variety of concepts to reveal its nature. Befu (1971), for example, uses the quality of *on*, which can be translated as 'duty', but which Hendry (1981) conveys more aptly as 'grace'. She also points out that the source of affection in the *ie*, called *aijō*, is principally defined by the relationship between parent and child rather than husband and wife. This particular relationship, discussed by Doi (1973) and Lebra (1976), centres on the idea of *amaeru* which means 'to make allowance for'. As Hamaguchi (1980) says in his study of *aidagara* (the quality of mutual relationship), relations within the family and in Japanese society as a whole have traditionally been described in terms of these two supporting concepts of 'duty' and 'allowance'. The idea of duty involves an inescapable feeling of indebtedness which must be fulfilled and which binds one person to another. Simultaneously, it is balanced by the indulgence of *amaeru*, mirroring the relationship of parent and child, and reflecting in an important way upon the nature of marriage in the context of the *ie*.

As Hendry (1981) emphasises, marriage is a continual theme in conversation, because it is within the institution of marriage that children are born and families are projected into the future. As outsiders it came as an occasionally irritating surprise to be repeatedly asked *why*, after a few years of marriage, we had no children. 'Surely', people said, 'you have children, perhaps in England?.' In the light of questions like this, the importance of children to the idea of the *ie* becomes very immediate. In European terms it can also be argued that this central concern is the source of strong relationships between husbands and wives. This can be seen in the popular saying *kodomo wa kazoku no kasugai desu*, or 'a child is the clamp which binds together the family'. But in the Japanese household the role of marriage and the significance of children can be attributed partly to the structure of the *ie* itself, but also to the experiences which that structure releases in the individual.

Living in the Tada *ie* suggested to us that it was not possible to understand family relationships by mapping the idea of parent–child relations from a Western viewpoint. In a situation where three generations live together the bond between parent and child, at least for the eldest son, is never broken. Most of his life will be spent in the company of his parents, under the same roof, and probably an equally large part will be spent in the company of his own eldest son, also under the same roof. Even after the death of his parents, the *butsudan* will be there as a tangible reminder of their continued influence. It is in the evidence of unbroken bonding of this kind, reflected in other aspects of life too, that the key to the *ie* seems to lie. Thus, in our own household, the strongest relationships were those between father and son, and mother and daughter. To some extent these two sets of relationships reflected common interests which were defined by outside values. The son, who would one day inherit his father's role in the household, obviously admired the older man's status and achievements. The daughter, on the other hand, knew that she was expected to marry out of the home and this gave her a common bond with her mother who had long ago done the same thing. None of this is to suggest that the parents did not share a warm relationship themselves, but the overwhelming impression was that this was defined by a common goal rather than something which stemmed from ideas of sharing, or fulfilment or equality.

Our own experiences confirm Lebra's (1976) assertion, that the Japanese 'are extremely sensitive to and concerned about social interaction and relationships'. Moreover, the kernel around which many of these wider 'social preoccupations' have developed seems arguably to have been the influence of relationships in the *ie*. In one sense, then, the *ie* serves as a model, or at least as an important point of reference, for the conduct of social relations generally. Simultaneously, the integrity of the *ie* is bolstered by the broader social environment of which it is a part. This means, for example, that it is difficult in rural Japan for a son or daughter to reject the values of family life. The same patterns of status which are identifiable in the home are applied in school and at work. The individual, therefore, is unable to escape into an alternative frame because the 'space' to do so simply does not exist. Thus school-life fosters a bond of group identity in the same way that domestic life does. It is achieved through the encouragement of extra-mural activities, through the persistence of *dōkyūsei*, and through the opportunities for developing lasting *sempai–kōhai* relationships. Most important of all, perhaps, is the powerful respect for hierarchy, viewed as a function of sex, or age, or social status. A vivid example of this occurred in the *dōkyūsei* group of *oniisan*. A former schoolfriend failed the council's entrance examinations and could work there only on a part-time basis. *Oniisan*, on the other hand, had been successful in the same examination and, like his father, was employed full-time. The outcome was that the 'frame' or group-background of *oniisan* and his friend were changed: the familiarity and equality of their schooldays was no longer appropriate and their social life thereafter was spent in the company of different peer-groups.

The constraint imposed by this respect for social hierarchies leaves little opportunity for the open development of personal relationships in the accepted European sense. This applies even to young men and women, who may meet informally as members of different-sex groups, but who seem to find a stronger bonding with their own group than with members of the opposite sex. Even in late teenage, for example, boys are very close and it is common to see friends walking together with the arm of one draped over the shoulder of the other. So it is that the traditional route to marriage is one that is arranged (*miai*), often with the help of a 'go-between' (*nakōdo*). Even after marriage the public socialising of man and wife is restricted. At the bar owned by *okāsan*'s friend, the Revoir, it was thus usual to see men arrive in groups to drink, to sing to taped music (the popular *karaoke*), and to dance with the 'hostesses' there. This was all perfectly respectable. The men felt no shame and no guilt, and the 'hostesses' bore no stigma for their work. For an outsider, raised in a quite different ethos, however, the conviviality seemed false: the open and frank mixing of the sexes merely disguised for a time the impossible barrier that lay between them.

Even in the house it seems common for some men to assert their authority over their wives, at least in front of friends. She may be treated, in the words of the popular saying, as simply a source of 'tea, food, bath and bed' (*ocha, meshi, furō, futon*). On occasion it was possible to see some of the anecdotal stories realised: a wife fetching her husband's newspaper though it lay within arm's reach, or a pregnant woman hurrying to serve her man whilst he proclaimed himself '*samurai*' in his own home. But it is an inevitably corollary of this kind of behaviour that the character of the wife's response can considerably damage her husband's standing amongst his friends. In a society which places such emphasis on these matters this is another source of intrinsic strength in the position of women within the *ie*. The role of obedient wife is played out, or so it seemed to us, because it is proper to do so and because it is in the interests of the *ie* as a whole.

There are times, of course, when the harmonious relationship of marriage is severely strained. Sometimes this leads to divorce, but in contrast to most modern countries the divorce rate in Japan seems to have fallen in the postwar period (Befu, 1967). Hendry's (1981) detailed study of Kurotsuchi found no recent divorces there and only a very low overall divorce rate since 1945. For Tōno we have no comparable figures, but we were able to observe a response to domestic stress which reveals something of the orderliness, openness and social relativism of rural Japan. The father of our household had once acted as go-between in arranging the marriage of a younger couple. He had become their *sempai* and when, after twelve years of marriage, the wife became distressed by her husband's persistent drinking and gambling, it was natural for her to turn to *otōsan* for help. Seemingly it was not the first time that her husband's behaviour had edged the family close to financial ruin and public humiliation. A meeting was arranged between the younger couple and the Tadas. Seated around the *kotatsu* in the best room of the house, the problem was discussed openly and without shame, and although we were not privy to the content of the meeting, it was clear from their subsequent behaviour that the warmth and trust between *otōsan* and his erring colleague continued unaffected.

One other, to us, touching sequence of events illustrates very clearly something of the relativism and the situational nature of *ie* life in rural Japan. From an early stage it was clear that the Tada children, the son and his younger sister, enjoyed a very close relationship, talking together often and sharing the gossip of their respective groups. Gradually we learned

45

that, during his time as a student at university in Tokyo, *oniisan* had received extensive help from his sister. She had cooked and cleaned for him and she had even supplied part of her income from evening work to supplement his diet and to enable him to participate fully in the important university football team. Such practical devotion, we thought, would be reciprocated when the sister moved to Tokyo to work. After all, we reasoned, she had moved in part because he had married and her room was part of the quarters of the young couple. We were wrong. Both sister and brother understood perfectly and accepted absolutely that their duties and responsibilities differed. The help which she had afforded was no more than the help which was due to the next head of the *ie*. For his part, the commitments of the *kōkeisha* did not include supporting relatives who were away from home. In so far as she relied upon anyone, *oniisan*'s sister relied upon her mother and grandmother, and neither sought nor expected assistance from her brother.

Being a member of the *ie*, therefore, entails an awareness of responsibilities and a consciousness of place to which the individual constantly refers. From our own experience the results were entirely harmonious, but at the same time they were far removed from our own Westernised ideals. There was no room for the individuality which might colour life with heated discussion. There was no room, either, for the passionate avowal of beliefs or for expressive emotion. In consequence, there was little opportunity for the development of alternative qualities, or values, or ideas, whatever their merit. Instead, there was a strong feeling of restraint, a degree of formality, and a recognition of duty which allowed the integrity of the *ie* to be preserved through the willing conformity of its members.

The Tada *ie* could not be said to be an example of a typical rural family. Both father and son were 'salary-men', employed in local government, and the mother runs a small shop and dressmaking business. Moreover, the father's position with the local council, called *shiyaku-shō*, is an important one: he is head of the finance department and in consequence enjoys considerable status in the town. Yet for all of them, the rural context of their life and work was very apparent. During the period of our stay, for example, *otōsan* was heavily engaged in preparing compensation claims and negotiating financial aid for the local farmers who had suffered severely as a result of a succession of poor harvests. The mother understood these problems only too well since she came from an influential family with a farming background. For his part, *otōsan* found most of his companionship amongst men who divided their time between council duties and farm work.

The ubiquity of these rural connections, even for so ostensibly 'modern' a family, seemed to enhance the consistency of other aspects of daily life.

Social relations in the household, for example, were governed very much by tradition rather than by expediency or wilfulness. To us, as outsiders, the implicit acceptance of relative status, which virtually eliminated conflict or dissent within the *ie*, was genuinely remarkable. Everyone combined expected roles and particular duties in a way which brought an element of formality to the domestic scene but which also conveyed a powerful impression of individuals subordinating themselves to the *ie* and actively striving for its common good. For the father and son in particular this service to the *ie* was largely rendered by fulfilling work commitments and preserving social affiliations that took them away from the house and away from their immediate family. In consequence both head and heir of the Tada *ie* lacked contact with the day-to-day matters of the household. These responsibilities devolved on the mother. But, again, our family was not necessarily typical. *Okāsan's* small dressmaking business and shop occupied a considerable part of her day and was a lively gathering-place for groups of women. In addition to ensuring the significance of her own economic status within the family, it also meant that in practical terms she drew heavily on the support of her mother-in-law in running the home. In this regard we were to observe none of the traditional 'conflict between the Japanese mother-in-law and daughter-in-law' (Nakane, 1967), although it needs to be said that *okāsan* had long ago assumed the status and authority of mistress to the *ie*.

Our family, therefore, was not typical in the sense that it was not a farming family. It was also a relatively affluent one, well known in Tōno, and respected because of the status of *otōsan*. The exceptional presence of *gaijin* also focused a degree of curiosity on the household that may not otherwise have been apparent. Yet the family remained very much a part of a rural community, reflecting in its relationships the surviving values of *ie* tradition which had an essentially rural origin, and conforming in its day-to-day routine to the same basic patterns of life that might be observed anywhere in rural Japan. Coming to terms with family relationships and with the ideas which underpin them is a slow process of revelation and realisation. Coming to terms with the routines of the day must, of necessity, be much more rapid. With growing experience, however, it is not difficult to see in the latter persistent echoes of the former.

On the farms in summer people are in the fields by five in the morning, able to enjoy three hours of cool at the start of the day. The Tada *ie* rises later, but still between 5.30 a.m. and 6.30 a.m. The first task of the day is to boil water to make green tea (*ocha*) and to fill a large thermos for the morning. Traditionally, it seems to have been the responsibility of the young wife to rise first and to set rice to steam over an open hearth in the outer kitchen. In most homes now electric or gas steamers work through the night, and the day begins with the thick, sweet smell of already-steamed rice. *Oba–san* rose first and usually placed the first bowl of rice and the first cup of tea on the *butsudan* altar. A little later both she and *okāsan* would pay their respects in front of the *kamidana* Shinto shrine by pausing, bowing, and clapping twice. One of their first jobs was to prepare lunchboxes. The ones that we saw most often were two-tiered and made of plastic. The lower tray was invariably filled with steamed rice, while the upper tray carried some complementary salted fish, or meat, or cold omelette with salt pickles. Sometimes a fermented plum, called *ume-boshi*, was set in the rice. Its vivid red stain was said to create a resemblance to the national flag.

Breakfast tastes varied. The older generation, father, mother, and grandmother preferred traditional Japanese fare of rice, raw egg, soya-bean soup and green tea, often using leavings from the previous evening meal. The son and daughter, however, liked European-style fried eggs (called *me-dama* or 'eyeball') with thick sliced bread, coffee, and yoghurt. On most mornings *otōsan* would sit at the low, heated *kotatsu* table whilst his son ate at the kitchen table. The women waited until the men had left before sitting down to their own breakfast. This timing fitted neatly with the first of the day's television serials, during which the evening meal was planned. The television was usually switched on very early in the morning. There are approximately eighteen hours of programmes on every channel, and television sets are to be found in shops, banks, offices, and railway stations. The early news reports, set against the background of the city commuter rush, enhance the feeling that throughout Japan the working day is beginning.

Although the grandmother in our family was in her seventy-seventh year, she still had a number of duties within the home which she started after *okāsan* had left for her shop. If it was a fine day she would air the *futon* sleeping quilts over the hot tiles of the lower roof. Other mattresses would be packed away and she would open room partitions and screens to the outside and sweep out the dust which came principally from old *tatami* mats. During the day, though, she had an opportunity to relax, sleeping or watching television at the *kotatsu*. Sometimes the rattle of screens would announce a visitor at the *genkan* (hallway) and send her running for slippers and out to the door exclaiming *Hai*! ('yes!'). After a brief formal greeting she would settle with her friend at the *kotatsu* to talk and enjoy green tea. Later in the day she would clean out the bath in readiness for the evening. Paraffin, for heating the rooms in winter and for heating the hot water boiler needed for the bath, would be carried in from the large storage tank outside. This chore also fell to her, even when her grandchildren were in the house. Indeed, it seems to be a general feature of Japanese

48

life that old people remain as active as possible for as long as health permits, particularly when there are young children in the family and where both parents are at work. In the farming *ie* it is common to see children in the fields in the care of their grandmother (Plates X, XI).

Early evening is one of the busiest times in the Tada *ie*. There were many visitors and they often brought gifts for the family, either to express thanks for a favour or to initiate a request for a favour yet to be granted. The exchange of gifts in this way is an important feature of daily life in Japan: people buy boxed sets of whisky, coffee, fine cooking oil, and the like, and these are set aside by the recipients and may even be re-used as gifts to others. Often, they are piled round the *butsudan*, partly in offering but also as a form of acknowledgement or display.

Early evening is also one of the few times when the entire family is gathered in one place as the women prepare and serve dinner. Most people seem to prefer fresh food, particularly fish, *tōfu* and vegetables purchased daily in lively local shops. Rice is the staple, of course, and this alone is usually delivered in twenty-kilo sacks. Together with soup, it is eaten from a bowl while accompanying dishes are served on small plates. Each person seems to have his or her own crockery and the men of the household have extra-large rice bowls called *donburi*. Partly by virtue of the way it is served, the preparation of food involves none of the skills of timing which are required to bring hot cooked meat and vegetables to the same plate at the same time. Western dishes, when they are served, are treated in the same way as Japanese ones, with the result that they are often cold.

It is clear, for example from the work of Cornell (1955) in the village of Matsunagi, that mealtime seating arrangements can be of considerable significance in reflecting authority and status within the *ie*. Our own experience revealed a greater degree of informality, although the women of the household certainly clustered at one end of the table in the 'humble' position nearest to the kitchen. The men never served themselves, and there was an element of competition between mother and grandmother in attending to the needs of *otōsan* and *oniisan*. My wife, too, was expected to treat me in the same way and any neglect on her part would summon a reminder from *okāsan* that she should pay attention to the amount of rice in my bowl, or beer in my glass. It was also possible to observe some rules of etiquette which have superstitious connotations. For example, it is bad luck for a couple to cross chop sticks when taking food from the central bowl, and in deference to the old Buddhist codes, food should never be pierced. There was a time when the enforcement of these codes forbade meat-eating entirely. This meant that families owned no frying utensils, but in the pragmatic way of country folk, we were told, meat continued to be cooked surreptitiously on farm tools like spades.

Of all the family members only *otōsan* was able to take a little food before the meal began. This always started with thanks to the gods, *itadakimasu*, meaning literally 'I will have some'. It ended with the phrase, *gochisō sama deshita*, thanking the cooks, and the reply *osomatsu sama desu*, or 'I hope it was not too bad'. In between, though, the eating was far from a leisurely affair. Despite the gathering of the family and the opportunity for conversation, food was disposed of quickly and with a minimum of fuss. The dishes, apart from the staple rice, vary with the seasons. Standard winter fare is the *oden* or *nabemono* stew. It is prepared with *tōfu*, *daikon* radish, *konnyaku* (devils tongue), eggs and vegetables. *Oden* is served with a small amount of fermented rice paste, called *miso*, which was once made in the home like *tōfu*, but which is now manufactured and sold commercially. The stew is simmered for some time to absorb the flavour of *shiitake*, or dried mushrooms, and enlivened with mustard. The *daikon* radish is a ubiquitous stew ingredient. It has a pungent smell and a strong taste, and it is credited with the quality of *i-no-sōji*, 'cleansing the stomach'. It is dried before pickling and, hanging in rows outside the houses, it forms a characteristic part of the autumn scene in the Isagosawa. There was a time, of course, when pickled *daikon*, or cabbage, or whatever, was one of the few supplements in a meagre rural diet of rice, and when commonplace dishes like *sukiyaki* seemed a luxury indeed. Today, when sugar, eggs, meat, and fresh vegetables are readily available, many families still enjoy the traditional taste of home-made salt pickle. Ours certainly did, and the kitchen reeked of vegetables and salt, pressed with a large stone, in the pickle barrel. The process produces a livid yellow scum, but washed and chopped the pickles are fresh and tasty.

In summer the diet is more varied and in keeping with the heat the family often ate cold foods. The most popular consisted of cold noodles (*soba*), rice, and *tōfu*, which were eaten with a salty sauce. Another summer speciality was smoked eel, believed to have health-giving properties at a time of year when the intense heat has debilitating effects. On special occasions raw fish (*sashimi*), or raw fish with vinegared rice (*sushi*) might be served and sometimes, on fine summer evenings, the family enjoyed an outside barbecue of whole squid (*ika poppo*). Delicacies like these, and like the river fish called *zakko* which was a particular favourite in spring, were obviously enjoyed for their flavour. For ceremonial activities, though, flavour came second to tradition and often to the symbolism of colour. This applied, for example, to particular annual festivals such as New Year and to specially joyful occasions (*o iwai*) like marriage. The preparations might not be especially tasty but they give pleasure of a different kind through the associations of their physical appearance. It was noticeable, too, that some seasonal pleasures like *hanami* (eating and drinking under the cherry blossom), or roasting lamb in the open air in autumn (called *gengis kaan*), often involved work groups rather than families.

The evening meal is eaten in the *ima*, or 'living room'. It is a small and intimate room and invariably smaller than the rooms given over to guests. It is also a *tatami* room, so there are no chairs. People remove their house slippers and sit on cushions on the 'platform' of clean, springy, *tatami* mats. The room is dominated by a low, central table, the *kotatsu*, the natural perspective of which is the eye-level of a person seated or reclining on the floor. It is around the table that the meal is taken and it is here, after the meal, that the family gather together in a group which conveys the most powerful visual image of the *ie* (Plate IX). The *kotatsu* itself reflects the role of the earlier central hearth, where smoke from a charcoal fire rose into the open rafters.

In the *ima* the family is surrounded by the paraphernalia of living. On one wall the Buddhist *butsudan* and Shinto *kamidana* shrine flank the telephone and a collection of oddments like calendars, books, letters, and piled boxes of gifts. Some of the objects were unusual to us, though they are common enough in Japanese homes: a rubber-headed hammer for pummelling and massaging the shoulders, for example, and a short bamboo spike used for cleaning out ear wax. This kind of assortment does a lot to dispel any image of the Japanese house as a tidy living space in which mere objects are not allowed to impinge on the 'flexible' use of plain matting or sliding panels. On the contrary, people like to have as much as possible within easy reach from the *kotatsu*.

One of the most important objects in the *ima* is the small stand containing utensils for preparing green tea: the thermos; a small one-handled tea-pot; and a bowl for dregs. Although it is not a ceremony in the formalised sense of *sadō*, the 'way of tea', the simple routine of preparing *ocha* has its own homely rhythm. With swift movements *okāsan* or *obāsan* would tap out the swollen leaves from the last pouring, and refill the pot with tea and hot water, serving it quickly to prevent the taste becoming too astringent. Sometimes, after an evening of drinking Japanese whisky, the father took a bowl of rice and fresh *ocha* mixed together, called *ocha-tzuke*. Drinking and offering tea is important and a useful metaphor for hospitality. One evening the family was discussing with a friend why it was that the home of a particular old carpenter was so popular and received so many visitors. The conclusion was that the old man always offered guests good quality tea, in contrast to some other homes where it was evident that the best was being set aside!

Sitting around the *kotatsu*, talking and drinking tea, may conform nicely to stereotypes of a Japanese family evening, but there is one other ingredient that is necessary to complete the picture. Television provides an

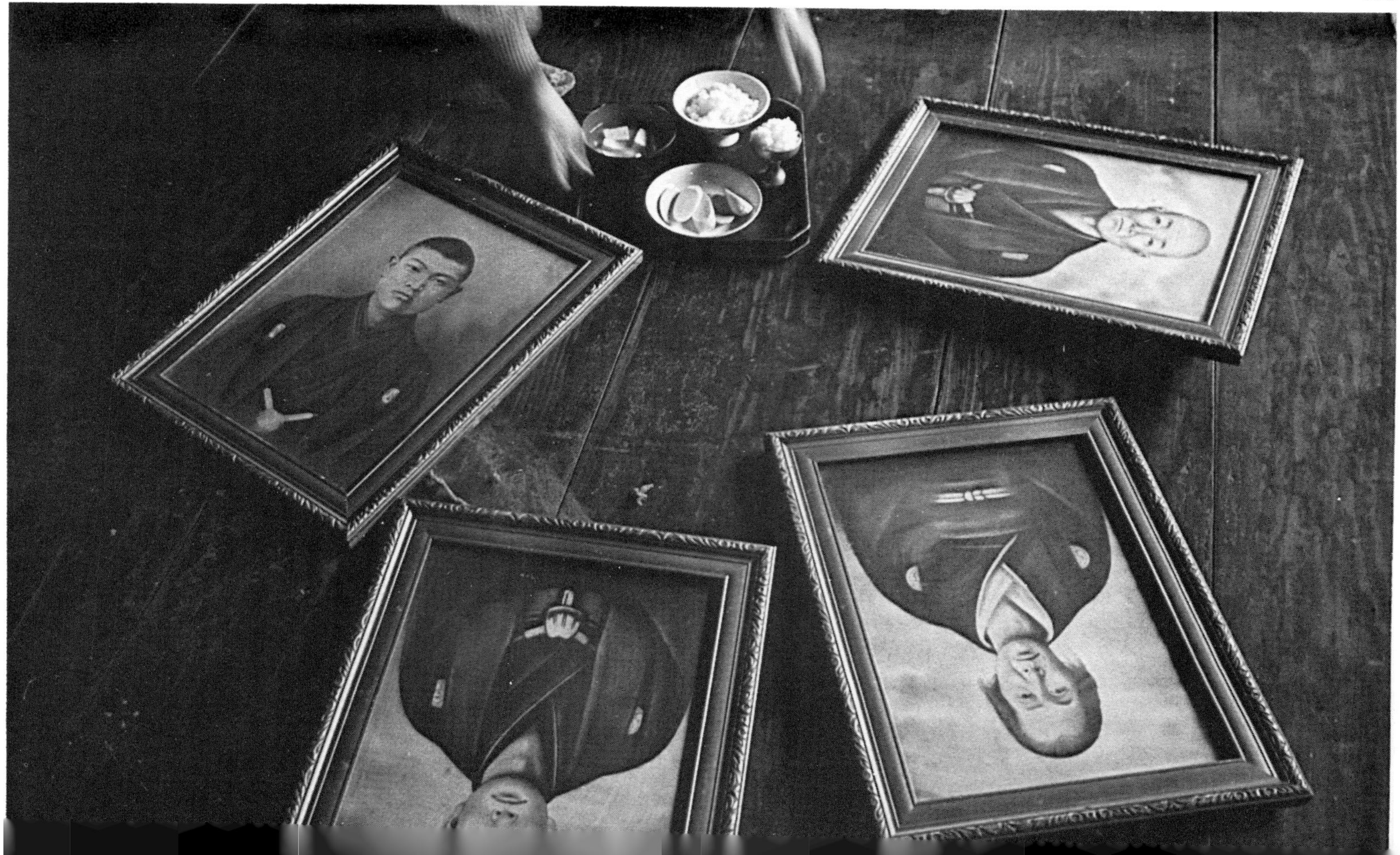

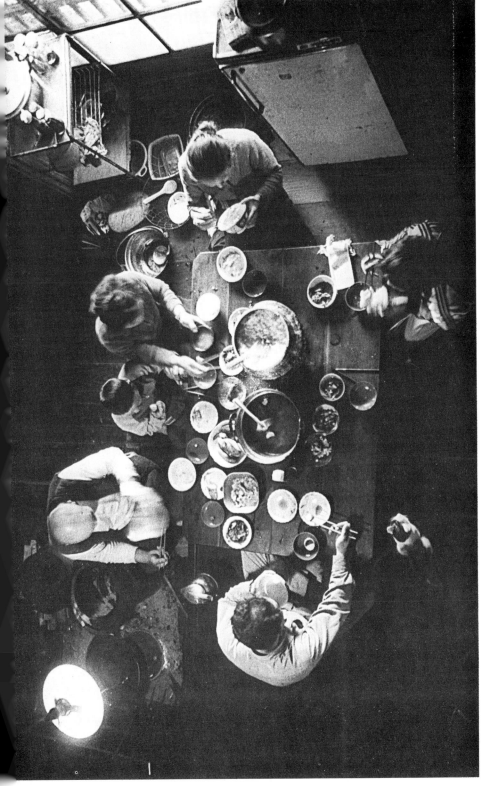

invariable accompaniment to the scene and plays a major role in the evening's entertainment. Its presence and its importance, in the same room as the *butsudan* and *kamidana*, highlights the juxtaposition of old and new in the *ima*. In our own household, televised baseball was a special favourite, and as the summer wore on the whole family became increasingly absorbed in the national championship for school teams. In between times, music is very popular, particularly folksongs. These musical programmes often involve an audience, and rather than listening quietly, the viewers too invariably join in the singing. Later in the evening attention switches to historical thrillers called *jidai geki* ('period plays') where the spirit of the *samurai* tradition is mixed with the action (and even music) of the American West.

Conclusions

It is difficult to generalise about the most basic and ordinary patterns of daily life in the *ie*. To distinguish between these 'ordinary' activities and other 'special' events, like annual ceremonies in the home, is itself an assumption. The small but significant routine of replenishing food in the *butsudan* shows how the unthinking and the mundane may easily blend into the more profound. Moreover, it is often trivial detail which exposes inconsistencies and contradictions in the *ie* and which serves to illuminate the bonds of affection binding the family. Thus, although everyone showed evidence of an awareness of formal duty, this formality did not amount to a code of inflexible rules within the home. For example, the grandmother had the last claim on the use of the bath even though it was her task to prepare it. Yet every night she would ask if anyone wanted to bathe (*ofurō ii desuyō*), and every night she would be told that she could go first. Since she had to rise early, and therefore slept first, it seemed unreasonable to deny her the first bath.

preceding pages

VIII Departed ancestors continue to live as real members of the *ie*.

IX The family gather together in a group which conveys the most powerful visual image of the *ie*.

X Old people remain as active as possible as long as health permits.

XI In the farming *ie* it is common to see children in the fields in the care of their grandmother.

The *ie* obviously amounts to much more than a set of rules and expectations. To us, it presented two different problems. First, it encompassed unfamiliar experiences and tastes which we slowly absorbed to the point of habituation. So, for example, the 'strange' taste of *daikon* and *miso* grew less and less strange until it was so commonplace as to evoke no response. But in addition the *ie* contains within its boundaries concepts, feelings, and structures which are far more difficult for the outsider to assimilate. These range from obvious things, like the contradictions between the traditional and the modern in the *ima*, or the contrasting roles of men and women, to things that are far less obvious. Of these, the most difficult of all is the question of locating the 'familiar' core of *ie* life for each of its members and of comprehending its meaning in the things that people did and the things that people said. We may observe a difference between those who are expected to prepare *ocha* and do so, and those who wait and are served with it. But whether we understand the meaning of this difference for the separate parties concerned is another matter.

3

Ceremonial and the *ie*

In rural Japan people pay little attention to such personal events as birthdays. On the other hand, they can recall very accurately the many ceremonial occasions which punctuate the year. A birthday, being an individual thing, is of little significance to a people whose socialisation is so heavily based on emotional dependence and group identity (Befu, 1971). Shared ceremonial observance, by contrast, emphasises the collective involvement which is at the heart of rural social organisation, and which envelopes not only the living but also the supernatural world and the spirits of the deceased (Dore, 1958). It releases,for the Japanese, 'the sentimental desire for the warm feeling of *ittai-ka,* or "oneness" which is expressed in their taste for "togetherness and sharing"' (Lebra, 1976).

However, the extent to which such ceremonial activity can be differentiated from everyday life, by using labels like 'religious' or 'ritual', depends largely on the viewpoint of the observer. In Western eyes the distinctions may seem clear enough, but Japanese commentators emphasise the blurred frontier between the supernatural and the everyday (Befu, 1962; Hori, 1968), and there can be little doubt that our identification of 'ceremonial activity' is, to some extent, artificial.

In much the same way the distinctions that we draw between the great religions of Japan, especially Shinto and Buddhism, can be misleading. Neither of them is an exclusive religion so that, although they may exist separately in terms of 'formal eclesia and doctrine' (Befu, 1971), at the level of folk belief their various features are blended together 'to meet the spirtual needs of the common people' (Hori, 1968). As the Tada *ie* illustrated, most homes have both Shinto and Buddhist 'altars' located at the centre of daily life. Their physical presence, often in the same room, is a tangible representation of the syncretic and complementary reputation of religious observance in Japan. The two shrines play different roles and cater for different needs, but they do so without conflict or tension. The Shinto shrine is the focus of immediate wellbeing for the family, the house, and the community. The Buddhist altar, on the other hand, is a reminder of *ie* lineage, of duty and responsibility, and a comforting link with the deceased (Plate XII). Together they secure the living and console the dead.

The folk beliefs of rural Japan, however, are not circumscribed or constrained by the traditions of these formal religions. Rather, the religions provide channels of mediation to an environment which is already imbued with its own spirituality. This resides in diffuse and ubiquitous *kami* deities: 'superior' entities which may inhabit either 'natural or man-made phenomena' and which have 'supernatural power of a benevolent or malevolent nature depending on the situation' (Befu, 1971). The *kami* may be anywhere, their influence at once vague but powerful, and their significance sometimes elusive for a Western mind. At a small summer festival in the Isagozawa ('Silver Sand Ravine'), for example, we were seated with a local farmer, eating and drinking under a canopy set among tall pines in front of the Ishigami shrine. The farmer was trying to explain the significance of Mount Ishigami in his life. He summed up the meaning of *yama*, the mountain, by saying that he had lived by its *okage*. This can be interpreted in different ways. The simplest translation is afforded by the rather clichéd 'in the shadow of', but a more appropriate one might be 'by the grace of', as in the phrase *okage sama de*, meaning 'thanks to your efforts'. In any event it became clear that he saw in the mountain a source of influences which were active rather than passive and which far transcended its existence as inert physical stuff (see Hori, 1968).

This is not to suggest that the Japanese anthropomorphise their world in any naive sense. Another anecdote makes this clear. In 1983 we were asked by the local Tourist Board to write an outsiders' view of Tōno for their annual handbook. It seemed to us natural to describe the atmosphere and environment near Tōno *machi* (a patchwork of rice fields and orchards) as having a 'friendly' quality. Amongst our friends on the Council, however, this personification of the natural world provoked much discussion and clearly presented some difficulties in translation. Eventually, and somewhat unhappily it must be confessed, they settled for 'nature is gentle as a friend might be' (*Tōno no shizen ga, tomodachi no yō ni, yasashii desu*).

Nevertheless, the diasporic souls and spirits which reside in the environment of rural Japan have a meaning which is tangible enough to find repeated expression in both daily ritual and annual ceremony. In addition, those occasions which are special for the rural *ie*, such as marriage or the building of a new house, also demand the appropriate recognition of influences which may be undefined but which are no less real for their lack of precision. In this chapter we report on those ceremonies and festivals which we were able to observe from the vantage of the Tada *ie*. We consider, first of all, the significance of the *butsudan* in daily routine and then describe the major ceremony of *obon* which centres strongly upon it. This is followed by an account of the New Year ceremonial which is associated particularly with the Shinto *kamidana*. We then describe a series of other ceremonies and festivals which have a locus primarily within the *ie*, and we conclude the chapter with a brief description of some of the communal festivals which we witnessed.

The *butsudan* and the festival of *obon*

In the older farm houses the Buddhist altar, called the *butsudan*, had its own special space. This was the *butsuma* ('room for the *butsudan*') and it was often located in an inner or rear part of the house (see also Smith, 1974). At the time of the major summer festival of *obon* nobody was allowed to sleep in the *butsuma*. In the more constrained spaces of modern houses, like the Tadas', the luxury of a separate room is not available. Instead, the *butsudan* is located at the very heart of daily activity in the *ima* or 'living room'. It is still probably the single most expensive item in the home (see Smith, 1955). A reasonable price to pay for a good *butsudan* in Tōno was 480,000 Yen (£1,920), but a specially designed model might cost as much as 2,020,000 Yen (£8,080). The most expensive part is the case itself (*soto no kiji*), which may cost between £1,000 and £6,000. Traditionally, it is made from hardwood, and *okāsan* pointed out the similarity between the character for *butsudan* (仏壇), and *tán* or 'hardwood' (檀). Although hard-wearing, the case has to be light enough to be removed easily in the event of fire or some other impending threat, and for this reason they are often made in two halves. In part, this also explained the popularity of modern plastic cases, which are not only lighter but also cheaper, though similar in appearance to hardwood versions. Indeed, plastic is very often used to imitate and replace expensive objects. It is possible, for example, to produce very convincing replicas of popular red lacquer ware, and it appears to be perfectly acceptable to substitute plastic for traditional materials when the cost of the latter is high.

The Tada *ie* is attached to the *Jishū* branch of the *Sodōshu* Buddhist sect, and the family *butsudan* contained features specific to this school. In general, however, *butsudan* follow a similar pattern: a shuttered case containing some image of the Buddha, surrounded by photographs and other objects commemorating the deceased, and spaces for offerings on its shelves (Table 2). It may also be extended into the room by an ornate low table, called the *mae tsukue*, with a cushion in front of it. As a repository for the souls of the dead (*tamashii*), the *butsudan* must not be replaced without some appropriate observance. We were told that ideally a new one should be purchased in each generation. The disused case is then placed in the care of the family temple and eventually cremated. This ensures that

Table 2: Cost of *butsudan* altar components (at 1987 exchange rates)

Name		Price (£)
Outer case (*soto no kiji*)	Hardwood	2,000–8,500
Small table (*mae tsukue*)	Often plastic	57– 111
Statuette of Buddha	Plain carved wood	116– 228
Mortuary tablet (*ihai*)	Plain wood or lacquer	31– 62
Candle holders (*rōsoku*)	Brass (pair)	15
Tea bowl	Red plastic with gold	5– 12
Rice bowl	Red plastic with gold	8
Lanterns (*okidōrō*)	Plastic	20– 69
Incense burner (*kōro*)	Brass	8– 28
Bell (*kanelriso*)	Brass (with cushion)	9– 31
Offertory stands (*kohai*)	Plastic or lacquer (large)	20– 49
	Plastic or lacquer (small)	8– 17
Tray for offerings (*rikuzen*)	Plastic	17– 62
Funerary flowers (*kinrenge*)	Plastic (with lights)	27
Prayer cushion	Embroidered	26– 191
	Total	2,382–9,425

the influence of any *tamashii* which remains in the old case is confined to the temple precincts. In Tōno *machi* many of the major temples stand alongside the Hayase river and it was not uncommon to find the ashes of old *butsudan* sprinkled on to the water.

The family explained that the most important object contained in the *butsudan* is the small tablet or scroll, called the *ihai*, upon which the names of deceased family members are written (see also Smith, 1974). Two copies are kept, one in the *butsudan* and the other in a simple shrine in the family temple. Should the *ihai* in the home be destroyed, there is still another record, standing alongside perhaps two hundred and fifty others in a small room at the side of the temple. The *ihai* records two things: the date of death and the name which is given to the deceased by the priest as a token of worldly success.

It was to the statuette of Buddha that *obāsan* offered tea and fresh rice every morning. As *hotoke*, deceased family members share the unity of Buddhahood. The anniversary of their death is marked simply by lighting a short stick of incense and spending some time in conversation or mediation in front of the *mae tsukue*. For this purpose the table has incense, a stand (*kōro*), a small bell on a cushion, and matches laid out in readiness. *Obasan* in particular used rosary beads while meditating before the *butsudan*, murmuring the low chant of the *amida nembutsu*. This is a simple repeated phrase, *namu ami dabu*, the 'name' (*nembutsu*) of the deity Amida (in Sanskrit Amitayus or Amithaba). The use of the *nembutsu* is associated with the beginnings of Buddhism as a popular religion since it is an appeal to the Buddha as a deity for help in the quest for enlightenment. On special occasions a relative visiting the home would kneel before the *butsudan*, lighting incense, and sounding the bell in two measured strokes. This action may be interpreted in two different ways. First it may be seen as a way of showing proper respect to the *hotoke* and simultaneously conferring this upon the family as a whole. Alternatively, it may be viewed as further evidence of the similarity of treatment which the Japanese accord to both the living and the dead. It is worth noting, too, that despite the many observations which record criticism of the irrelevance or indifference of Buddhism to matters other than 'death and the dead' (Smith, 1955), we personally encountered none of this (among others, Smith, 1955, 1974; Befu, 1971).

Apart from personal mementoes like photographs, the *butsudan* in some *ie* hold special tutelary deities specific to that particular home. Because the doors of the case are kept closed it is normally impossible to see them. It was with considerable pride, therefore, that the local museum was able to hold an exhibition of these *uchi-gami* (home deities) in 1982. There is considerable doubt as to their origins and significance (see Smith, 1974), but many of them had apparently been so carefully concealed that their presence was unknown even to the closest *dōzoku ie*. We can add nothing to the debates summarised by Smith (1974) except to outline the forms of the *uchi-gami* collected by the museum. There were thirty-five examples in all. Most of them resembled Indian Vedanta Buddha figures, seated with arms upstretched and palms outwards. But there were also a few unusual forms: for example, a twisted branch carved with the head of a horse which is a familiar element in Japanese mythology. There was also a tea bowl containing a very tiny seated figure. But the most interesting consisted of a variety of cloaked dolls which represented the characters of the *oshirasama* legend. Though we have no way of knowing, it seems possible that these dolls were once in the possession of *itako*, blind women mediums who practised their blend of art and shamanism in the north-east of mainland Japan. Certainly Blacker (1975) records their use as one of the 'instruments of power' which allow the *itako* to summon the *kami* which will take possession of her.

It is an indication of the syncretic nature of Buddhism in Japan that the *butsudan* should house *uchi-gami* which probably have their roots in primitive Shinto (Hori, 1968). Another interesting connection which we were able to observe was the arrival each month of a small packet from the family temple (*otera*). It consisted of a charm inside an envelope, printed with a flowing character from the special script of religious language. The charm inside was invariably a five yen coin, marked by its distinctive central hole. The charm, or *mamori*, articulated the idea of 'luck' which is usually associated with the important concept of *en*, having the significance of 'karmic destiny' (Hendry, 1981). The father explained to us that *en* was associated with the Shinto shrine, but he saw no inconsistency in the Buddhist employment of the same symbolism. The use of the five yen coin in this context is also interesting in consequence of its phonetic associations. In Japanese *yen* is pronounced 'en', and *go*, as well as meaning 'five', is also an honorary prefix. 'Five yen' (*go en*), therefore, can also mean 'revered good fortune'.

Obon is a major annual festival celebrated throughout Japan on 13–15 August. Because it occurs late in the year, the demands of agricultural work are usually slack and most people are able to take the festival as a holiday. It also occurs in midsummer, so that relatives and friends often take advantage of the warm weather to return for an annual visit, ensuring the popularity of the occasion. The purpose of *obon* is to mark the return of the souls of deceased forebears to the *ie*, and in Smith's (1974) words it is 'by far the most elaborate of the ... seasonal rites directed to the collectively of the ancestors' (Plate XIII). To the literal Western mind, of course, *obon* seems to present a contradiction: how can it be that the spirits of the dead are located in the *butsudan* where they receive daily offerings and yet have to be guided home at the midsummer festival? Our own family was unable, or perhaps unwilling, to attempt an explanation, possibly because they doubted the ability of a *gaijin* 'to understand what is going on' (Smith, 1974). The festival itself has been described many times and it is clear that the detail varies from place to place (among others, Hori, 1968; Blacker, 1975; Hendry, 1981). Our own experience, though, relates only to Tōno and to *obon* seen from the perspective of the Tada *ie*. It is this perspective we describe.

Despite the sombre association of *obon* with the spirits of the dead, there was a distinct holiday atmosphere in Tōno in August 1982. Streets were decked with lanterns and in playgrounds or other open spaces stands were erected in readiness for the dances (*bon odori*) which mark the end of the festival. In the countryside *dōzuku*-related *ie* take it in turn to clear the graveyard of the local temple, though we found no evidence of the custom of *bon-michi-tsukuri* ('making of the *bon* road') described by Hori (1968). Bon is also a time to acknowledge past favours with the giving of gifts. The Tada *ie* received fruit, coffee, *sake*, and salted rice biscuits called *osembe*. It seems that offerings of fruit and vegetables, never meat, were also once made in front of the *ie* tombstone. The word *bon* itself means 'bowl' or 'tray' and symbolises this idea. Sometimes the offerings were placed on reed mats and raised up on crossed bamboo canes to preserve them from scavengers, but though the matting is still on sale in the supermarkets, the practice itself seems to have disappeared.

The Tada family spent the first day of *obon* at home, preparing the *butsudan*. It was carefully cleaned and the mother brought out the large offering stands (*kōhai*) and the tray (*rikuzen*) on which a symbolic meal would be served. The family also decided to buy a paper lantern and arranged this with an electric light above the altar. These lanterns are sold only at this time of year. The Tadas also removed the two mortuary scrolls from the *butsudan*, hanging one on each side of the altar. The scroll placed to the left contained an intercession to the divinity Kannon (the Buddhist goddess of mercy) on behalf of the father's sister who had died in infancy. It contained the word *mushin*, which can be variously interpreted as 'intercession', 'detachment', or 'innocence', together with the *Amida nembutsu*. The second scroll was dedicated to the deity Dainichi or Daihi (the Great Sun Buddha) who is associated with light, life and creation. It recorded the names of deceased *ie* members and the date of their death in the manner displayed on the tombstone. The ancestors were called *jōbutsu*, persons who had successfully reached Buddhahood. Our attempts to probe the family on the nature of 'awakening' and the implications of Buddhahood, however, met with little success.

The three-day festival entails welcoming the *tamashii* back to their *ie*, feting them there, and ensuring their return. On the first evening, therefore, the father went out and cut some branches of green wood to make a bonfire which would send up clouds of smoke. This fire, called the *mukaebi* or 'welcoming fire', is intended to serve as a beacon to the spirits to guide them back to the *ie*. In addition, as *otōsan* explained, it also had the practical value of discouraging mosquitoes, so that everyone was able to sit indoors with the window screens open, watching the plumes of smoke from the fire and enjoying the stillness of the evening.

Amongst the farms of the Isagosawa a custom still continues which Yanagita noted in 1910. If an *ie* has suffered a bereavement since the last *obon*, the festival is specially marked as *hatsubon*, the 'opening' *bon* for that person's soul. As Smith (1974) notes, it is only after the end of the spirit's first *bon* that its ties with the world of the living are severed and its place amongst the ancestors is secured. As if in recognition of the bewilderment of the wandering spirit, therefore, tall poles are erected to aid its return. They are topped with the white *heisoku* papers and the sprigs of pine that feature so strongly in Shinto ritual: this at the height of the major Buddhist festival!

We have no way of knowing whether the pole-raising practice is repeated in other parts of Japan. There is, however, another ceremony in an outlying area of Tōno *shi* called Tsukimōshi *machi* which certainly has close parallels elsewhere. Again, it marks a *hatsubon* and in some details it is similar to the ceremony reported by Bernier from the coastal village of Sone in Mie prefecture (Smith, 1974). In Tsukimōshi the ceremony is called *fune'ko nageshi* ('launching the boat'), and like the Sone festival it is a communal affair. It begins with a dance in the grounds of the local temple and moves to the riverside where the boat, constructed from rice straw, is to be launched. The launching begins as small paper lanterns are placed in the stream at some distance from the assembled crowd. For every villager who has died in the past year a lantern is contributed by each of the forty-eight village *ie*. The boat is launched by the young men of Tsukimōshi, dressed in *fundoshi* loincloths, and as it is guided down the illuminated stream it is burned. In Smith's (1974) view it is the community involvement which distinguishes the Sone festival. He views it as 'the last of the cycle of corporate acts directed to the individual as a member of the community'. 'Thereafter', he says, 'the person's soul is left to the care of his own household.' The same may probably be said of Tsukimōshi.

Happily, there was no *hatsubon* for the Tada *ie*. On the first evening, before lighting the fire, the family visited the graveyard of their temple. The visit had a particular significance, though, since the father had just succeeded in having the gravestone moved close to home. In the fading light every temple graveyard was filled with people. Some were engaged in quiet meditation, or else, like the Tadas, tidied the grave and conversed with friends. The atmosphere was relaxed, respectful but convivial. The family took water from a tap near the temple entrance, using one of the plastic containers provided and, with a small ladle, poured it over the black tombstone. Although some people had their own traditional wooden bucket for this purpose, many had brought any available utensil, often a kettle. It surprised us that *oniisan* seemed unsure of the proper procedures and observance which was required. The father gave everyone in the party five sticks of incense (one for each deceased ancestor commemorated by the tomb), and in turn we stepped forward, lit them, placed them in a hollow on the plinth, and bowed and clapped once in acknowledgement. *Obāsan* then placed fresh flowers by the stone and everyone busied themselves tidying the area. *Okāsan* gave out small sweet rice cakes which were ostensibly for the deceased. In fact, they were eaten and said to be a protection against bad teeth!

It must be stressed that the atmosphere in which these simple acts were performed, although respectful, was never melancholy or sombre. The graveyard had become the scene of an ordered but informal social gathering. Like the family, others strolled through the temple paths and precincts, exchanging greetings or pausing to mark an important tomb. The houses which flanked the paths had their screens open so that in the gloom the lanterns above their *butsudan* were clearly visible.

On the second day of the festival the *ihai* scrolls were again taken from the *butsudan* and opened to display the names of the deceased. Gifts were piled on the *mae tsukue* table and the mother prepared a simple meal to be served on the *rikuzen*. She explained that the characters comprising *rikuzen* (六月喜) signify the joyful nature of the occasion, as the character 熹, called *yorokobi*, indicates. The remaining components, meaning 'six' and 'month' (六月) were, she thought, a possible reference to the traditional timing of the festival.

The offering of food is called *osegaki* meaning literally 'feeding the hungry ghosts'. It must never include any meat or fish, although this prohibition did not extend to the diet of the family. The *rikuzen* supports five red lacquer bowls in which the mother served pickles (vinegared *daikon*), boiled vegetables (*nitsukemono*), a *miso* soup, salt pickles (*utsukemono*), and steamed rice sweetened with red beans (*sekihan*). In the middle she placed some green tea. The *rikuzen* even contained a pair of small chopsticks which were placed along the edge of the tray nearest the *butsudan*. This meal was renewed on the following day.

The offertory stands (*kōhai*), which resembled red lacquer but were actually plastic, were placed in pairs within the *butsudan*. The larger pair held watermelons which the family eventually ate. On the smaller, inner, pair the mother arranged a display of moulded pale pink sugar lotus flowers. These are sold in confectioners' at this time of the year, but the Tadas kept theirs wrapped for subsequent use.

The three days of *obon* are a holiday, and on the second and third evenings the main street of Tōno *machi* was closed to traffic and became the scene of a small fair. The scale of these festivities did not rival the September celebrations, but there were stalls, many shops remained open, and the streets were filled with families enjoying the cool evening. There was the usual range of snacks to be had: grilled squid, rice-flour dumplings with octopus, sweet-bean cakes (*manjū*) and candy floss. And of course there was *sake* and 'draught' beer. But, sadly, or so it seemed to us, the traditional summer *kimono* (*yūkata*), which are tied with a colourful sash and worn with wooden sandals (*geta*), were not much in evidence. They have given way to popular informal Western styles of dress, notably jeans and tracksuits.

The spirits of *ie* ancestors are said to leave the house on the third evening of *obon* and their departure was traditionally marked by communal dancing called *bon odori*. Hori (1968) believes that the dances evolved from the *odori-Nembutsu* which were dances performed by magic-religious figures (*hijiri*) and which were intended to soothe 'revengeful and angry evil spirits' (*goryo*). To *okāsan*, however, the *bon odori* were simply associated with 'seeing off' (*miokuri*) the souls of ancestors and were not dignified by any particular religious ceremonial. Smith (1974) has observed the declining interest in the *bon* dance throughout Japan, and its popularity varied greatly even within Tōno *shi*. Our own experience confirmed Smith's (1974) more general description in that we saw no musicians or singers and the only accompaniment was provided by a solitary drummer. The dancers themselves were mostly older women whose husbands had retired to bars and to coffee shops to play electronic mahjong. The dances are performed at walking pace around a central dais occupied by the drummer and decked with red and white streamers. The movements are slow and synchronised and suited to the restrictions of movement imposed by the *yūkata kimono*. Those dancers who actually wore the *kimono* tied their sleeves back in the manner which was common when the *kimono* was worn for work. Indeed, we were told that many of the dance movements were derived from the work routine, like digging in the earth, and most of the refinements of the dance are in the precision of hand movements and in the co-ordination of the dancers. An innovation in 1983 was a new *odori*, the *shinkansen*, which had been invented to mark the opening of the new 'Bullet train' link with the north-east.

The summer festival of *obon*, therefore, provided us with an opportunity to observe the continuing role of the *butsudan* within *ie* life. It may not be a feature of all Japanese families, since it is significant only when a son has succeeded his father in the role of *ie* head. But within most of the households that we saw it seems to be a natural focus of everyday routine. As the *bon* festival emphasises, the *butsudan* provides a tangible link with the important 'hidden' side of the *ie*: the past and the future which guide family behaviour and responsibilities. At the same time, the informality of *bon* shows again how reverence blends easily with the natural attitude and becomes just one more part of the accepted order of things.

New Year and the *kamidana*

Yanagita (1970) believes that the midsummer festival of *bon* has origins that pre-date the introduction of Buddhism into Japan. In his view the Festival of the Dead has simply 'acquired the scent of Buddhism from long years of incense smoke', obscuring an earlier folk observance. Whether he is right or not, there is no doubt that *bon* finds 'a perfect counterpoint' in the Shinto celebration of the New Year (Smith, 1974). Throughout Japan it is a time of great significance, both in relation to agricultural practices and within the ceremonial year of the *ie*. In effect, there are two celebra-

67

tions: one for the Gregorian New Year called *shōgatsu*, and a 'lesser' one for the Lunar New Year called *koshōgatsu*. Knowledge of the traditional practices associated with the latter, however, seems to be fading fast, even though some farming *ie* still follow the 'old calendar' (*kyūreki*).

There are two basic systems of Shinto belief. One is called *uji-gami* and the other *hito-gami*. *Uji-gami* centres on the family or clan, each one of which had its own shrine dedicated to a particular ancestral spirit. Nurturing these deities, therefore, was a family responsibility rather than a communal one and *uji-gami* observances were necessarily private and particular (Hori, 1968). The *hito-gami* type, on the other hand, is not aligned with individual *ie* or *dōzoku* but instead reflects a communal recognition of individual Shamans and their association with special *kami*. It is these *hito-gami* beliefs which constitute the public expression of Shinto and which are rich in expressive ceremonial and symbolic paraphernalia. It would appear that the New Year now has a strong *hito-gami* orientation which has largely replaced the traditional *uji-gami* observances (Yanagita, 1970).

Most of the household Shinto god shelves (*kamidana*) that we saw were dedicated to the central Hachiman shrine in Tōno: a *hito-gami* shrine associated with the deities Gion, Sumiyoshi, Tsushima, Inari, and Kitano. The contents of the *kamidana* seem to vary little and since general house-cleaning is a feature of New Year preparations throughout Japan, we were able to observe them quite closely. Indeed, the cleaning and preparation of the Tadas' *kamidana* was carried out by the father and the *gaijin*. It contained a symbolic replica of the main shrine consisting of a model of the Hachiman's principal sanctuary facade (*shaden*). The models vary considerably in size and in expense. The more elaborate may cost as much as £300 and have multiple roofs and railings which are capped with metal. In addition, and despite Smith's (1974) observation that 'there is no image of the deity', on the god shelf, the rear wall of the Tada *kamidana* is covered by three large printed papers, each depicting a deity of the main shrine (Fig. 2). Other *kamidana* may have as many as five of these prints. In an arrangement of three, though, the paper on the left showed Ebisu sama, the guardian deity of wealth. On the right was another deity of good fortune, Daikoku sama, the god of Five Cereals, who is known in Sanskrit as Mahakala. Ebisu and Daikoku are both rotund and jovial figures with the enlarged ear lobes associated in popular belief with wealth and well-being. In one hand Ebisu carries a fishing rod and under the other arm he holds a huge fish. It is likely that the fish is a sea-bream: they are often linked with festive occasions in Japan partly because of their red colouring and partly because their name, *tai*, has phonetic links with the congratulatory greeting *omedetai*. Ebisu sits on a rock with waves foaming at his feet

68

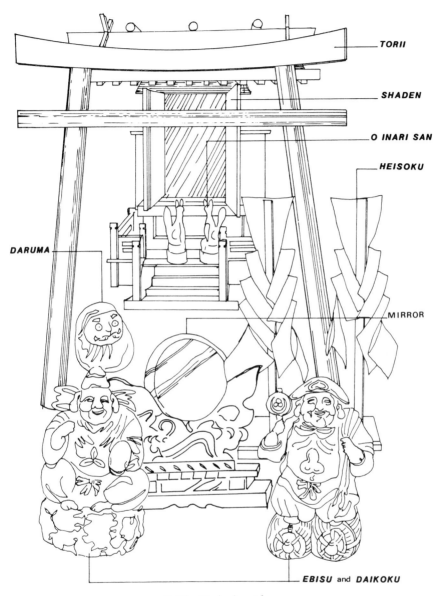

TORII

SHADEN

O INARI SAN

HEISOKU

DARUMA

MIRROR

EBISU and DAIKOKU

2 The Tada *kamidana*

(Fig. 3). Daikoku sama stands upon two rice-straw barrels of grain. In his hand he carries a mallet, called the *uchi de no kozuchi*, from which he shakes out wealth and good fortune. In confirmation, gold coins of the traditional oval shape rain down around his feet, and mice and rats scurry amongst the scatterings of grain. The background to the prints of Ebisu and Daikoku consists of pine sprigs and plum blossom respectively. Both of them are connected with ideas of good fortune and together with bamboo they constitute the traditional *shōchikubai* depiction which often accompanies gifts or celebratory decoration.

Of the remaining Shinto deities, the Tada *kamidana* contained a print of the god of longevity, Jurōjin. He is shown seated beneath a large gateway (*torii*), wearing a hat which suggests Tibetan influence and surrounded by a circular halo which may be a direct representation of the sun, or its indirect symbolisation in a mirror. Arranged before the deity are objects involved in the New Year ceremonial: the entrance decorations called *kadomatsu*; offerings of rice cake (*mochi*) and fish, and white cut papers (*heisoku*) which are widely used to mark Shinto ceremonials. A scroll hanging from the gateway invokes charms for a plentiful harvest and safety in the home, both of which are popular themes at New Year.

There are other deities who occasionally find representation on papers hung about the *kamidana*. The goddess Benten or Benzaiten, for example, brings good fortune, and there are other gods of wealth and fortune like Bishamonten and Fukurokuju. The most endearing of them, perhaps, is the deity Hotei whose principal feature is echoed in the common phrase *hotei bara*, meaning 'pot belly' or 'large stomach'. The specific genealogy of these deities and their links with Indian and Chinese mythology are not generally recognised by most people; it is enough that they all have a traditional association with wellbeing within the *ie*.

Ebisu and Daikoku are depicted in other forms within the *kamidana*. At the Tadas', for example, they were modelled in heavy red glaze and flanked the shrine, again with Ebisu to its left and Daikoku on the right. The small shrine, or *shaden*, also has its own specific guardians in the form of white china foxes (*kitsune*) called o-inari-sama. Much has been written on the significance of the fox in Japanese folk tradition (Blacker, 1975). It is said that the first sprig of rice travelled from China to Japan in the mouth of a fox and the *inari-sama* sometimes hold rice ears in reflection of this. But the fox also has a sinister reputation as a possessor of souls. It can be placated and won over by the offer of delicacies which it is usually denied. One of these, as Blacker (1975) notes and as we observed, is fried soya bean curd: an offering made by tradition at the New Year.

The white-glazed foxes which guard the *shaden* are matched by other white-glazed objects which emphasise the theme of purity in the shrine:

jurojin

ebisu　　　　　　　　　　　　**daikoku**

SCALE

3　　6　　9
|　　　　　　　　| centimeters

3 Shinto papers in the Tada kamidana

pairs of shallow dishes, for example, cups for *sake*, and stands for *heisoku* papers. There might also be a conical white china object which is said to represent the 'seed' of primeval fire and life, an 'egg' often depicted in the claw of a fearsome dragon.

A central feature of the *kamidana*, placed directly before the *shaden*, is a small round mirror called *Yata-no-kagami*. In the Tadas' it was mounted on a stand carved with motifs of fire and flanked by small lanterns to enhance the perspective effects of the *shaden* and to pick out certain of its features. Like the fox, the mirror also has considerable significance in traditional folklore. It symbolises the sun, and with the *sakaki* tree, it is a sacred treasure of the Imperial Court. Moreover, as Blacker (1975) notes, the mirror is believed to act as an inviting inducement to the *kami* and an enticement to their guardianship.

The final element in the basic ornamentation of the *kamidana* is provided by *heisoku* papers. They are easily made by making three cuts in a piece of folded paper and reversing each fold. Instructions are provided in the almanacs, but at some *ie*, like the Tadas', a past favour merits a special visit from the priest who performs the simple duty. *Heisoku* in the Tada *kamidana* were set on small stands in two pairs, while four more were hung across the front of the shrine. Usually, the number four has inauspicious connotations because it may be read as *shi* and thus recall the *shi* of *shinu*, which means 'to die'. In keeping with a general preference for odd numbers, therefore, four in avoided when making up a gift or a guest list or whatever. In the *kamidana*, however, the four papers were said to represent the four quarters of the compass, an important theme in extending the beneficial influence of the shrine throughout the home.

The *kamidana* may also contain small wooden tablets which depict on one side the symbol of the current year: in 1982 this was the Dog (*inu*), and in 1983 the Wild Boar (*i-no-shishi*). The reverse of the tablets which we saw depicted a horse with its head high and its belly low set in the cantering pose which appears in the earliest pictures preserved in the area. The shrine also contained a *daruma* doll: a specifically Buddhist symbol which again indicates the syncretism of family religious observance. The dolls are fashioned in *papier maché* and painted red or white with large expressive faces. Their significance derived from the legend of the Zen patriarch Bodhidharma (circa 470–543), who taught that the Buddhist Absolute may be grasped intuitively without the false mediating reality of words and language (Saunders, 1964). As a result of protracted seated meditation, Bodhidharma is supposed to have lost his legs, and it is this which is at the source of the *daruma* doll. Its legless, rounded base means that it cannot be knocked over and it thus combines the exalted goal of devoted meditation with the more tangible Japanese quality of resilience in the face of adversity. The dolls are also eyeless when they are purchased and these are painted in, one to make a wish or request, and the other when it has been granted. One-eyed *daruma* may therefore express the hope of a safe journey, or the birth of a child, or whatever: in 1982 the victor in Tōno's local elections triumphantly painted in the second eye of a large *daruma* doll (Plate XIV)!

These observations record the contents of a particular god-shelf in a particular house. We saw others in Tōno, and in the Isagozawa generally, and although all of them differed in the detail of their contents, they were all devoted to rounding out the theme of wealth and plenty in the *ie*. The New Year, of course, is the time when this theme receives particular reinforcement and when the influence of the *kamidana* is most strongly projected through the *ie*. In part this is achieved through a variety of objects which are specifically associated with the seasonal festivities. For example, the deities Ebisu and Daikoku are depicted on brightly coloured plastic displays which the Tadas attached to a bamboo rake. Using the rake, the family literally 'rakes' up symbolic good fortune. This symbolism is extended to personal wishes for specific fortune through ornate arrow-heads with triple feathers. They are so built as to emit a wailing sound as the arrow flies, its fading noise reminiscent of the declining tone used by priests in incantation. Tied to the arrows are charms asking for *ka-nai-an-zen* ('safety in the home'), or *ju-sai-shō-fuku* ('preservation from cala-mity'). Another popular New Year charm and decoration which is not confined to the *kamidana* consists of a fan of rice straw hung from a short rice-straw rope. These again carry plastic depictions of the deities Ebisu and Daikoku, charms against household disaster, and a moulded arrange-ment of plum, bamboo, and pine (*shō-chiku-bai*). Throughout the town they deck shop frontages, doorways, petrol pumps and even earth-moving equipment idle during the holiday. Some objects may be depicted within the *kamidana* and also distributed about the house. This enhances the impression that the god-shelf serves as a focus for forces which are spread throughout the *ie*. In the Tada home paper charms (*mamori*) were placed in the toilet area, by the gas burner in the kitchen, and beside the inner post of the *genkan* hallway.

In the Tada *ie* the imminence of New Year was signalled by the arrival of the priest from the Hachiman shrine. He came to perform some simple purification rites. His involvement, though, was unusual and reflected the fact that *otōsan* had acted as go-between in arranging the marriage of the priest's son. Even though his presence honoured a past favour, however, it was still proper for him to receive something for his trouble: a bottle of *sake* wrapped in red and white paper and a similarly wrapped envelope containing ten thousand yen (£43). For the purposes of the ceremony the basic equipment of offering – a candle, small dishes of rice and salt, and a glass of water – were set on a table below and before the *kamidana*. The family then knelt, father foremost, then the son, mother, and finally grandmother, in the small area between these offerings and the television. The ceremony, with its incantation (*norito*) delivered by the priest, is brief and ends as the family members step forward in turn to bow and clap reverently at the shrine. It is important, however, that the good fortune for which the act interceded is adequately distributed about the physical precincts of the house. Thus the father took the water and symbolically threw it 'over the roof' (actually a lower part of the front porch). The salt was carefully divided between the kitchen, the drains at the front of the house, and the toilet area. Finally, the purified rice was mixed in with that being steamed for the evening meal. In this way the blessing was spread about the house and amongst its members.

Preparation for the New Year is also a period of intense activity for the women of the *ie*, since offerings of specially prepared foods play an important role in the general renewal of spiritual ties. The traditional practice used to be for each *ie* to produce its own rice cake (*mochi*) for the festival season. Steamed rice was pounded into a sticky cake on large wooden pestles and then fashioned into slabs to construct the three-tiered decoration which forms the standard New Year offering (Plate XV). These days few households follow the old traditions. The wooden pestles can be seen abandoned in farmyards and most families order their cake well in advance from the local bakery. The three-layered displays arrive at the end of December. They are called *sanko mochi* ('three-tier mochi') or *osonai mochi* to distinguish them as a sacred offering. Often the topmost layer is replaced with an orange (*mikan*) from the Satsuma district of the south. This practice has its own significance and lore, and it is bound up in the theme of renewal which draws together the major preoccupations of family life at this time of year. The symbolic link is provided by the orange colouring of the *mikan*. The words *oranji-iro*, meaning 'orange colour', may be read alternatively as *daidai*, thus corresponding to the *dai* of 'generation' (see Hendry, 1981). This association between the physical object and the idea of longevity and continuity of the family line is reinforced in the phrase *daidai sakaeru*, meaning literally 'flowering of the orange/generations'. Alternatively, this may be rendered *mi-ga-naru* ('appearance of a new bud') when referring to the establishment of a new branch of the family through marriage. The traditional wedding greeting *hana to nare, mi-to nare, minoru ki to nare* which reflects the idea of flowering, fruition and seeding is thus symbolised in the *sanko mochi*.

The Tadas had four *sanko mochi* displays: a large one and three small ones. The large one was placed on a wooden tray called the *sanbo* just below the *kamidana*, together with a bottle of *sake* and a candle. This display remained undisturbed until the official end of the festival on 15 January. A smaller display was set in the *butsudan*, another in the mother's shop, and a fourth in the rear window of the family car. After the end of the New Year festival *obāsan* placed the *sanko mochi* on a window ledge outside, leaving it to desiccate and grow dirty. It was left in this way until *setsubon*, the official end of winter, when the remains were powdered and added to the soup of an evening meal.

The mother explained that in her childhood the New Year was a traditional holiday for the young bride of the *ie* and a rare opportunity for her to return to her parents' home. She would usually take a gift of *mochi* weighing perhaps ten kilograms. The round slabs earned the name *kagami mochi*, a reference to the mirror which would have been one of the bride's few personal possessions. The holiday itself was called *me shōgatsu*, 'the woman's New Year', because of its importance for the young wife and because it normally took place at the end of family festivities (see also Hendry, 1981). *Okāsan* also recalled a small festival at the end of December devoted specifically to Ebisu sama, when the family was served with *tai* (sea-bream) and *sashimi* (raw fish), pickles and *sake*, and when each child received a gift of money. For this simple festivity the family had observed seating in strict order of *ie* hierarchy by sex and age.

Though we observed neither the *me shōgatsu* nor the festivities for Ebisu sama, the Tadas still continue the traditional practice of taking a first meal of the year on New Year's Eve (*toshikoshi*). As Yanagita (1970) observes, the Japanese normally conceived of a day from evening to evening rather than morning to morning, and so the first meal of the New Year is actually taken on New Year's Eve. The period before the meal is one of strict abstinence until the first sounds of the temple bell at eleven o'clock could be heard around the town. When they were younger, the children of the household had then paid their respects to their grandparents and received sweets in return called *toshi dama*. The family then ate a meal of Japanese noodles (*toshikoshi soba*) and a large stew of the usual winter fare: potato-starch noodles, fried bean curd, eggs, *tōfu*, *daikon* and *shiitake* mushroom flavouring.

We shared two of these *toshikoshi* meals with the Tadas. The first, in 1981/2 was doubly special since the year marked the recurrence of *oniisan*'s birth sign (the Dog). To honour the occasion the meal was taken in the best room of the house, the *Nihon ma* or 'Japanese-style room', which was heated for the event. They also invited some of *oniisan*'s cousins and served extra dishes of sliced squid, tuna, pickled herring, anemones and sea squirt, washed down with liberal quantities of hot *sake*, whisky and beer. They also produced a large red plastic drinking bowl

75

called the *taihai* which was passed from hand to hand so that everyone might drink. The following year, however, the family reverted to the normal practice of having the *toshikoshi* meal in the living-room. *Okāsan* placed the father's meal before the *kamidana*, thus offering his food symbolically to the guardian deities, and the family as a whole shared the *sake* from this offering.

It is worth digressing for a moment on the subject of food, since the New Year period is not generally a time for very appetising preparations. The season is called *osechi* and *osechiryōri* is prepared in quantities sufficient to last the family through the first five days of the New Year. In effect, this frees the women of the responsibilities of food preparation for a short time. The mother thus prepared a grey stew called *onishime* or *umani*, using a mixture of grains and beans. Traditional ingredients are black beans (*kuromame*), *namasu* (called *mameshiku* and designed to promote health), *kinpira*, burdock root (*gobō*), *tarako*, a small sweetened fish called *tatsukuri*, fish roe (*ikura*), and white beans (*kinton*) mixed with chestnuts (*kyūri*). Using these ingredients reflects a traditional three-day period of abstinence at the start of the New Year as a mark of respect for the guardian deities. The period is called *san-ga nichi-bun*.

The main event of New Year's Eve is the visit to the local Shinto shrine called *ganchōmairi*. In 1981/2 and in 1982/3 the New Year was accompanied by the onset of bitter winter cold. The trip from the warmth of the *kotatsu*, therefore, had none of the relaxed pleasure of the *obon* devotions. Dress was uniformly western, but at least most families seemed willing to brave the weather and to join the queues waiting to ring the bell of the shrine and to throw some coins in the offertory and make a wish for the coming year. It is apparently permissible to make these devotions at any time up to the seventh day of the New Year. Why this should be so is not clear, though Yanagita (1970) has suggested that the *kami* may have been thought to depart on the sixth day.

The stalls at the shrine Hachiman *jinja* did a good trade in charms for the coming year. The Tadas, for example, bought wooden tablets and arrows for the *kamidana*, and lottery tickets which gave advice on fortune in the new season. On the way home we also called at the family's Buddhist temple to exchange greetings. Here visitors share in the task of ringing the temple bell one hundred and eight times to sound out the Buddhist cardinal sins, called *bonnō*. Each stroke is marked by placing a bean in a box. The Tadas also collected an almanac for the coming year before hurrying home to drink the thick, sweet *sake* called *ama-zake*, which is made from the wine tailings, and to enjoy a hot bath.

On the second day of the New Year it is customary to make a 'first

writing' called *kakizome*. Often this consists of a single character express-
ing greeting or celebration, and they are frequently used to decorate kites.
The days following the New Year are also a time of some activity as
families sift through the greeting cards they have received and compare
those to the list of those sent. It seemed perfectly acceptable to send a
card after the New Year if someone had been accidentally omitted. Each
card is the same, a standard postcard with some message written on one
side, usually a variation on the standard greeting (*akemashite omedetō
gozaimas*) and reply (*kotoshi mō yoroshiku onegai itashimasu*). In 1982/3,
the son with his new bride bought a home printing set to design more
personal greetings and even indulged in a humorous copy of the national
post office lottery number which most cards carry. Altogether the family
received about three hundred cards and despatched a similar number,
reflecting something of the extent of ritual duty and expectation which
binds individuals and *ie*, and which must be renewed at this time of
year.

On the seventh day, once the *kami* have departed, it is traditional to
make a preparation of 'grasses' called *nanakusagayu*, or simply *okayu* (see
Hendry, 1981). Popular belief is that these purify the body after the
excesses of the festivities and prepare the soul for the coming months. The
seven grasses that are used are: *seri*, or water celery; *nazuna*, or shepherd's
purse; *gokyō*, or cotton weed; *hakobera*, or chickweed; *hotoke no za*, or
dead nettle; *suzuna*, or Chinese rape; and *suzushiro*, or garden radish
(Uemichi, 1984).

Officially the New Year festival ends on 15 January. As Yanagita
(1970) has shown, the traditional end of the festival varies from the 15th
to the 16th in different parts of Japan. In the *hito-gami* context it is
marked in Tōno by a small ceremony held at the Hachiman shrine. People
bring old decorations and the redundant contents of *kamidana* to be
ceremonially burned in the shrine grounds. The fire is called *dondoyaki*
and its purpose is to release the influence of demons from the objects
which are burned and to confine them to the Hachiman precincts. In this
sense it is very similar to the cremation of *butsudan* and the controlled
release of *tamashii*. The objects which are to be burned are first topped
with sprigs of pine and *heisoku* papers and blessed by the priest. Then the
fire is lit and people crowd as close as they can to 'bathe' in its purifying
smoke. Rice-cake dumplings are toasted on sticks and distributed amongst
the worshippers.

We were told that the *dondoyaki* ceremony has declined in popularity
in recent years, fewer and fewer people bringing offerings to the fire. At
least part of the reason seems to lie in the alternative attraction of the

seijinshiki ceremonies which are held on the same day. Since the New Year brings the communal advancement of one year in age for all Japanese, it brings one group of *dōkyūsei* ('same-year classmates') to the significant twentieth birthday. Seemingly under the auspices of the council, this has been developed into a major ceremony. It is, of course, of some personal significance too, since it marks the end of the close ties which will have dominated this group through the school and adolescent years. Many will already have left Tōno and future links will be confined to *dōkyūsei* reunions and to holidays. To us it seemed that the town was filled with young people hurrying between the civic hall, where the ceremony takes place, and photographers' studios and restaurants. Perhaps because the commemorative photo is such an important part of the event, the girls are all dressed in their finest *kimono* (Plate XVI).

The atmosphere pervading the Tada *ie* throughout the New Year festival was one of relaxation combined with a sense of duty. The start of the year as a time of renewal is marked in a variety of ways: by attention to the guardian deities of the *kamidana*; through the symbolism of genealogy portrayed in *sanko mochi*; and in the communal advancement of groups defined by age. It is also a time of heightened spiritual awareness that may seem to the Western eye to be superstitious. Small events, however, are magnified by the portentous atmosphere of the season. The first dream of the New Year, for example, is traditionally held to have special significance. Known as the *hatsuyume*, people would once try to influence its content by placing a picture of a ship bearing wealth and good fortune (called the *takarabune*) under the sleeper's pillow. In this way it was hoped to encourage images of plenty and the smiling influences of Ebisu and Daikoku.

Our own family did not report any *hatsuyume*, but there was an event which illustrated something of the sensitivity of the season and which dominated domestic conversation through most of the New Year. On New Year's Eve in 1981 *oniisan* took the family car and, accompanied by his fiancée, went to meet his sister at the main line station as she came home from Tokyo for the break. When they returned to the house all three were unusually quiet and subdued. *Oniisan* said at first that the car had skidded. Later, after much conversation with his father, it was revealed that they had seen a train from one of the mountain roads in a place where no train could run. It was also too late for any more trains to be travelling to Tōno. All three car passengers insisted that they had seen the train twice, and even that they could hear its sounds. Various explanations were canvassed, including the idea that they had seen a string of cars, but none of them could dispel the feeling that this was some kind of omen, perhaps concerning the son's forthcoming marriage.

The Lunar New Year and traditional practices

When Smith described the agricultural community of Kurusu in 1955, New Year was still celebrated there according to the lunar calendar. Today, even in remote rural communities like those of the Isagozawa, the new calendar has come to dominate the timing of festival observances. Nevertheless, remnants of traditional folk practice persist, even though they may find a modified expression in accepted modern forms. It is easy, of course, to see a decline of belief in the dilution or disappearance of the older ways of doing things. Yet such an assumption must take account, not only of present-day practices, but also of the resilience of a folk tradition that still affords significant remnants of an earlier time. The lunar new year (*koshō-gatsu*) is one of these. Its date varies, but in 1981/2 it fell on 25 January and in 1982/3 on 14 January. The festival observances usually last for five days. Unlike the *hito-gami* festival of the Gregorian calendar which is directed to the theme of renewal in relation to the guardian deities, the Lunar festival in rural areas was principally concerned with the idea of fertility. It is an idea that finds a variety of expressions, some of which were recounted to us and some of which we were lucky enough to see.

One of the surviving observances of the lunar new year in the Isago-zawa appears to be the festival of *Oshira sama*. It is based upon a legend which probably originated in China and which exists in a number of different versions in Japan. But whereas it remains no more than a folktale in China, it has assumed the significance of a sacred ballad (*saimon*) for the Japanese (Blacker, 1975; Hori, 1968). It purports to explain the origin of silkworm culture in Japan, and its preservation, according to Hori (1968), can be ascribed to the blind shamanesses of rustic north-eastern Honshū (see also Blacker, 1975). There are many puzzling features of the *Oshira sama* legend and the observances that accompany it that we are not adequately qualified to discuss. In particular it was recounted to us in the context of *koshōgatsu* celebrations, whereas Hori (1968) suggests that *Oshira sama* are worshipped 'usually around the vernal equinox', that is about 20 March. We have no explanation for the discrepancy except to observe that, just as the story itself varies from place to place, so too it seems does the timing of the rituals connected with it.

The version of the *Oshira sama* legend which prevails in the Tōno area was recorded by Yanagita in 1910 (Morse, 1975). It is sufficiently interesting to recount at length.

'In present day Tsuchibuchi village there are two households called *daido* (i.e. having household deities). Mannojo Ohara is the master of the *daido* in Yamaguchi now. His mother, named Ohide, is over eighty and still healthy. She is Mr Sasaki's elder sister. Skilled at witchcraft, she has

79

shown Mr Sasaki how she can cast a spell and kill a snake or drop a bird that is perched in a tree. Last year, on 15 January by the old calendar, the old woman told this story: "Once upon a time there was a poor farmer. He had no wife but did have a beautiful daughter. He also had one horse. The daughter loved the horse and at night she would go to the stable and sleep. Finally she and the horse became husband and wife. One night the father heard of this and the next day, without saying anything to the daughter, he took the horse out and killed it by hanging it from a mulberry tree. That night the daughter asked her father why the horse was not anywhere around and she learned of the act. Shocked and filled with grief, she went to the spot beneath the mulberry tree and cried while clinging to the horse's head. The father, abhorring the sight, took an axe and chopped off the horse's head from behind. Then all at once the daughter, still clinging to the horse's head, flew off to the heavens." It was from this time that *Oshira sama* became a *kami* (deity). The image of the *kami* was made from the mulberry branch on which the horse was hanged.'

Some days later, the story continues, silkworms descended from the sky to the farmer's mulberry tree where they began to spin cocoons. Believing the silkworms to be incarnations of the daughter, the father nurtured them with great care to establish the tradition of silkworm culture in Japan.

Like many of Yanagita's 'legends', the biographical details in which the story is embedded enhance the matter-of-fact tone of the narrative. The story brings together common features of the pattern of rural life which probably persisted widely in Japan until 1945: sericulture, for which mulberry groves were established, and horse-breeding which led to the development of the distinctive *magariya* farmhouses of the north-east. The worship of *Oshira sama* as the guardian deity of sericulture seems once to have been led by the blind *itako* (shamanesses) and to have been observed 'mainly by housewives, organised on the basis of *dōzoku* groups, small territorial groups, or groups of relatives' (Hori, 1968). As it was presented to us, however, no *itako* were involved and the simple ritual merely consisted of placing a new layer of clothing on *Oshira sama* dolls, one representing the horse and the other representing the girl. This is done on the eve of the New Year; the dolls are set out on a low table with offerings of *sanko mochi* and *sake* wine and the legend is retold. It is interesting that the simple square of bright material that is used to clothe the mulberry stick dolls is not removed and replaced, but merely added to each year (Plate XVII). Blacker (1975) records examples with as many as ninety to a hundred layers of cloth 'the undermost ones rotting away with age'. In most places, as she also observes, the clothing actually covers the head of the doll, but in Iwate the carved head is allowed to protrude through a hole (Plate XVIII). This certainly accords with the images which we saw and which had a forbidding appearance, enhanced as it was by the black polished mulberry wood. Some of the horse dolls have pointed ears, some of the girl dolls have a high pointed hat, but otherwise the carvings are crude and difficult to distinguish.

In an extension of the *Oshira sama* tale which was told to us by *okāsan*, the story was linked to the mountain deities of the Isagozawa. In this version the disappearance of the daughter produced three sister *kami*. One day, the sisters were travelling in the area of Tsukimōshi and as evening fell they went to the temple to rest. During the night each of them had the same dream in which the Buddha blessed them with a lotus flower. The youngest of the three was the first to awake and, finding a lotus bloom on the sleeping form of her eldest sister, she took it for herself. When they had all wakened, the sisters agreed to part company. The youngest, since she had the lotus flower, went to dwell on the highest mountain, Mount Hayachine. The eldest took the lowest mountain, Mount Ishigami, and the third sister went to Mount Rokkōshi. Thus, Tōno became home to three sister-*kami* mountain deities.

In their turn, of course, these mountain deities must be worshipped, and festivals are held at the New Year and in summer at the temples which flank Mount Hayachine. The temple ceremony, presided over by a mountain priest, centres on the *kagura* dance in which the dancer wears a *shishi* mask to depict a fearsome lion or a deer (Plate XIX). In the course of the dance, the jaws of the beast are brought together in a hollow 'clack', while an assistant holds a trailing black tail under which people would pass in search of protection from the deity. Offerings of *sake*, rice, and salt are made, and in acknowledgement the *kagura* bows its head and brings its teeth together. We were told that it was once the custom for the beast to circulate amongst the houses of the nearby mountain villages. At present, though, the significance of the *kagura* as a New Year observance seems to be declining, at least in Tōno. By contrast, though, on the northern flank of Mount Hayachine the dances have not only been preserved, but have been considerably elaborated into a tourist attraction. They have brought a measure of unaccustomed prosperity to the upland village of Take and the wealth and splendour of the mountain temple there contrasts sharply with its poorer counterpart in Tōno *shi*. We found it interesting that even in a household like the Tadas, who had no *Oshira sama* dolls and who seemingly attached little significance to the *uji-gami* traditions of secretive house deities, nevertheless had the mask of a *Gonge sama* deity permanently on a shelf below the *kamidana*. The *gonge*, with flaring nostrils and a fearsome array of teeth, recall the lion-like beasts of the *kagura* dance and the lingering, mystical influence of the mountain *kami*.

Most of the domestic *koshōgatsu* observances seem to have disappeared

81

from the Tōno area. We do not know how many households still recount the *Oshira sama* legend and dress the dolls, or how many recognise the mountain deities through attendance at the *kagura* dances. But we were specially fortunate to meet a farming *ie*, the Shirahatas, where the eve of the Lunar New Year is still greeted in the traditional way of decorating a tree within the house. The tree is called the *mizu ki*, meaning literally 'water tree'. It is a species of dogwood associated particularly with the waterlogged margins of streams and ditches. The preparations began in 1981/2 early on the morning of 14 January. The entire three-generation family took four hours to complete the decoration, setting slender branches of *mizu ki* on an upturned quern in the outer kitchen of the *magariya* farmhouse and decking it with rice flour dumplings called *dango* and *mochi*.

The scene inside the old *magariya* conveys a powerful impression of the stern realities of earlier rural life in north-eastern Honshū. The outer kitchen area, set between stables and living quarters, has no ceiling; the bare rafters are blackened by smoke from the large open hearth which dominates the boarded room. The height allows for an impressive *mizu ki* display, while its blackness serves as sombre contrast to the cheerful pink and white balls of rice flour (Plate XX). As the preparations begin the inside scene is dominated by steam rising from the large two-tiered pot (*kama*) and from water boiling on the hearth. The women prepare *mochi* outside in the yard using the *kama* supply of freshly-steamed rice. Following traditional practice, the preparation of *mochi* is hard work. One person kneads the rice in the polished bowl of a heavy wooden mortar, called *usu*. She times her work with regular blows from a long-handled pestle wielded by a helper, moistening and rolling the sticky dough in between beats.

In the meantime, the men work on the tree itself. It seems likely that the *mizu ki* preparations are simply a variation on the more widespread traditional practice of decorating branches of pine (*kadomatsu*) for the eve of the New Year. The pine was formed into two posts, bound with rice straw and bamboo, and joined with a length of sacred rope. The rope was marked with four *heisoku* papers and sometimes with a piece of kelp wrapped in white paper and bearing three open circles. The *kadomatsu*, or 'door pine' seems to have been placed inside the main entrance to the house and to have been the point at which guests were welcomed on New Year's Day. It was sometimes called *Ichiyamatsu* or 'one-night pine', since the decoration was dismantled on the first day of the year (Yanagita, 1970). In our own experience, however, the *kadomatsu* now seems to have little relevance other than an ornamental one and its artistic arrangements of thick bamboo, rice straw, and plum blossom replicas are purchased rather than made.

For the Shirahatas, though, the *mizu ki* celebrations retain their original significance. The base of the tree is bound with rice straw and rice-straw rope, and fronds of bamboo are set at its centre. When this is done, small oval dumplings in white or pink are fastened directly to the tree, or arranged in fan-like displays on lengths of rice straw which are then hung from the branches. The rice straw is braided into knotted clusters, each with eight strands, and dumplings are attached to its head and four to each strand. These displays are called *awabo*, and five of them were hung on a piece of rice-straw rope across the corner where the *mizu ki* stood. The display was completed by placing a low lacquer table in front of the tree with two offerings of *sanko mochi* and two bottles of *sake* with cups. A centrally-placed candle was lit and the family took is in turn to come forward, bow and clap. Then, with their guests, they settle at the *kotatsu* where the women serve a stew and *mochi*.

The Shirahatas had no doubts that the significance of the *mizu ki* decoration is associated with preparations for the coming agricultural season. The rice flour dumplings may be said to resemble both heavy ears of rice and large silkworm cocoons. The theme of fertility, moreover, is supported by a second piece of ritual which engaged the Shirahatas later on the same day. Called *o ta ue*, literally 'transplanting', this second ceremony anticipates the first work of planting small rice seedlings in the paddies in early May (Plate XXI). The place of the rice, however, is taken by small sprigs of pine, 'planted' in rows in the snow, and accompanied by offerings of rice cake and *sake*. Marking the start of the lunar new year in these ways at least establishes links between the agricultural cycle and the lunar phases which were thought to be one means of predicting the weather.

In some *buraku* communities the theme of *koshōgatsu* as an anticipation of the agricultural year is celebrated as a communal, social event. We attended one of these at a small hilltop shrine dedicated to the deity Haguro. The spot is marked by some distinctive boulders cleft by the growth of tall pines. At the lunar new year the small group – there were twenty-one in 1982 – gathered at the shrine in the evening to eat and drink and to discuss projects for the coming year. Most of the participants are men. They arrive with offerings of *mochi* and *sake* and bow and clap at the small shrine within the building. The few women who are present are in charge of the food. They make the climb first to open the building, to take out a slat in the side for illumination, and to light a fire in the central hearth. Soon there is a stew of *tōfu*, noodles, *daikon*, and *miso* bubbling over the fire. When the men arrive the atmosphere develops quickly under the usual influence of *sake* and beer (Plate XXII). Friends circulate, pausing by the low tables and offering their cups in traditional greetings. Communal projects (*yui*) are discussed and plans may be laid to clear river weed, for example, or to demolish an old house. But undoubtedly the high point of the evening was the preparation of rice-flour dumplings in a variety of authentic male and female sexual forms. These are then boiled and eaten in an atmosphere of ribald hilarity. In this way the theme of fertility is again reiterated, but without formalised ritual beyond the inevitable commemorative photograph which was taken to mark the end of the gathering.

In Tōno itself communal gatherings are also held to mark the end of the old year. The parties are called *bōnenkai*, and are followed a few days later by a *shinenkai* for the advent of another year. They seem to be a recent phenomenon and although superficially they may appear to be trivial and light-hearted affairs, they again reflect something of the Japanese need for group identification and group effort. Like their rustic counterpart, they have a purpose which lies at least partly in the mutually supporting roles of men who work together; their goals may be different but their drives are the same despite the urban veneer of *bonenkai* activities.

Teachers at the main Junior High School held their *bonenkai* at the best restaurant in town, the Mizumoto. The strict hierarchy of age and seniority was reflected in the order of seating around the low tables which flanked the *tatami* room. The headmaster's table was at the end furthest from the entrance. The formality of the introductory speeches, however, soon began to contrast with the atmosphere of excitement fostered by large quantities of whisky and *sake*. In Japan, of course, alcohol seems to play a singularly important role in social gatherings of most kinds. It is an acceptable means of breaking down otherwise impossible barriers of status, and drunkenness in front of one's colleagues carries no stigma. Indeed, part of the purpose of *bōnenkai* is to air grievances in an open atmosphere and to say aloud all those things which would be inappropriate in normal circumstances. Yet even here, and in the context which we describe, the gathering still retained a formal sense of purpose. At the end of the evening, before the group divided for still more drinking in local bars, everyone joined in a circle with two of the younger members of staff in the centre. The 'master of ceremonies' – another junior staff member noted for his entertaining manner – then began to bellow out a rhythmic chant based on the theme of *gambare* ('try hard'). The chant was taken up by the whole group, its volume increasing to a crescendo of shared purpose and energy.

These seemingly trivial gatherings, some of which took place in bath houses or nearby hot spring centres, and some of which had as 'themes' such apparently vulgar notions as eating competitions, have become an effective urban counterpart of the more traditional rural ceremonies. The extent to which the individuals involved recognise the combination of a dependent tradition in a modern form is not really clear, and certainly the *bōnenkai* are quite divorced from the spiritual purposes of the older ceremonies. Yet the web of social dependence which those older ceremonies reinforced remains sufficiently strong to require physical expression even in the 'new' context of modern urban society, and it sits comfortably enough alongside the ritual duties of the Shirahatas, the formal observances of the Tadas, and the earthy humour of the Lunar New Year at the Haguro shrine.

Further annual ceremonial

In addition to the great religious festivals of *bon* and the New Year, the rural Japanese calendar observes a broad spectrum of other ceremonies which punctuate the year. Some of them are essentially domestic and find their principal expression within the *ie*, whilst others are dominantly communal. It is difficult, though, to make a firm distinction between them since important group relationships often overlap or compete with *ie* ties. As the celebration of New Year shows, for example, a strong communal quality can exist alongside an observance which probably has its roots in the private domain of the household. The theme of domestic renewal thus finds an echo in the communal advancement of age, and the lingering elements of an *uji-gami* tradition sit comfortably enough with the public devotions of *hito-gami* beliefs. In the final section of this chapter we consider some of the other ceremonies and festivals that we saw or heard about in Tōno. We begin with those which are overtly communal. The list is not exhaustive and our description is only brief, but perhaps it will serve to give some impression of the resilience of a deeply-ingrained tradition.

Even in the case of *ie* celebrations, of course, their personal significance may be modified by the fact that they occur at prescribed times of the year. The knowledge that others are sharing the same experience, therefore, means that even life-cycle events take on something of a public flavour. This is certainly the case for the first of the annual ceremonial events following the New Year. This is the age celebration which takes place on 15 January. We have already described the *seijinshiki* which acknowledges the entry to adulthood of all twenty-year-olds in Japan. But there are other of these *toshiiwai* ('year celebrations') which are picked out for their special significance. These derive from traditional beliefs about the mystical power of certain numerical combinations (see Hendry, 1981). For men, an important landmark is the forty-second year. The number four is thought to be inauspicious through its phonetic association with *shi*, meaning 'death'. The number two also has unfavourable implications since it is the first of the even numbers. when they are placed together, at the age of forty-two, the year becomes a *yakudoshi* or 'bad-luck year'. It is in the nature of Japanese thinking, however, that the time should be marked by celebration since it is reasoned that a man needs the support of his family and friends in his *yakudoshi*. The equivalent time for women occurs at the age of thirty-three, called *onna-no-taiyaku* ('women's calamity') and it is marked by supportive gatherings of women friends. The effect of *toshiiwai* celebrations of this kind at least has the merit of bringing a continuous stream of business to the restaurants of Tōno, keeping them lively and full well after the end of the New Year holiday.

Much later in the year, on 15 November, the Japanese celebrate another age festival, the *shichi-go-san* or 'seven, five, three'. Children who have reached the age of seven, or five, or three, are taken to the local shrine where parents express their gratitude to the tutelary deity and invoke continued blessing for their offspring (de Garis, 1934). The blessing is called *yakubarai o shite-moraimasu*, literally 'receiving a cleansing of demons'. As Hendry (1981) notes, the *shichi-go-san* is a recent amalgamation of a number of traditional rites signalling changes in the way in which children were dressed. In Tōno, and no doubt elsewhere, the main activity of the day seems to centre on beauty parlours and photographers' studios. The boys wear the wide traditional *hakama* 'trousers', and the girls wear their first *obi* sashes. They emerge from the beauty parlours as elaborately costumed, powdered and even bewigged miniatures of their parents. They also receive gifts of long, brightly decorated envelopes carrying pictures of the stork and turtle which symbolise longevity, and filled with sweets. In Kurotsuchi, Hendry (1981) notes, the occasion was treated rather casually, but in Tōno, as far as we could judge, it still retains a widespread recognition.

The period between the New Year and the official start of spring (4 February in the Gregorian calendar) is the period of *kangeiko*. In north-eastern Honshū, of course, it remains very cold and it is a testing time when the body and the spirit may be toughened in the practice of martial arts. Nevertheless, the start of Spring (*risshun*) is acknowledged even in the bitter cold by a simple domestic ceremony aimed at driving out any lingering demons. In the Tada *ie oniisan* performed the ceremony, taking peanuts (once red beans) and throwing them from every door and window with a cry of 'demons out, luck in'! By tradition he was then required to eat the number of peanuts equivalent to his age. The person who performs this simple act was described to us as *toshiotoko*, the 'man of the year', but it can also be translated as 'New Year man' and it is clear from Yanagita's (1970) account that the duties of the *toshiotoko* used to fall upon the head of the oldest branch family. They began at New Year with the setting up of the sacred rope (*shimenawa*), the *heisoku* papers and the *kadomatsu* pines. The Tadas were also aware of another duty that traditionally fell to the *toshiotoko*: this was to draw the first water (*waka mizu*) from the household well. According to Yanagita (1970), however, this was a New Year practice restricted to the remote village of Akka in northeastern Honshū, and the water was used to make the year's first offering of boiled rice. The least pleasant of the traditional duties that used to fall to the *toshiotoko*, we were told, was the *susu harai*, literally 'cleaning the soot' from the open beams and rafters of the old farm houses. It is interesting that this has now found a formal urban equivalent, at least in Tōno. At the beginning of spring the local council conduct an inspection of the houses in each ward, a visiting official taking a perfunctory glance at the drains and the kitchen area and marking his attendance by placing a small sticker on the doorpost. Over the years, these are accumulating!

In the farming *ie* the beginning of spring finds further recognition in the festival of the spring winds. It takes place according to the Lunar calendar, but in official terms it fell between March 2 and 4 in 1982. Its purpose, we were told, is to encourage the onset of the first warm breezes of the year bringing the beginnings of the thaw to the hard frosts of winter, and also to afford some degree of protection against pestilence for the farmers' crops. Again the observance is a simple one involving the construction of straw dolls (*wara ningyo*). The dolls themselves echo something of the rural concern with fertility: they are made in male and female pairs with exaggerated sexual organs, and the male doll carries a protective stave. Both dolls have fearsome faces painted on paper and are made to stand at the entrance to farm tracks throughout the growing season (Plate XXIII).

At about the same time of year, on 3 March, the dolls' festival, or *hinamatsuri*, is held. It is celebrated throughout Japan and not surprisingly it has a special significance for girls. Beyond seeing the Tadas' own set of dolls, which were old and of considerable value, we had no personal experience of the *hinamatsuri* and, indeed, Smith noted its virtual disappearance from Kurusu as long ago as 1956. *Okāsan* said that no particular ritual is attached to the day except after the birth of a girl when the family will invite the parents of the bride to a small celebration (but see de Garis, 1934). Nevertheless, it was noticeable that local shops were displaying and selling doll sets from about the middle of February, and that some of them cost as much as £200. The dolls themselves reflect the traditional hierarchy of Japanese society with a feudal lord and lady on an upper tier and a gathering of courtiers, advisers, artisans, and servants below them. In addition, the sets also contain a selection of miniature artefacts including artificial offerings of the celebratory *mochi*. The equivalent day for sons of the *ie* is celebrated on 5 May in a festival known as *Tango-no-sekku*, which might be interpreted as 'The First Day of the Horse'. It is also known sometimes as *Shōbu-no-sekku* or the 'Iris Festival'. The significance of the horse, of course, lies in its perceived qualities of bravery and strength, and the *shōbu* iris is said to resemble a sword-blade in shape (see de Garis, 1934). Traditionally the festival involved the boys of the family paying solemn respects to the heirlooms of warrior ancestors. The day was marked by erecting balloons or streamers on a long pole set outside the house, usually one for each son (see Smith, 1955). The balloons took the form of a carp which is much admired for its qualities of determination, strength, 'and the will to overcome difficulties' (de Garis, 1934). These days it seems that the festival has lost much of its significance, though in Tōno carp streamers, costing as much as £100 each, can still be seen fluttering in the spring breeze on 5 May.

There is another ceremony in May which is still observed in some of the farming *ie* like the Shirahatas. It is known as *hachijūhachiya* ('eighty-eight') and it takes place on the 2nd of the month, just eighty-eight days after the official start of spring. The number eighty-eight has a significance which derives from a linguistic association with rice and rice-growing. In Chinese loan characters (*kanji*) eighty-eight is written as a sequence of eight (八), ten (十), and eight (八). These may be seen as the dissembled parts of the character for rice, *kome*, which is written as 米. This association is not confined to the *hachijuhachiya* festival alone, but also provides impetus for the celebration of a person's eighty-eighth year. In this way rice-growing has developed from being a means for living into a symbol for life and growth itself. The actual festival is intended to serve as a protection against late frosts which could significantly damage the young rice seedlings (*ine*) at a time when they had been transplanted in the paddies. It involves setting small paper flags on the earth banks of the rice fields. The flags often depict the horse, which is said to be a source of powerful protection.

Summer begins officially on 22 June and on the following day, in anticipation of the taxing heat to come, there is the *ie* festival of *shōbu* and *yomogi*. We have already mentioned *shōbu*, the Japanese iris, a sweet flag or rush which grows in abundance amongst the rice fields, and which symbolises in its sword-like leaf the courage and determination of a warrior. This is given added significance by its botanical name which is pronounced in the same way as 'warlike spirit'. The connection of *shōbu* with *yomogi*, however, is not at all clear. *Yomogi* is a mugwort or wormwood (*Artemisia indica*). In a European context, as its botanical name indicates, it is taken to be a symbol of fertility since the tiny flowers of the plant resemble a cluster of female breasts. It may be, given the timing of the festival and the coming rice harvest, that the significance of *yomogi* in Japan derives from a similar association. Certainly the ideas of courage and fertility figure largely in the minds of the rural Japanese. Unfortunately, we have no evidence whatsoever for this particular interpretation. The explanation which we were offered came from *okāsan* and lay in a story which she took great relish in telling. It is a salutary tale of a young man who married a girl of great beauty, particularly noted for the length of her hair. Soon after the marriage the husband began to notice that however hard he toiled and however much he supplied his home with vegetables and rice there never seemed to be enough to go around. His wife was dutiful, apparently hardworking and respectful, but she did not seem to be able to manage the domestic budget. Things came to such a pass that the husband decided to conceal himself and watch his wife as she worked. What he saw filled him with fear. His wife, believing herself to be alone, took down her hair, which had been piled high for work, to reveal a gaping mouth into which she put dozens of rice cakes, pickles and vegetables. The man had married a mountain demon! He was saved only by hiding amongst the tall spiked banks of *shōbu*, the fronds of *yomogi*, and the treacherous sands which they concealed, into which the demon was afraid to enter.

Whatever the origins of the *shōbu* and *yomogi* festival, it was widely observed around Tōno. Sprigs of the two plants are placed under the highest point in the eaves of the house, and sometimes at windows and above the front door. The Tadas also placed large bunches around the *butsudan*. Finally, *shōbu* leaves are placed in the evening bath and the bather ties a length around his or her head to enhance the infusion of strength which it symbolises. In this way, at the start of the most demanding season of the year, the *ie* in its physical, spiritual, and family form takes on the symbolic strength of the warrior.

The onset of summer heralds a time of hard labour in the fields: rice paddies need constant attention as grasses and weeds flourish in the heat and humidity, and there is the continual labour of cutting animal fodder from the banks of the fields. There is, therefore, something of a lull in festival activity until *obon* in mid-August. Nevertheless, the year is punctuated by a total of sixty-nine documented festivals, including national holidays, most of which seem to be specific to a particular shrine or temple.

Given the multiple influence of great religions like Shinto and Buddhism, and the way in which their beliefs are intermingled, it would be the task of a specific study to describe in detail the history and development of even one communal shrine festival, to illustrate how they combine social life and religious observance, and to account for the obvious decrease in participation at all but the most important. Superficially at least it is difficult to avoid the impression that traditional festivals are continued by those who have, by virtue of status or personal commitment, some attachment to the past. But the centralisation of the main force of festival activity, partly by the local council and partly by the school curriculum, tends paradoxically to obscure their significance for the individual whose participation becomes increasingly vicarious. In the Aozasa area of eastern Tōno, for example, there is a long tradition of performance of the *shishi odori*, the 'deer dance'. Originally it was a form of expressive folk-art, linked to the rice harvest and to the protection of the mountain gods (see also Smith, 1955), and in this form it still survives in the Isagozawa. But in Aozasa the picture has changed radically. Older men are still called in to play the complicated drum and flute accompaniment to the dance, but the performers themselves are now all members of the Junior High School. They learn the steps of the dance progressively as they move through school grades, but they probably stop dancing altogether when they move to the senior school at sixteen. Nevertheless, a 'team' of dancers now parade their skills not for the gods, but for audiences in America and China as well as throughout Japan. They make their own elaborate masks which are decorated now with the insignia of the Junior High rather than of the village of Aozasa. The pride which a family might once have felt at having an accomplished dancer at its head is now transferred to a child who becomes a member of the school troupe.

In the more remote areas, though, the *shishi* dance still retains some of its old authenticity and its religious and social significance. For example, a small festival is still held annually on 7 August at the shrine on Mount Ishigami in the Isagozawa. About a third of the seventy-seven families from the four *buraku* in the valley assembled to enjoy the food and drink prepared by local wives and to seek the protection of the gods in the traditional way. It was raining and a large sheet of blue polythene had been strung between the tall trees to give some shelter to the celebrants. Without exception these were the older men of the *buraku*. They took off their shoes and sat on more polythene sheets in the shadowy blue light cast by the canopy. To begin with, they adopted the formal kneeling *hiza* posture, but as representatives of the council, the co-operative, the village elders and family heads each in turn made offerings of pine sprigs at the delapidated shrine, the atmosphere began to relax. Settling into the more comfortable cross-legged *agura*, the gathering began to enjoy their food and drink and to anticipate the *shishi*. The dance was led by Suzuki Kaoru *san*, a farmer from the lower valley who is a skilled performer. He was accompanied by two other characters: the *tengu* with a long-nosed bright red mask, high clogs, and a staff, and the fool whose mask is twisted and pouting and who wears a towel tied around his head. Unlike the leader, the other dancers performed with an awkward self-consciousness that contrasted sharply with the polished accomplishments of the Aozasa Junior High. Yet it was probably always so with these festivals. Their purpose, after all, lay in the interweaving of close community ties and the powers of the deities rather than the creation of spectacle or entertainment.

The rice harvest is also anticipated by the main Tōno festival, held between 14 and 16 September at the Hachiman shrine. Again, compared with the small rural gathering on Mount Ishigami, this is a magnificent occasion when competing villages show their skills in dancing, archery, and in carrying the palanquin (*omikoshi*). *Oniisan* had been involved in the preparation of the council palanquin, an arrangement of three straw-wrapped barrels surmounted by a thick padded red and white rope. It symbolises the ark of the deities which is kept in the Hachiman shrine. Altogether it weighed over 500 kilos and it was carried by a team of twenty-four volunteers, three to each projecting arm. The *gaijin* was one of the volunteers. We were dressed in a traditional costume of white breeches (*fundoshi*), a short 'hapicoat', and straw sandals. We were also tightly bound about the midriff with ten feet or so of cotton sheeting to give support for the day's work. Although there were some brief pauses, the work of carrying the *omikoshi* continues throughout the whole of the first day of the festival, the bearers becoming progressively inebriated from seemingly endless supplies of *sake* and beer. Eventually the palanquin seems to move with a will of its own, carriers on one side having no knowledge of the behaviour of those on the other. It suddenly careers at speed from one side to the other of the narrow streets, or swings up and down with a crushing force as the group seems to find a common purpose. It is, without doubt, a most exhausting way of seeking the protection of the gods!

The parades and palanquin bearing of the first day are followed on the second by a family assembly in the grounds of the Hachiman shrine. They eat and drink and watch more parades and a series of competitions beginning with horseback archery. *Shishi* dances are performed in a competitive atmosphere, and the energy and commitment of the dancers sometimes draws a response from a member of the crowd who might, after a little too much to drink, join in with his own version of the dance. The festival reaches its climax in a parade and dedication of the Hachiman *omikoshi*, distinguished by its fine golden cockerel. But the *shishi* dancers continue to perform into the evening, dancing in small groups for their friends or circulating the houses of important contacts in the town and dancing in their honour.

The climactic Tōno festival is a time for sheer enjoyment, growing out of religious practices but adapting and elaborating them to serve modern tastes for organised spectacle and display. As on the many other occasions when we witnessed festival activity, there was no apparent tension between religious observance and personal or communal indulgence. Indeed, there was no effective separation between them. This applies even at Christmas (called *Kurisumasu*). We met no Christians in Tōno, but Christmas Eve is acknowledged and the main street of the town is decked with Christmas trees and reindeer displays. It has become an accepted part of the winter holiday, a slightly 'special' day to be recognised with a little more *sake* and beer than usual. But the Tadas admitted that without the presence of *gaijin* they would have given it little attention. Its significance, they thought, was primarily commercial and principally confined to the southern cities.

Conclusion

Our final impressions of the festivals and ceremonies which we saw, or which were recounted to us, is that they exist on a variety of different levels and fulfil a range of needs all at the same time. None that we can recall can be entirely divorced from the mysteries of folk religion but all of them seem to serve a social purpose as well. These influences, though, are seldom overt. No one could tell us with authority, for example, how the *shishi odori* developed or what particular meaning it has. It is connected with the rice harvest. It has always been so. It is an expressive plea, a form of thanksgiving, an invitation to the deities, and so forth. But for the participants, the meaning and excitement probably lies in the performance itself. For the observers it lies in the entertainment of an occasional spectacle. If there are deeper connections, then they remain deep for the ordinary folk, not open to articulation, but certainly not open to rejection by an outsider.

The quality which distinguishes this kind of activity for us is that it is set above the normal routine while simultaneously remaining a part of the everyday pattern. They demand no self-conscious veneration and they inspire no air of mystery. On the prescribed day, and in the correct manner, the ceremony is performed. But family life, or village life, does not subsequently revert to 'normal', since these events are part of the normality of an unquestioned world of belief. There is some scepticism amongst the young, of course, but perhaps there always was. And *oniisan*, who queried some of the ceremonial acts he was required to perform, still shared a common awareness of powers that were beyond the corporeal.

XIII

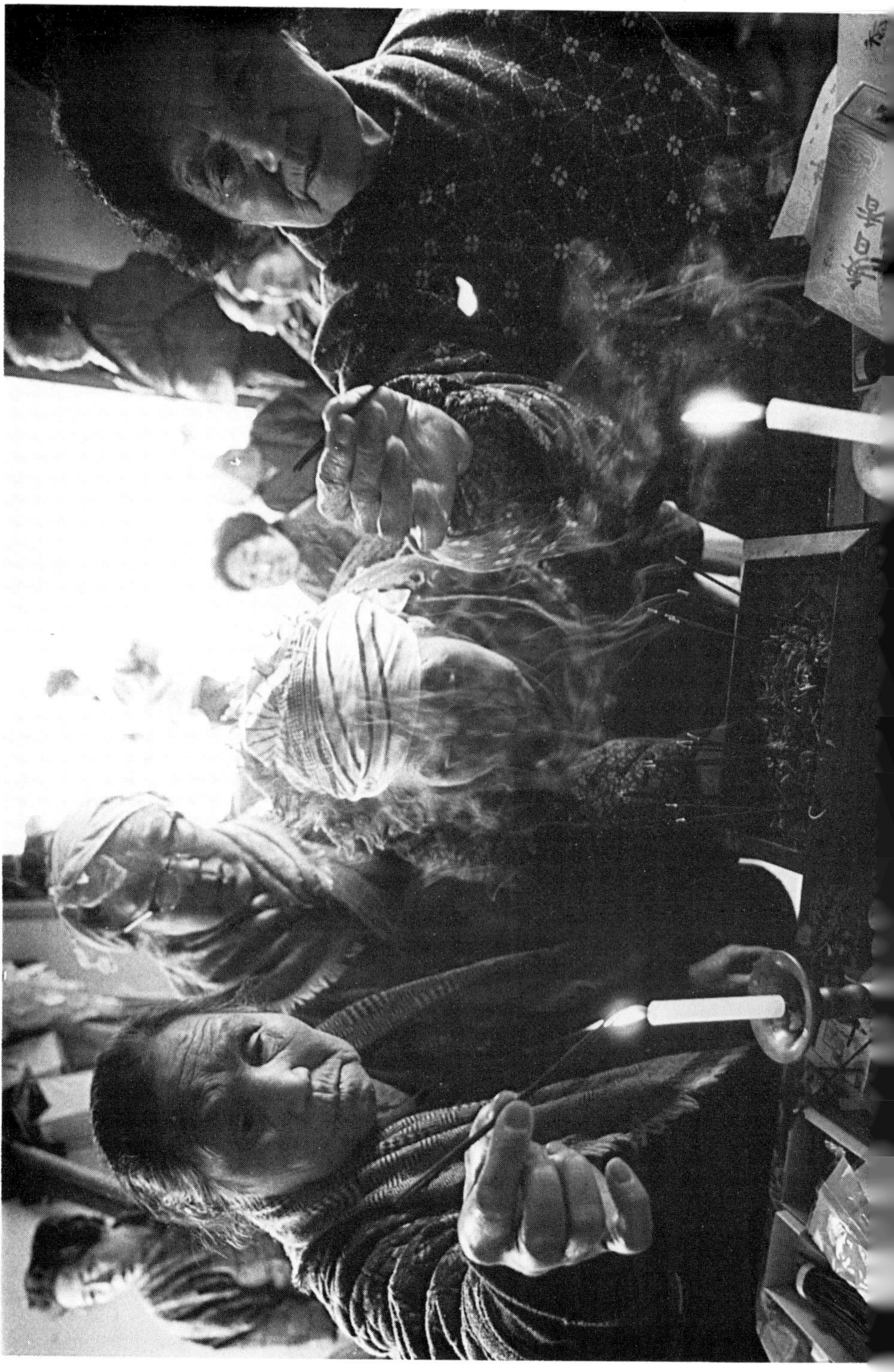

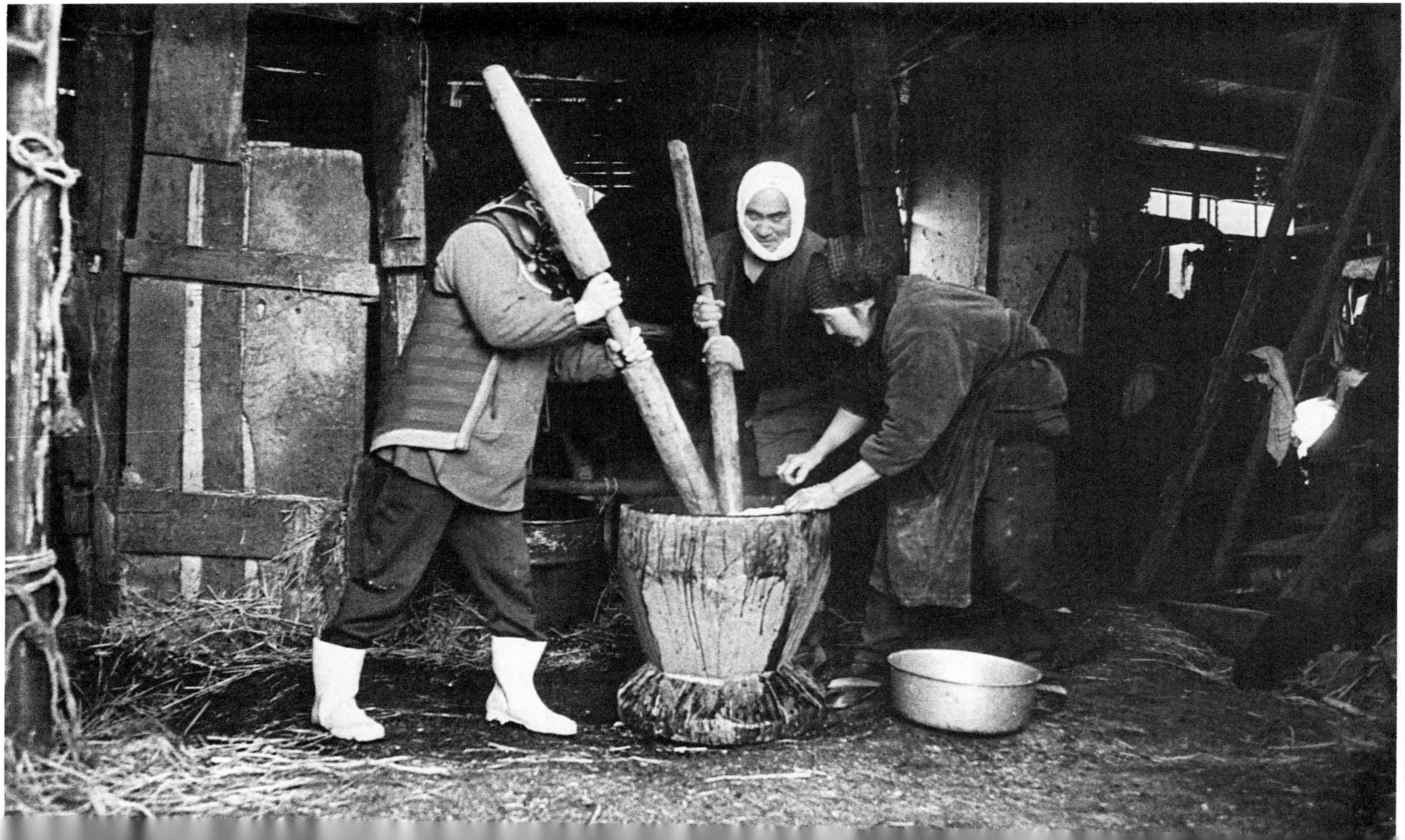

XVII

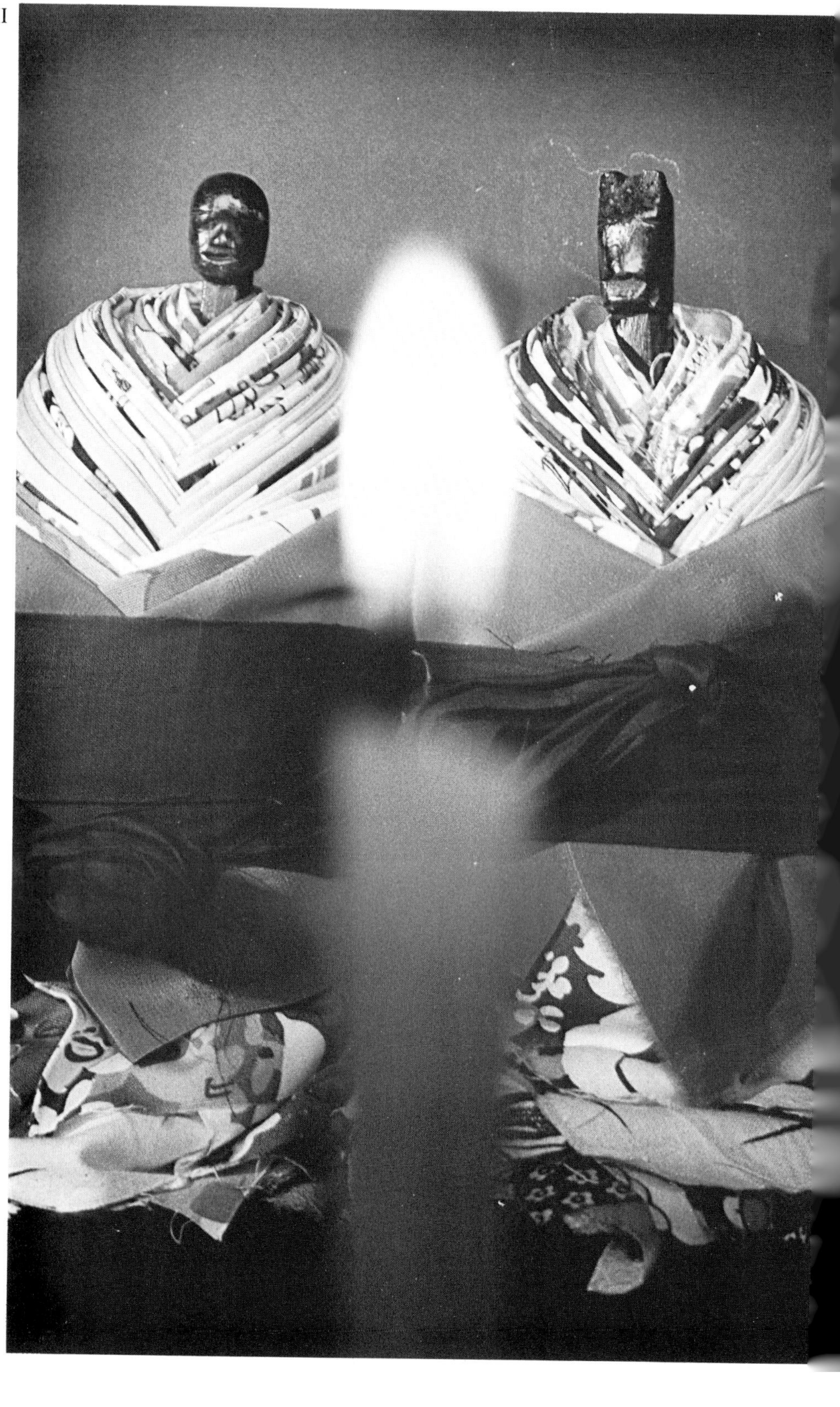

XIX

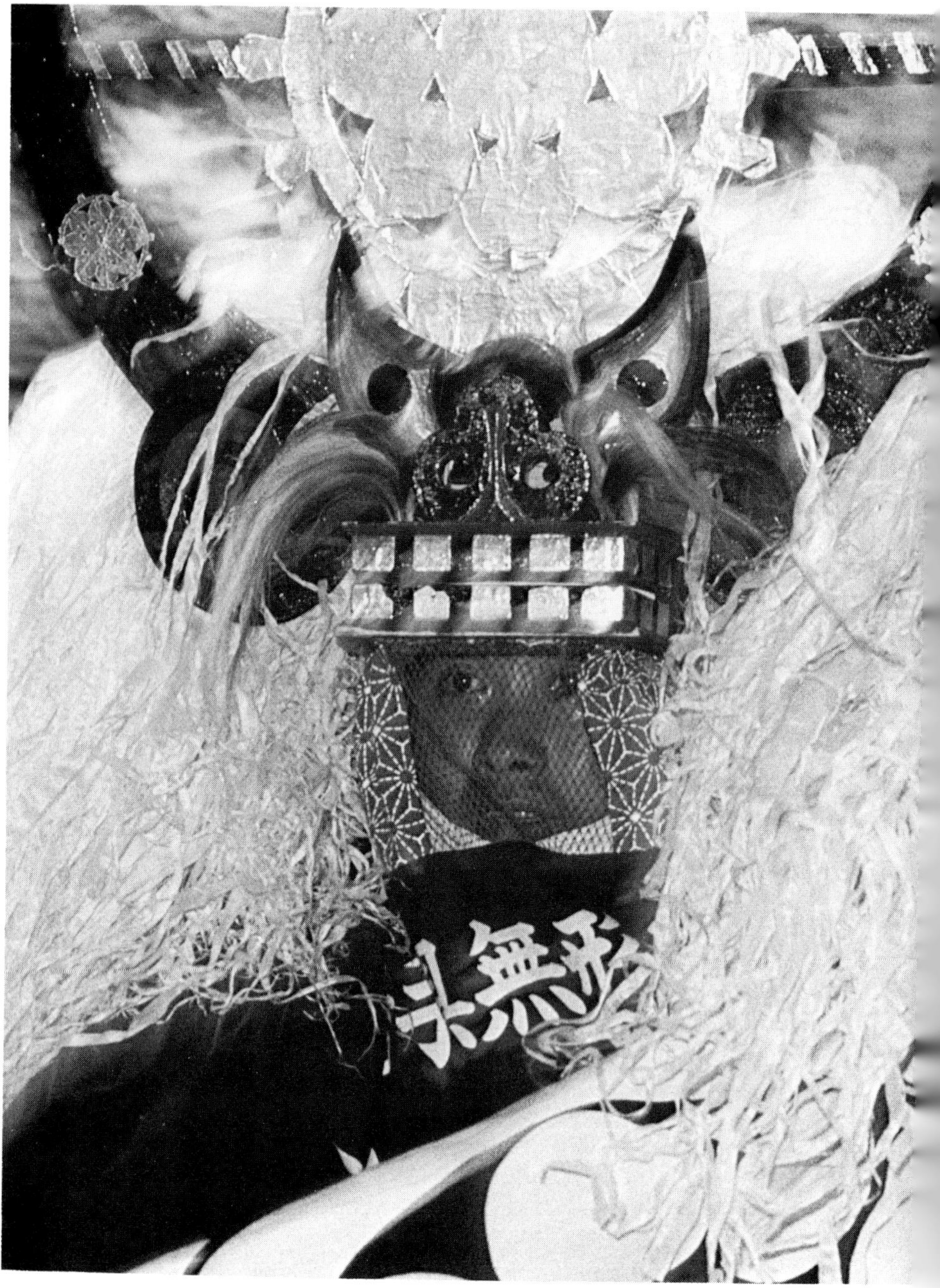

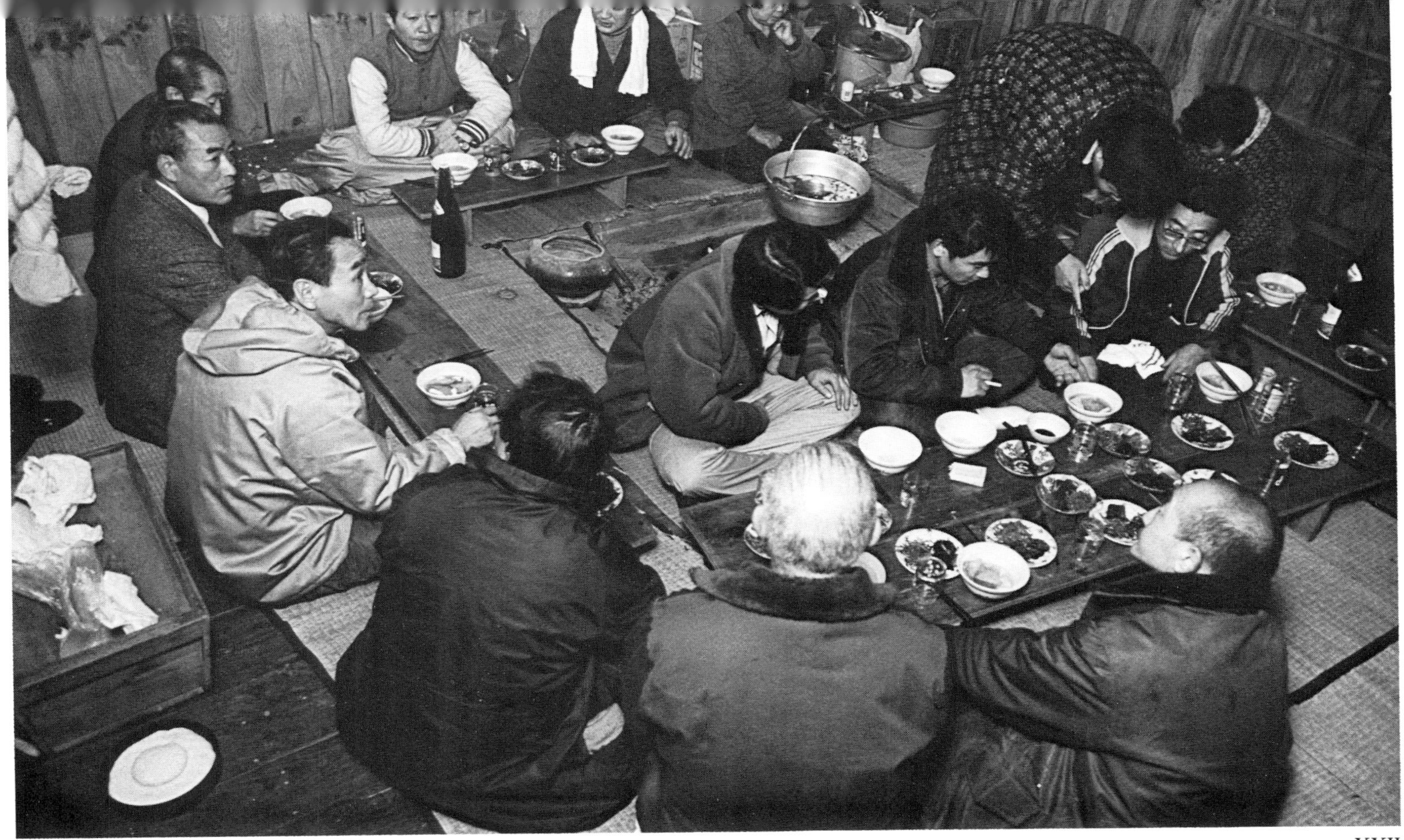

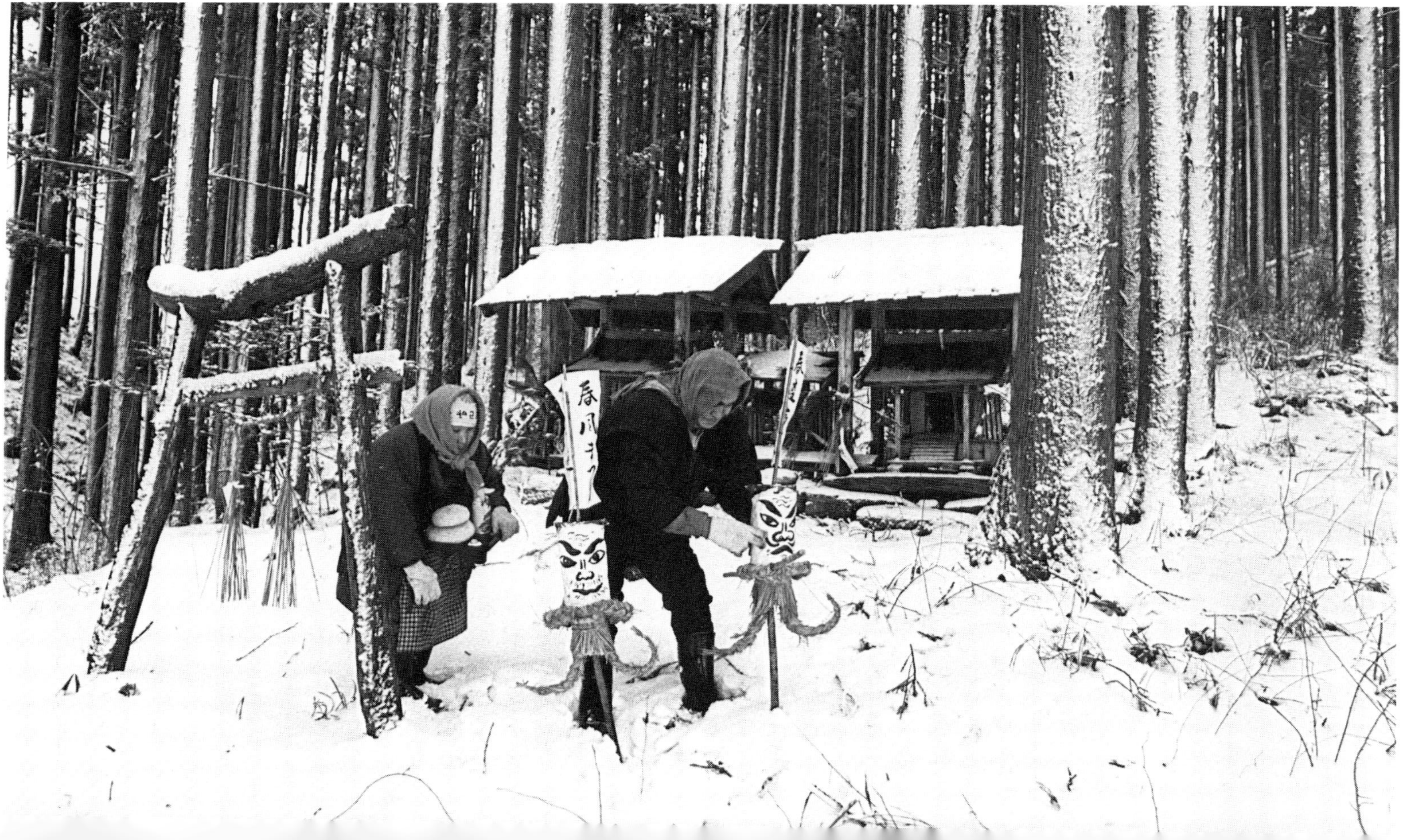

The incident on New Year's Eve was a good example. On another occasion, driving through the Tsuchibuchi district, he confided an unease which he believed confirmed the area's historical notoriety.

The annual round of ceremony and festival, therefore, are so much a part of rural life that they draw the individual unremarkably through the year. No sooner is one event over, it seemed, than preparation for the next one is beginning. But there are times in the life cycle of the *ie* which do stand outside the routine. This is because they are those critical points at which the *ie* is redefined in its internal relationships and its relations with the outside world. They are marriage, birth, death, and housebuilding. Living with the Tadas gave us an opportunity to observe two of these important junctures. *Oniisan* was married during the latter part of our stay and in the summer of 1982 our carpenter friend, Horiochi *san*, constructed a new house.

preceding pages

XII The Buddhist altar is a reminder of *ie* lineage.

XIII The purpose of *obon* is to mark the return of the souls of deceased forebears.

XIV In 1982 the victor in Tōno's mayoral elections triumphantly painted in the second eye of a large *daruma* doll.

XV Steamed rice was pounded in large wooden pestles.

XVI The girls are all dressed in their finest *kimonos*.

XVII The simple square of bright material that is used to clothe the mulberry stick dolls is not removed and replaced, but merely added to each year.

XVIII In Iwate the carved head is allowed to protrude through the hole.

XIX The dancer wears a *shishi* mask.

XX The height allows for an impressive *mizu ki* display, while its blackness serves as sombre contrast.

XXI 'O ta ue' anticipates the first work of planting.

XXII When the men arrive the atmosphere develops quickly under the usual influence of *sake* and beer.

XXIII Both dolls have fearsome faces painted on paper.

Marriage in the *ie*

Since the ending of the Second World War the *ie* pattern of household organisation has been under great pressure. For Japan as a whole it has ceased to be the predominant form of family organisation, and even in those instances and those areas where it survives this depends upon increasing accommodation to ideals which are alien to its traditional character. In Morioka's (1986) view, one of the principal causes of *ie* breakdown is to be found in the 'privatisation' of family life. In essence this means that marriage sees the beginning of a family and the death of one spouse sees its end. Under the old system, of course, marriage was simply an element in the ongoing *ie* continuum, necessary for its survival but by no means sufficient for its definition. The consequences of the privatisation of family life have an important bearing on social relationships generally. According to Morioka (1986), it has led to the breakdown of mutually supportive neighbourhood relations, to the weakening of obligatory kinship ties, to the slackening of discipline in the public sphere of child behaviour, and to the realignment of parent/child relations from the traditional father/son coalition to a coalition of mother/children from which the father is excluded.

The shift to privatisation, however, is by no means complete and the traditional *ie* values, though certainly the subject of scrutiny and reflection, are not always readily abandoned even amongst the young. Our own family gave us ample evidence of the propensity for survival which the *ie* can display under the threat of modernisation. Tōno is not Tokyo, of course, and in the rural areas of Japan the pressures to conformity slacken less readily. Nevertheless, in the marriage of *oniisan* the household faced an important test. In its successful resolution the Tada *ie* was preserved, at least for another generation.

The trend towards nuclear families, consisting only of parents and dependent children, is an inevitable corollary of the growth of marriages made out of mutual love. The Japanese call such marriages *ren'ai*, and in their nature they emphasise the precedence of individual choice. Between *ie*, however, the traditional form of marriage is one which is arranged and which the Japanese call *miai*. This is essentially a bond between 'houses', a merging of lineage, and a promise of co-operative association. Hendry (1981) has shown how *miai* marriages, which once typified the union of only the grander Japanese families, gradually spread through the nation as a whole during the Meiji period (1868–1912). Ideally, they pay scant regard to the wishes of the individuals concerned, centring instead on the benefits which will accrue to the *ie* from an appropriate match. The major concession to prospective bride and groom is the arrangement of a 'mutual viewing' when both the couple and their respective families have an opportunity to assess each other. It is from this mutual viewing that the name *miai* is drawn.

The business of arranging a *miai* marriage is a delicate one: in a very real sense it is a matter of matching the qualities which each *ie* will bring to the other. For this reason, the work of creating the match is often entrusted to an experienced third party, called *nakōdo* (go-between). *Otō-san* was a prime example of a *nakōdo*, since his position of authority made him available to the approaches of junior staff who were already predisposed to trust the soundness of his judgement. Another friend who served as *nakōdo* during our stay was Horiuchi *san*. He was involved in arranging the marriage of a policeman as a *muko yōshi* and from him we learned something of the go-between's role. For both partners to the match he had obtained lengthy *curriculum vitae* which contained details of physical appearance, educational background, occupation and interests. He organised the first *miai* at a restaurant in Tōno which, he explained, was a 'neutral' venue. The subsequent negotiations leading up to the betrothal took several months during which he made a total of fifty-three contacts between the respective *ie*. To compensate for the frequent visits, the telephone calls and his own personal contribution to the negotiations, Horiuchi *san* received 50,000 yen (£212).

The marriage of *oniisan*

For *oniisan* the question of marriage was a sensitive one. Before we arrived to live with the family he had already made one request to marry. This request had been refused by his parents and *oniisan* had accepted their refusal. In the light of traditional *ie* marriages the grounds were common enough: the other *ie* in question had suffered disgrace through the business dealings of the grandfather. He had given his personal stamp (*hanko*), akin to a signature, to a business partner who had then used it to obtain false credit. The not inconsiderable social standing of the Tada *ie* would have been compromised by such a match and, whatever the feelings between the principals involved, *oniisan* bowed to the wishes of his parents. His second

107

request to marry took place in no less difficult circumstances and once again threw into sharp relief the unfolding tensions which *ren'ai* can create within the *ie*. On this occasion he asked to marry his cousin, the daughter of *okāsan*'s brother. This time, however, his own determination was such that he was prepared to leave the family home, and to forsake his rightful place as its future head, in order to marry the girl of his choice. For her part, too, the girl was equally determined. Together, they sought medical advice regarding the genetic implications of the match and talked at length about the favourable results which they received. But the social implications of the marriage of two close relatives remained and *okāsan* in particular anticipated the gossip that would certainly come on the periphery of her circle of friends. *Otōsan*, on the other hand, showed great patience and restraint, and it was clear to us that uppermost in his mind were the consequences for the *ie* should his son leave to live in Tokyo. Faced with such a stark choice the essential pragmatism which forms the basis of *ie* continuity allowed the parents to bow to the wishes of the *kokeisha*. Once the decision was made, however, *oniisan* himself was happy to see the marriage unfold according to the proper *miai* sequence. Thus, although it was quite unnecessary in this case, the Tadas approached an old acquaintance of suitable social standing to perform the duties of *nakōdo* on the wedding day, and to arrange the two ceremonies which precede the wedding itself. The first of these is called *saketate* (literally 'offering *sake* wine') and it signifies the successful outcome of *miai* meetings with a preliminary discussion of the terms of the dowry. The second is the betrothal ceremony, which is called *yuinō*. In the remainder of this chapter we will describe these ceremonies and the wedding of *oniisan*. We make no claims for the generality of our observations; indeed it is difficult to see what could be added to Hendry's (1981) comprehensive study. Instead, we merely report the things which we saw and were told from the intimate vantage of the Tada *ie*, drawing attention to differences in practice where these seem apparent.

Hendry (1981) observed that in Kyūshū the ceremony of betrothal was prefaced by a meeting called *kimeja*, or 'decision tea'. An alternative name is *kugicha*, or 'nail tea', which symbolises the binding nature of the decision. To settle the agreement the family of the prospective groom offer gifts to the family of the bride. These gifts consist of tea, a large sea-bream, and a bottle of *sake*. Much the same kind of meeting takes place in Tōno, except that tea is omitted from the list of gifts and the ceremony is known as *saketate*. The omission of the tea, we were told, reflected a potentially inauspicious phonetic association between the word for green tea (*ocha*) and *cha-cha ga ireru*, which means to interrupt, to pour scorn on another person's ideas, or to gossip. In keeping with the custom that the number of

108

gifts should always be an odd one, therefore, it is the practice in Tōno to take two fish.

Mindful of the importance of timing in these matters, *okāsan* explained that in the six-day Buddhist week the meeting was best held on *daian*, 'great safety', or *tomobiki*, 'pulling a friend'. Often the *sake tate* would involve two *nakōdo* and the father of the groom, again in keeping with the Japanese preference for odd numbers. In the Tadas' case, however, *oniisan* himself attended, necessitating the presence of both parents. Dress was strictly formal: traditional black *kimono* with family crest (called *mon*), or alternatively a black suit and tie for men. The tradition of wearing black for any formal occasion, celebratory or otherwise, recalls a time when people were too poor to afford more than one 'special' dress. Things are different today, of course, and *okāsan* had a range of beautiful kimono to grace any occasion, some of them costing in excess of £1,000.

As in other ceremonial, detail conveys much of the weight of symbolic meaning. The choice of sea-bream, for example, reflects their name, *tai*, which has a phonetic link with *omedetai*, meaning 'congratulations'. An acceptable alternative, it appears, would have been the variety of scorpion fish called *kichiji*, which also means 'auspicious event'. The fish themselves were labelled with a character that appears often in marriage tradition: this is *shimeru*, which means 'to tie up', and it is related to the notion of *engumi*, which implies the binding together of the important destiny of the respective *ie*. A similar expression is *enmusubi*, which derives from the action of tying a *kimono* sash, and indeed the character comprising *musu-bu*, 'to tie', is also used in the common word for a wedding, *kekkon*. The fish were offered on a plate made from red lacquer, its colour again signifying an *iwai* or celebration. Around the rim were depictions of the crane and the turtle, symbolic of longevity that recur often in the marriage theme, and that are conveyed in the word *tsuru-kame*. In Kyūshū, Hendry (1981) tells us, the same symbols decorate the specially-boxed gifts of tea. The fish were also offered with their stomachs placed together in an explicit reference to the fruitfulness of the union. *Okāsan* called the purpose of this *fuku awase ni-shite dasu*, 'to bring out great happiness'. Placed back to back, clearly, the implications would have been very different.

The meeting itself, as it was recounted to us, was an extremely simple but scrupulously correct occasion, marked not so much by the things that were actually done but by the way in which they were done. When the Tadas' party arrived at the house of the bride-to-be, their hosts opened the sliding screens from the polite kneeling position, placing the left hand on the edge of the panel and pushing with the right. On entering the *tatami* mat room the guests took great care not to tread upon the edges of the mats. The panels were then closed by placing the right hand above the left, while taking great care to face the guests all the time. Formal greetings were then exchanged and *okāsan* demonstrated the way in which she had knelt, gathering in the hem of her *kimono*, placing her hands fifteen to thirty centimetres away from her, palms flat on the *tatami*, thumb and index finger touching, and bowing her head to the floor. Movement from this position and on to the cushions provided, she said, must always be initiated by bringing the right foot forward. Once on the cushions, the parties to the meeting adopted the formal upright kneeling posture called *tate hiza*, rather than the relaxed cross-legged *agura*. Seating order was important since it reflected status and indicated proper deference. The two *ie* heads, therefore, sat together beside the *tokonoma*, their wives beside them, then the couple, and finally the two *nakōdo* nearest the entrance. The father of the groom then offered his gifts, saying, *Kochira no ojōsan o kudasai*, 'Please give (this) your daughter'. The reply was a simple assent couched in polite language, *Hai, yoroshiku degozaimasu*. From this point, the meeting relaxed, a meal was served, and details of the forthcoming *yuinō* (betrothal) and subsequent wedding were discussed.

The ceremony of *saketate* is simply a foretaste of a much more elaborate betrothal ritual which Hendry (1981) called *honja* ('main tea'), but which we came to know as *yuinō*. It is essentially an occasion on which the family of the groom again offer gifts to the family of the bride. This time, however, the gifts are far more extensive and elaborate and are at least partly designed to contribute to the bride's trousseau (Hendry, 1981). It is a sign of the times, however, that *okāsan* bought the gifts in a packaged set accompanied by a comprehensive booklet detailing the symbolic significance of the articles, and describing the origins of *yuinō* as:

> a social courtesy in the form of a public announcement that a couple wish to marry. It is not connected with a personal search for a partner, nor is it a reflection of feelings of love. According to the folklorist Yanagita, the functions of marriage as expressed in the *'yuinō'* are threefold; to create a mutual relationship between households, assure the family line, and gain social approval for the match. The name *'yuinō'* is thought to have its origins in *'yuimono'*, meaning 'gifts of betrothal' and in associated ideas of the strengthening and renewal of family ties noted by Yanagita. It is also a derivation of *iui-ire* meaning to propose or suggest. (Own translation.)

Whatever its derivation, and Hendry (1981) favours an etymology based on *iui-ire*, it is clear that detailed practice varies in different parts of Japan. In some areas, for example, there may be a return exchange called *yuinō kaeshi* from the parents of the bride to the family of the groom. This was not the case in Tōno, we were told, and Hendry (1981) says that it does not occur in Kurotsuchi either. The gifts from the groom's family comprise

Table 3: The yuinō betrothal gifts

Item	Name	Number	List number
contents list	*mokuroku*	1	0
cord	*naganoshi*	1	1
money	*yuinō kin*	3	(2)
cord or hair	*tomoshiraga*	1	3
fans	*suehiro*	2	(4)
cuttlefish	*surume*	5	5
kelp	*konbu*	2	(6)
sake barrel	*yanagidaru*	2*	7
dried fish	*katsuobushi*	2	8
ring	*yubiwa*	1	(9)

* The barrel contains two *shō* of sake (3.6 litres)

three groups: money, *kimono* material and symbolic objects. Together there were ten items excluding the *kimono* material in the *yuinō* set purchased by *okāsan*. But again in keeping with the Japanese preference for odd numbers, some of the gifts were amalgamated and counted as a single offering to avoid arriving at an even number total. *Okāsan* believed that the preference for odd numbers lay in the fact that they could not be divided equally and therefore had the significance of a number 'which could not be cut' (*wari-kirenai kazu*). The association was with a destiny, *en*, which would continue as an unbroken thread. There is one exception to this general rule, though, and this concerns the number eight. Possibly because of its links with the character for rice, eight is thought to augur well, as in the phrase *oiwai wa hitoe de naku, futae ni mo, ya-e moto no kasande* ('neither once nor twice-fold auspicious, but eight-times lucky'). In the context of marriage it is taken to be a reference to the prospect of a large family.

Most of the gifts were wrapped in open hexagonal envelopes, with white outer surfaces and red inner ones. They were tied with ornate designs in gold-coloured thread and decorated with images of the crane and the turtle. The first item on the list purchased by *okāsan* is called the *mokuroku*, or 'list of contents'. *Okāsan* could not explain its significance as a gift, but Hendry (1981) gives an explanation which fits in well with the fact that most of the objects derive their symbolic significance from etymological association. *Mokuroku*, she notes, may also be written with characters which have the meaning 'long-lasting greenery' implying plenty and fertility for the couple (Table 3).

Gifts in Japan are traditionally tied with *noshi*, which is dried abalone, and in the *yuinō* this binding itself comprises one of the offerings when it is called *naga noshi*, literally 'long *noshi*'. Once again, Hendry (1981) records an explanation for its inclusion: since fish is prohibited to people in mourning the *noshi* symbolises the absence of death or misfortune on the happy occasion. Offered with it was the money, sealed in a plain white envelope. It seems to be generally accepted that for an employed groom an appropriate sum would be three or four times his monthly income. In *oniisan*'s case this meant that the envelope probably contained between 116,000 and 174,000 *yen* (£493–£740). Sometimes, *okāsan* said, a higher amount might be agreed and if it could not be paid initially then a 'deposit' called *soba* might be accepted. A smaller sum might also be suitable if the balance of the money was spread to be included in the purchase of costly *kimono* materials. These traditionally consist of a roll of red material and a roll of white material, called *kōhaku*. *Okāsan* compromised, however, with two rolls of white silk shot with pink and with a third roll patterned to her own choosing and intended for the bride's mother.

The third of the gifts in the *yuinō* set is called *tomoshiraga* and comprises characters which mean 'together' and 'white hair'. The symbolism is obvious and in Tōno it is usually signified by using a length of hemp (*asa*) which is used to bind wooden clogs (*geta*). The implication is of a bond which cannot be cut and which again reflects back on the central idea of *en* destiny, as in *en ga kirenai*. Enumerated singly, the next offering would be the fourth in the *yuinō* set. The number four, however, has extremely undesirable connotations in this connection and it is avoided with the typical pragmatism to which we have already referred. The gift itself consisted of two fans but they were offered together with the *tomoshiraga* to make up gift number five! Each fan, called *suehiro*, was white and they were offered closed to symbolise the happiness and prosperity which would open out with the marriage.

The next two gifts were also counted together to avoid the ill-luck of the number six. These were dried cuttlefish and dried kelp (*surume* and *konbu*). Their significance is largely derived from the loan characters which may be used to match the sound of the words. Thus *surume* can be written as 寿留女, which means 'female longevity', and *konbu* as 子生婦, or 'child-bearing woman'. They were accompanied by two pieces of *katsuobushi*, the dried fish which is flaked and used as seasoning. Finally, amongst the *yuinō* gifts, was the *yanagidaru* or 'willow-wood barrel' full of *sake*. It is a traditionally-styled red-lacquer bucket with long wooden handles, but again its real significance in the *yuinō* is symbolic. *Yanagi* is normally written as 柳 and barrel as 樽, but for the purposes of betrothal it is rendered as 家内喜多留, which is a charm against a wasteful wife within the *ie*. The *yanagidaru* made in fine red lacquer can be extremely expensive and it was not included in the packaged set bought by *okāsan* at a cost of 35,000 yen (£148). Instead she borrowed one from a cousin who had a wine shop on the understanding that eventually it would be returned.

In addition to the money and the *kimono* material, the *yuinō* set was rounded off with a ring; in effect, an engagement ring. This is a relatively recent innovation reflecting Western influences, but it lends itself well to the overall symbolism of the betrothal ceremony. Normally, *yubiwa* is written as 指輪, which represents 'finger' and 'circle', but used in the context of the *yuinō* this becomes 結美和 which is a combination of the characters for 'bind' (結), beauty (美), and 'peace' (和). Occasionally, *okāsan* said, the set of gifts might also be supplemented by a black *kimono*, called the *tomosode*, and by some make-up. These are essentially extra contributions which recognise the extensive and costly preparations that are in store for the bride.

As for the event itself, this follows a similar pattern to the earlier *sake tate*. It was held at the home of the bride's family, in their Japanese-style guest-room (*Nihon-ma* or *setsuma*), and seating arrangements were decided by proximity to the most socially-elevated place, the 'picture-recess' (*tokonoma*). This has an 'upper' side, which was offered to the Tadas as guests, and a 'lower' side occupied by the family of the bride. Within this arrangement, however, pride of place is given to the respective *ie* heads, then their wives, then the couple, and finally the male and female *nakōdo*. Table 4 illustrates the arrangement which was actually used and an alternative which, *okāsan* said, would be equally acceptable. Both parties were prepared to recognise the auspicious connotations of eight persons at the gathering. We were not present, of course, and we can merely recount the sequence of events as it was told to us.

On entering the bride's house, with a minimum of formal greeting, the Tadas went straight to the *tokonoma* and set out the *yuinō* gifts. The act itself has a traditional name, *torikawasu*, and is accompanied with the brief exchange, *Yuinō o torikawasu, omedetogozaimasu*, and *Shuken ni haraimasu*. Only then were formal greetings exchanged, after which *oniisan*'s *nakōdo* said, 'This is the *yuinō* from the Tada *ie*, please accept it eternally (. . . *sama kara no yuinō degozaimasu, ikuhisa osome kudasai*). For his part, the bride's father replied, 'We eternally accept it', following which he inspected the inventory and gifts. Sometimes a receipt is included, and it is at this point that it would be given by the bride's parents to the groom's *nakōdo*. On formal acceptance of the receipt the ceremony is concluded, an act called *yuinō o kawasu*, and the guests are offered food. The gifts themselves are left on display in the *tokonoma* until the

Table **4**: *Yuino* seating arrangements

(1)	Recommended *picture recess*			
1	*yuino* gifts	2		
		4		
		5		
		6		
	3	7		

Key:

- 1: 'upper side'
- 2: 'lower side'
- 3: go-between
- 4,5: groom's parents
- 6: bride's representative
- 7: groom

(2) Tada *yuino* seating			(3) Acceptable alternative	
picture recess			*picture recess*	
1 *yuino* gifts	2		1	2
3	5		10	9
4	6		5	3
7	8		6	4
9	10		*entrance* 8	7

Key:

- 1: 'upper side'
- 2: 'lower side'
- 3: groom's father
- 4: groom's mother
- 5: bride's father
- 6: bride's mother
- 7: groom
- 8: bride
- 9: male go-between
- 10: female go-between

If members of linked senior and junior *ie* are also present these would be seated between 10 and 5, the senior nearest the recess. Sometimes there are other guests, and *okāsan* thought these would probably occupy a place 'below' 7. 'Upper side' and 'Lower side' are specified terms of social status

wedding. The formal ceremonial content, therefore, is minimal, a simple exchange handled in polite language. As is often the case, however, it is in preparation and arrangement that people show their awareness and concern. The Tadas thought it unfortunate that the *yuinō*, like other aspects of the wedding ceremonial, had become commercialised and so expensive.

The wedding

Hendry (1981) records two practices which pre-date a wedding in Kurot-suchi, but which we were unable to observe in Tōno. The first is called *hanamuke* and involves the receipt of gifts of money by the families of both the bride and groom. The gifts are given by relatives and neighbours. The second is called *wakare* and is a farewell party for the bride attended by age-mates, relatives, and perhaps by neighbours. If *hanamuke* gifts were received into the Tada household, we were unaware of them, and clearly we were in no position to observe or attend the bride's farewell from her family home. On the other hand, we did see the arrival of the clothes, the furniture and the utensils that normally accompany a Japanese bride when she takes up residence in the groom's *ie*. As Hendry (1981) implies, it is difficult to know how best to regard this assortment of goods which may have considerable value. 'As they are regarded as her part of the inheritance of the household', Hendry writes, 'they may be compared to a dowry.' She goes on to say, however, that since they are 'mostly for the personal use of the bride' they are best regarded as a trousseau.

In any event, they arrived at the Tada home in early June, some three months before the wedding, and they necessitated considerable adjustment in the household, not least out of simple pressure upon space. The young couple clearly intended to establish a 'private' area of their own. This is common practice and the departure of *oniisan*'s sister gave scope for the enlargement of his own room. Into this room, the bride brought a selection of furniture. This included a heavy wardrobe, called *tansu*, which was bound with the black iron-work (*nanbu tekku*) for which Iwate is known. In keeping with tradition, she also brought a mirror which was incorporated as part of a small dressing table. Then came a stereo-system, a table, sofa, and a traditional display unit for tea ceremony utensils (*cha tansu*). The final item of furniture for the couple's now crowded room consisted of a bed and signalled the end, for *oniisan*, of sleeping on *futon* quilts. The bride also made her presence felt in the kitchen, very much *okāsan*'s domain until this time. Into the already limited kitchen area she introduced a large new refrigerator, a rice dispenser, and a microwave oven. All this was accomplished without fuss, and *okāsan* in particular made great efforts to accommodate the new *ie* member and some-day mistress of the home. For her part, of course, the impending move to Tōno meant great changes for the bride-to-be. The separation from her parents would evidently be painful and she had yet to be introduced to *oniisan*'s colleagues and friends. She would be expected to show deference to his favourites and to recreate her own social life from *oniisan*'s circle alone.

The wedding was set for 26 September, 1982. It was a Sunday and the auspicious *dai-an* day of 'great safety'. The previous day had been a busy one, greeting guests, notably relatives, and preparing the wedding gifts that are traditionally given to each one. The Tadas had decided to offer boxed sets of linen and these arrived at the house wrapped in celebratory red paper. Unfortunately, the supplier had neglected to label each box in the customary way, with the name of the bride and groom and the words *kekkon iwai* ('wedding greetings'). Four uncles were pressed into service, crouched over the piles of boxes with paper and brushes to make good the omission, whilst others ferried the newly-labelled gifts aside to dry, even using a hair-blower to speed things up. Meanwhile, on the same day, the bride and groom had their photographs taken in full wedding costume at a studio in town.

Early the following day, the long business of dressing for the wedding began all over again. It is most difficult for the bride, of course, and her preparations and subsequent changes of clothing were supervised by a dresser. Her hairstyle conformed to the traditional oiled and piled shape, but it was achieved with the aid of padding and a wig (in Tōno, at least, they call the style *bunkintakashimada*). Her make-up was also the customary white, since beauty is equated with a fair skin. Her lips were red and her eyelashes strongly exaggerated, so that the whole effect was to make *oniisan*'s bride almost unrecognisable. The wig was topped with a white hat called *tsuno-kakushi* ('horn hider') which Hendry (1981) explains as a symbolic reference 'to the bad traits of a woman's character which must be hidden to signify future obedience to her husband'. The *tsuno-kakushi* not only protects the hairstyle and signifies compliance, but it also serves to allow the display of small ornaments, usually plastic replicas of jade figures or sprigs of rice. When the white *kimono* is added, the bride, thus attired, is called *hana yome* or 'flower bride' (Plate XXIV). It is clear, again from Hendry's account, that there are different interpretations of the significance of the white *kimono*. Sometimes it is equated with 'purity' in the Western sense, but more traditionally the association seems to be with the concept of a new beginning. In this interpretation the *kimono* has the same significance as the white clothing of a new-born baby or the white robes in which the dead are dressed.

The *kimono* is protected by a wide-sleeved outer gown called the *uchikake*. The one worn by *oniisan*'s bride was decorated with fine red and gold depictions of storks. *Okāsan* told us that the bride's preparations were incomplete without the addition of seven other objects which she would carry with her on the journey, by foot, to the place of the ceremony. These, called *hakoseko*, comprised a needle and thread, a fan, purse, mirror, comb, and a pair of scissors. Sometimes, too, she might carry a short sheathed knife called a *kaiken*, which is intended to surprise anyone who might attempt to prevent her reaching the wedding place. Altogether, *okāsan* explained, the business of preparing and dressing the bride was an expensive one: the hire of the wig and the application of make-up cost about £110; the hire of the *uchikake* and the *tsuno-kakushi* added another £55.

By contrast, *oniisan*'s own preparations seemed minimal. He hired a pair of the customary wide trousers (*hakama*) striped in bronze and grey and wore a short inner *kimono* and an outer coat bearing the Tada crest on each shoulder at the front, under the arm folds at the back (called *osode*) and in the centre of the back. In the white tasselled cord which fastened the inner *kimono*, he carried a fan. Nevertheless, as the couple walked the last hundred yards to the *shikijo, oniisan* led his bride by about three strides (*sanpō gurai mae*). Constrained by her new *kimono* and slippers, the beautifully-dressed bride shuffled behind, establishing from the outset the proper place of husband and wife.

There are a variety of wedding ceremonies, conducted according to Shinto (*shinzen*), Buddhist (*butsuzen*), or civic (*kōminkan no kekkon*) patterns, but they vary little in their basic form. The act of marriage itself need not be performed by a priest, and in the past it was usual for the go-betweens to conduct the ceremony at the bride's house. The Tada wedding, appropriately enough, took place at the modern civic centre under the auspices of a 'registrar' called the *kanchōsan*.

The actual ceremony is privy only to close relatives and the *nakōdo* and, once again, we can merely recount its character from the descriptions afforded by *okāsan*. As in preliminary ceremonials, the two *ie* face each other in the small room. The most senior members, father then mother, sit nearest the altar (*saidan*) furthest from the entrance. Next to them is the eldest son, then grandparents and other children. The stages in the simple ceremony may be announced by a *shinko jin*. The couple are waited upon by two attendants: in the Shinto service these are girls clothed in white and called *omikosan*, but in the civic service there is a boy and a girl, dressed in red and white respectively, and called *ochomechosan*.

The marriage rite consists of the sharing of *sake* which is served from a nested set of three cups. It is called *san-san-ku do* ('three-three-nine times'), a name for which Hendry (1981) offers a variety of explanations, all of which hinge on different interpretations of the prescribed manner in which the couple share the wine. In the Tada wedding, so we understand, the attendant filled the smallest cup from the groom's side, pausing slightly three times. *Oniisan* then drank the *sake*. The sequence was then repeated, still on the groom's side, until all three cups had been used. The centre of attention then switched to the bride, who was served in the same way by her own attendant. *Okāsan* described other forms of *san-san-ku do*. Some-

117

times, she said, the bride follows the groom but starts with the second cup. Alternatively, she may begin with the third and final cup so that, as she drinks, the cups may be replaced in sequence. Whichever form is taken, after the bride and groom have finished, the *nakōdo* and then guests take a sip of *sake* from a cup which is passed around. As it was recounted to us, this was the end of the formal ceremony.

The Tadas then assembled thirty-four relatives for the important wedding photograph including, as temporary members of the *ie*, their foreign guests. As in other circumstances, seating arrangements reflected status and affiliation. The bride and groom sat centrally at the front, he on the left, with the male and female go-between flanking them. Next came their respective fathers and mothers, and finally other relatives clustered to the respective sides of the family. In all cases, of course, the menfolk took the most central places.

The major organisational piece of the wedding had taken place some time before. This was the preparation for the wedding reception, called *yorokobi* or *hirōen*. These days it is a major part of marriage ceremonial and there are many groups which must be represented. Originally, of course, it would have been held in the home where sliding screens would be removed to turn virtually the whole area under the farmhouse roof into a single room. Guest numbers now, though, far exceed the capacity of a single house. A friend of the Tadas, for example, hired a local sports hall for a guest list of 248 people, the top table being arranged underneath one of the basketball nets. As an employee of the town council, however, *oniisan* felt obliged to use the civic hall and catering services, placing an effective limit of 187 on the number of people who could attend.

The list of invitations always involves certain obligations which must be fulfilled regardless of preference. In particular, there is an obligation to invite immediate neighbours, even though social contacts with them might be few. This was the case with the Tadas. It is expected, too, that representatives of any major school, club, or work group to which the bride and groom belong will also be invited and will offer speeches in the course of the reception in honour of the couple. The final seating arrangement was printed on a large, decorated card which was scrutinised carefully by the guests to ensure that the proper rules of status had been observed. Thus, the seating plan is often annotated for clarity, for example with *itoko* ('cousin') or with the title and position of a notary. The directions of social gradient are provided by the high table, furthest from and facing the entrance, and by the recognition of an 'upper' side on the left, as we described in the *yuinō* ceremony. On this occasion, however, the parents of each of the couple always occupy seats nearest the entrance, as if to reflect the minimal attention which they receive at the *hirōen*.

The basic seating plan for the wedding of *oniisan* required the bride and groom to be on display at a high table, flanked by the go-betweens, selected family representatives, and guests of honour (Fig. 4). We were told, as well, that the high table may also include a representative of the couple's close friends called *otsukai no erai hito*, or 'trusted loved ones'. To us, as outsiders, the most surprising feature of the invitation list was that it tended to involve only single representatives (most often the male head of an *ie*), or a group directly linked to either bride or groom, but seldom incorporating spouses.

Like the guest list, the invitations themselves are handled with great seriousness and efficiency. Apart from the usual details of time and place, they also state the important *kaihi*, or 'entrance fee', which each guest is expected to pay just before the *hiróen* begins. We are tempted to see this as a variation on the *hanamuke* gifts which Hendry (1981) reports, but in fact we have no evidence to support the connection or to establish the origins of *kaihi* payment. We can merely observe that a suitable sum seemed to be 7,000 *yen* (£30), and to record that the couple received cash gifts which certainly exceeded 1,400,000 *yen* (£6,000).

The reception itself, as we experienced it, was at once a formal and lighthearted affair. Beginning with the honoured guests, in this case the mayor of Tōno, the assembly was treated to a succession of speeches from each of the groups represented at the gathering. They all reiterated a congratulatory theme allied to snippets of biographical detail, such that the *hiróen* became virtually a catalogue of the couple's school and personal achievements. Set against the formality of the speeches themselves, though, the other guests continued to eat, to drink, and to talk very loudly. When the couple left the hall to effect the bride's first change of dress (*iro naoshi*), some of *oniisan*'s friends treated the assembly to an amusing slide-show depicting facets of his childhood and later life.

When the couple returned the bride had changed into a vivid red kimono in celebration of her new status, and the festivities became generally more animated as guests lined up to sing, dance, or to give stylised displays of martial arts skills on a small stage near the entrance. The groom changed into soccer kit, after which he was addressed by his team mates and made to exercise amidst ribald humour. Finally, he 'kicked' a ball which was ceremoniously carried to the bride at the other end of the hall to cries of 'goal!'.

In recent years, as Hendry (1981) says, elements of Western wedding ceremony have crept into Japanese practice. Sometimes, it seems, couples have a many-tiered wedding cake, usually costing around £250, which is in reality a hollow plastic construction decorated with real icing and provided with one small 'cake' section which the couple may cut. The

Mayor	Go-between	Groom	Bride	Go-between	Honke
Local Government Dignitaries		Tada relatives and honke	Close relatives of the Bride		Local Government Dignitaries
Groom's work colleagues and sempai			Groom's University colleagues	Groom's friends	Tōno soccer club organisers
Ski club members		Tada neighbours		Bride's workmates	Close friends of the Tada Ie
		Members of Groom's Ie	Members of Bride's Ie		Same-age friends of the Groom

4 Translated Tada *hirōen* seating plan

Tadas had decided against having such a cake, but a Western influence still made itself felt at the *hirōen* when, towards the end, the bride changed for the third time. This time she emerged wearing a white European wedding dress. Together with *oniisan*, who was now attired in a suit, she performed what has become known as the 'candle service'. This involves the couple visiting each table to say a few words to the guests and to light a small candle from a larger one carried by the groom. We could find no explanation for the candle service and it is not recorded by Hendry (1981). It seems possible that, like the white wedding dress and white suit that is sometimes worn by the groom, it has no real significance beyond a visual enhancement of the occasion.

The Tada *hirōen* ended emotionally. Significantly, the bride and groom stood not together, but on either side of their parents on the stage, as the father of the groom gave his personal thanks for the work involved in the celebrations. The couple then left through a tunnel of arms formed by the guests, and after some lighthearted antics outside, they were driven off to start their honeymoon in Hawaii. The guests then wrapped up their gifts and the trays of red and white celebratory rice-cake provided for the occasion and departed, the parents coming home exhausted to a small family gathering.

Marriage and the *ie*

Although the arrival of the bride's trousseau meant some major physical upheaval in the home, the real effects of the marriage were ones of gradual assimilation rather than formal change. The couple preferred to spend their time privately in the upstairs 'apartment' they had created. This showed itself in small things: the young wife would fill their thermos with hot water for tea and friends would be invited upstairs rather than, as in the past, sharing the family *kotatsu*. The parents accepted this, remembering perhaps the days when they too yearned for some privacy. But they also expressed the hope that in time things would change and communality would come back into living.

To us, the most noticeable and unusual feature of the marriage was that *oniisan* continued his private life much as before. His wife, possibly intimidated by the close-knit community outside, spent the bulk of her time indoors, upstairs, and alone. There was, of course, a certain amount of obligation involved in *oniisan*'s continued presence at drinking sessions with work colleagues. But there is no doubt either that this remained a pleasurable outlet for him rather than merely a dutiful one. Moreover, it is also important to observe that his frequent absence did not reflect in any way any apparent failure or disharmony in the marriage; rather, so it seemed to us, it reflected accepted roles.

Although the potential for competition over the menfolk between *okā-san* and the young bride sometimes called for mutual restraint, the reiteration of a familiar pattern drew the two women together. The young wife, anxious to make a good impression and still obviously conscious of her status, would pay close attention to the mealtime needs of both her husband and father-in-law. To a mother used to catering for both husband and son this meant some re-adjustment. The bride also had to learn to accept family friends, some of whom, given their rural background, she may not have liked. She found it impossible to wait for the New Year when traditional practice would have allowed the first return visit to her parents. Instead, she travelled to see them often as the process of adjustment continued.

Recent developments

For a time after the wedding it seemed that the Tada *ie* was evolving in a very traditional way. The daughter had left home to work in Tokyo and the house was shared by grandmother, parents, a married son, and his wife. In due course the couple had a daughter and the household sheltered four generations. Early in 1985, however, *oniisan* and his new family left Tōno. Ostensibly their departure seems to threaten Tada *san*'s conception of *ie*, but as the reasons were explained to us it became clear, yet again, that this was another example of the kind of flexibility which helps to preserve principles whilst simultaneously assimilating change.

One thing is abundantly clear: *oniisan*'s decision had nothing to do with tensions that were internal to the *ie*, that is with tensions that were within the house itself. On the other hand, as we have indicated, the concept of the *ie* extends beyond its definition as a roof, or an address near the river in Tōno. It extends beyond the interpersonal relationships of the people who share the house as well. It exists also in an intricate web of social linkages, obligations and expectations which have their origins in the wider community outside. Paradoxically, *oniisan*'s departure owed most to his father's position and to the dignity of the Tada *ie* in the wider community of Tōno. The position and importance of his father within the administrative structure of the town gave him an inevitably high political profile, but also militated against *oniisan*'s own career within the same administration. Promotion and personal advancement, if they came at all, could only come slowly lest allegations of nepotism besmirched the name of the *ie* and compromised the value of that promotion. In consequence, he was confined to relatively insignificant posts, dealing with sports and leisure, but well away from the powerful education committee and finance department, from the library and from the museum. To the extent that *oniisan*'s career was constricted, so too, in the longer term, was the status and advancement of the *ie* as a whole.

All of this was well-recognised by Tada *san*. Discussion and decision, we have since learned, took place in the same atmosphere of careful equanimity that characterised the earlier discussions of the marriage. At its centre was the survival and dignity of the *ie*. Basically, this required two things: that *oniisan* should be successful in whatever new career he chose and that he should return to Tōno with his success independently achieved. As far as we are able to tell, his progress to date makes this vision a tangible one. He began by using his legal qualifications to secure a job with a company engaged in land development for leisure purposes in the Tokyo Bay area. He was particularly concerned with local government liaison on the delicate and vital matter of land development regulations. He was, of course, ideally suited to the work, having an excellent grasp of the legalities and a wide experience and natural skill in dealing with administrators and the administrative machine.

His next move, however, was the most significant one and the one on which he will ultimately depend for the fulfilment of *ie* ambitions. In 1986 he left the original company and founded, with a partner, a company of his own. This, too, is concerned with leisure development services and it seems most likely that in the coming decade such services will be in considerable demand in Japan. Certainly the government will be forced to consider ways of developing the domestic economy, making adequate leisure provision, and eventually tackling the difficult question of Japan's obsolete land laws. It may be significant, too, that Tōno is initiating a major environmental improvement programme. In part it involves re-modelling streets in the manner of the traditional pattern and at its centre is Horiuchi *san*, the builder and master carpenter who is a close friend of the Tadas and whose work we discuss in the final chapter. The development of associated leisure facilities and the establishment of Tōno as a holiday centre therefore seems to offer the kind of opportunities which will coincide well with *oniisan*'s intentions.

For the present, he has established a home in Chiba prefecture, near Funabishi, which lies at the head of Tokyo Bay and within an hour's commuting distance of the city centre. He lives in a standard block of flats (*danchi*) conforming in reality to the stereotype of cramped living conditions much-satirised by foreigners. Like many other urban Japanese, however, his ambition is to own his own house and even, perhaps, some land. Return to Tōno, he knows, offers him the best hope of fulfilment in an environment of family and friends.

Oniisan's decision to leave Tōno probably reflects the same kind of thinking that has prompted the move to southern cities by so many other young people. In one sense it seems to be a surprisingly 'modern' response from a family which, experience taught us, places great store by tradition. But we are persuaded that the move has not fragmented the family in any deep sense. Recent visits confirm the confidence and momentum of the *ie* in spite of *oniisan*'s move and the recent retirement of Tada *san* in April 1987. The father remains a substantial figure in the politics of Tōno and the son is laying the groundwork for his eventual return. The changes that have occurred have been practical, physical ones, principally of location. But they do not seem to have affected the structure of respectful ties that operates in the *ie* as we saw it. The changes come not out of a desire for something different, or out of rebellion, or out of any perceived need to assert a particular independence. Rather, they stem from the circumstances of *oniisan*'s position in Tōno and the belief that only by searching out appropriate change can more important things remain the same.

House-building in Tōno

In Tōno as in most of rural Japan people prefer to live, if possible, in the same place and to rebuild the family home rather than buy another one on a different site. There is, therefore, no mechanism for house sales since it falls within the range of most families to save or borrow enough money to construct a new house of their choice. This is a major event in the life of the *ie*, which may be repeated in alternate generations. Until very recently most of the farmhouses in Tōno were of the thatched L-shaped *magariya* or straight *sugoya* type. In some cases these had stood for two hundred years. Since 1947, however, they have been replaced by a variety of designs. Some of the newer houses follow traditional patterns but others incorporate a range of modern influences. The effect of this mixture has been to change the rural scene considerably.

Rebuilding a house in Tōno is the responsibility of the head of the *ie*. It is an occasion of great importance for a variety of reasons. Most obvious-ly, it represents a major financial outlay for the family, in excess of £50,000. At the same time the extent of this outlay is a physical expression of the current status of the household within the community. But in addition to these material concerns the rebuilding of a dwelling also represents a reorientation of the *ie* in the natural world. Since this world is filled with fickle *kami* spirits the design and orientation of the new house traditionally involves the employment of geomancy. In Japan this is called *kasō*. It may be seen as an intercession with the spirit world through the 'phasing' or orientation of the house.

The ceremonies of *kasō* liberate the site of the house by the appease-ment of the *kami* deities. They are followed by other ceremonies during the period of house construction. These include the initial 'ground-breaking' ceremony, called *jichinsai*, and the important 'ridge-pole raising' ceremony of *tatemae, muneage* or *jōtōshiki*. The *tatemae* ceremony marks the completion of the roof of the new house. It then remains to give rooms their substance and to incorporate construction and decoration. In this chapter we consider these ceremonies, most of which we were able to witness as a result of our friendship with the master-carpenter Horiuchi *san*.

House-building ceremonies

Traditionally, both the plan and the alignment of houses impinged on the destiny of the *ie*. For this reason the first stage in house building always involved the services of a diviner (*ogamiyasan*). Though the influence of *kasō* seems to have waned considerably in modern Tōno, few people are willing to ignore it altogether and most still pay some attention to the suggestions of *ogamiyasan*. To some extent the level of *kasō* involvement may depend on the sympathies of the builder who, in the process of house-building, often develops close and influential ties with the family. Where a diviner is involved, his role is to introduce the proposed plan of the house to the spirit world of *kami* and to align its physical form into an auspicious spiritual one. Like other forms of divination in Japan (*tesō*, palmistry; *ninsō*, fortune-telling), *kasō* also conveys the idea that a particular physical structure is merely a transient single form in a succession of past and future states.

Some of the basic rules of *kasō* are spelled out in the widely-used *unseikoyomi* 'fortune almanacs', and have been elaborated by Seike (1981). Strictly speaking, however, the details of divination remain the province of *ogamiyasan*, since only he has the spiritual status and power to act as a mediator with the *kami*. To some extent, therefore, the process of divination remains shrouded in mystery as do the spirits to which it is directed.

The standard *kasō* chart, used by both diviner and layman, reflects the work of successive interpretations in which the influence of Chinese cosmology is very clear. The chart divides the compass into a total of twenty-four sectors. Reflecting Chinese tradition, north appears at the bottom and is a direction which has generally inauspicious connotations. The principles of *kasō* reflect the Chinese Taoist cosmology in which opposing but interlinked forces, the yin and yang, dominate man's relationship with the natural world. The popular labels 'female' and 'male' are used to encapsulate the various, but dependent, characteristics of these respective forces, but they also have wider implications. Fung Yu-Lan (1937) goes so far as to draw a parallel between ancient Greek philosophy and yin–yang cosmology, when he writes that 'If we examine the series of the ten pairs of antinomies enunciated by the Pythagoreans, such as Limit and the Unlimited, it is evident that what they call Limit corresponds fairly closely to what the exponents of the Book of Changes call the yang, while the

Pythagorean Unlimited similarly corresponds to the Chinese yin'. In Japanese, where yin is rendered as *in* and yang as *yō*, Nelson (1962) has identified their varied attributes as follows.

In: negative; female; melancholy; north side of the mountain; sex organs; secret; shadow; south side of a river; earth; bottom; back; inactivity; cloud up; be obscured; *kage*, shade; *okage*, indebtedness, favour, help, patronage, support.

Yō: positive; male; heaven; daytime; sun; top; movement; facing the sun; sunshine; south side of the mountain; openly, publicly.

There are a number of ways in which the *in–yō* duality may be expressed. One of them is in the form of the familiar black and white diagrams shown in Figure 5. But it may also be expressed in matrices of nine numbers in the basic pattern:

	south		
	4	9	2
east	3	5	7	west
	8	1	6
	north		

The four cardinal compass points are initially represented by odd numbers which change according to the pattern outlined by Seike (1981). Within the initial matrix the sum of any column, row, or diagonal, will be fifteen. The mathematical perfection that is apparent in this static matrix, however, becomes ambiguous as a cyclical element is introduced into the derivation of individual numbers. For example, numbers representing the cardinal points are said to be derived from the multiplication of each cardinal number in turn by a factor of three beginning from north = 1, and moving in an anti-clockwise direction. Thus,

$$1 \times 3 = 3 \quad \text{(east)}$$
$$3 \times 3 = 9 \quad \text{(south)}$$
$$3 \times 9 = (2)7 \quad \text{(west)}$$
$$3 \times 7 = (2)1 \quad \text{(north)}$$

The 'accommodation' that is evident in the manipulation of numbers in this way indicates something of the mystery of the exercise and at the same time its 'fundamental aim of creating a truly inclusive system of thought – one which would embrace and explain all the phenomena of the entire universe' (Fung Yu-Lan, 1937).

To understand the alignment of emblems that the *kasō* chart combines

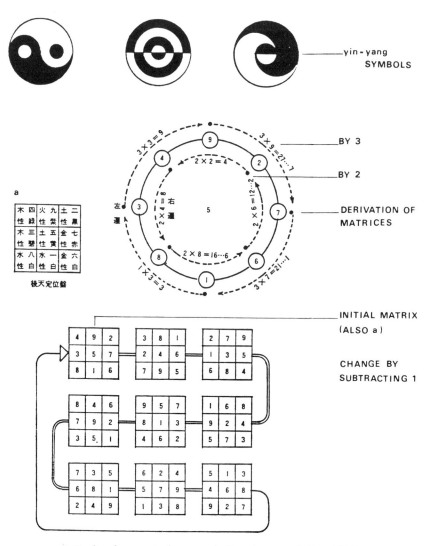

5 Cyclic changes in *kaso* symbolism (source: Seike, 1981)

it is useful to begin with the association of numbers, elements, colours and directions employed by Chinese cosmology. These are:

number	element	colour	direction
1	water	white	north
2	earth	black	south-west
3	wood	blue	east
4	wood	green	south-east
5	earth	yellow	central
6	metal	white	north-west
7	metal	red	west
8	water	white	north-east
9	fire	purple	south

Seike (1981) adds that in earlier times the numbers also had directed significance for human qualities and traits; for example, two denoted rest and lust, and four, hope and thought.

In addition to the spatial or directional qualities that are evident in yin–yang cosmology, there is also a temporal element derived from two things. First, the twelve-year zodiac cycle of Buddhism, called *jūni-shi*, which is represented in a series of animal signs. They are: rat (*ne*); ox (*ushi*); tiger (*tora*); hare (*u*); dragon (*tatsu*); snake (*mi*); horse (*uma*); sheep (*hitsuji*); monkey (*saru*); cock (*tori*); dog (*inu*); and wild boar (*i-no-shishi*). Second, the ten signs of the Buddhist calendar (*jikkan*). These are based on the elements wood (*ki*), fire (*hi*), earth (*tsuchi*), metal (*ka*), and water (*mizu*). Each one of these is represented in two phases, an 'elder' and 'younger' brother phase. The 'elder' component is denoted by the suffix *e*, and the 'younger' by *to*; thus, wood (*ki*) = *ki-no-e* and *ki-no-to*. The five elements therefore yield a total of ten signs.

In the *jikkan* system each element is identified with particular qualities. They are:

wood tactile sense, penetration of the earth, springing from the earth, faces the rising sun, heat of the south, warmth and thus life;

fire moulds and changes, representing the south, heat and incubation;

earth exuding or 'returning', the process of ripening and interplay of late summer;

metal a barrier or end, beginning of retreat, autumn, the low sun, harvest and income;

water the horizon, level and equal, peace and tranquility, cleansing, winter, stored food and the calm of *komoru*, shut away from the world.

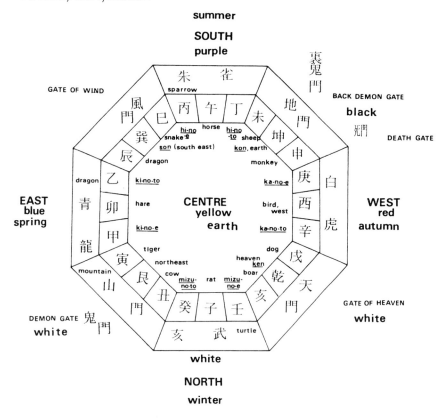

6 Summary of *kaso* symbolism

Each element is linked to the others, in the manner of *yin* and *yang*, by cause and effect. It is this linkage rather than any external temporal reference that gives the *jikkan* system its particular sequence. This sequence derives from two cycles called *sōjō* and *sōkoku*. In the former fire consumes wood, wood becomes ash and earth, metal condenses water in the earth and wood grows again from water. In the *sōkoku* cycle water extinguishes fire, but fire melts metal, wood requires earth, and earth channels water. One is therefore a cycle of growth or positive change, whilst the other acts negatively or indirectly. By the final phase of development in *kasō* cosmology the ten *jikkan* elements have acquired both temporal aspects and directional qualities (Fig. 6, 7). These can be summarised (Seike, 1981) as:

kinoe: rise and fall (fluctuation), east;
kinoto: growth, impermanence, east;

130

Implications of kasō divination according to the chart, for each of the
twenty four sectors of the compass and elements of house design indentified.

Household feature	S	SW	W	NW	N	NE	E	SE
kamidana shrine	. . .	X X X	g x .	. G g	. . .	. X .	. . .	. . .
butsudan shrine	. . .	X X X	G g .	. G g	. . .	. X .	. . .	. . .
well	o X x	X X X	g g g	o g G	x . x	x x x	g . g	. . x
kitchen	o X x	x x x	g g g	o g .	x X x	x x x	x g x	x X x
toilet	o X x	x x x	. G g	o . .	x X x	. x x	x x x	x X x
bathroom	o X x	x x x	. G g	o . .	x . x	. x x	x . x	x X x
window	. . .	. . .	. . .	. g .	. x .	x X .	x g .	. g g
entrance	g . .	. x x	g o g	x G g	. . .	. . g	. . x	g G g
stairs	. . .	. x x	. o o	x G o	. . .	o x o	. x x	x o x
store/barn	. . .	. g .	. . .	g g g	x . x	G g .	. . .	g g g
guest room	. . .	. . .	. . .	. g .	. . .	. . .	. . .	. g .
picture recess	. . .	. g .	. . .	. G .	. . .	. . .	. . .	. . .
pond	x x x	. . .	g g G	. . g	. . .	. . .	. . .	. . .
gateway	g . .	. . .	. . .	. . .	. . .	. X .	. . .	. . g
extension	. . .	. . .	. . .	. . .	x . .	. . .	. . .	. . .
shoin recess	. x x	x x .	. . .	. . .	x . .	. . .	. . .	. . .
garden	. x x	. . .	g g G	g . .	g g g	. . .	. . g	. . .
garage	. . .	. . .	. . .	. . .	. . .	g g g	. . .	g . .

Key

X	prohibited
x	inauspicious
o	requires care
g	favourable
G	recommended
.	no advice given

7 Summary of *kaso* advice

hinoe:	flourishing, maturation, south;
hinoto:	end of growth, south;
tsuchinoe:	end of growth, centre;
tsuchinoto:	end product, centre;
kanoe:	change, west;
kanoto:	death and renewal, west;
mizunoe:	birth, north;
mizunoto:	development, north.

Ordinary people, including many builders, have only a limited knowledge of *kasō* practice, and even those details which are available do not fully account for the complex interaction of emblems, numbers and qualities which will eventually ensure that the house is properly aligned. Builders who are both interested and informed in the ways of divination may still be faced by a bewildering array of alternatives for each of the eight major compass directions. They are all, for example, associated with 'gates' of influence through which *kami* may access the house. Some of these influences are benign. North (*kyūmon*), for example, indicates the gate of rest, but south (*shōmon*) indicates the gate of injury. Most feared are the 'demon gate' (*kimon*) in the north-east, and the 'rear demon gate' (*urakimon*) in the south-west. To avoid offending the *kami* it is quite common for the *kasō* charts used by builders to be accompanied by very practical notes. For example:

> This is a copy of the traditional divination chart used in house planning. On inspection you will see twenty four divisions which are called the 'twenty-four mountains'. The chart may be used by placing it at the central point of the house plan and aligning the four compass points. The lines of the chart are then projected over the plan and these traced to the advice contained in each sector. For example if the projected lines of the 'rat' sector (true north) include a toilet or drain then the chart predicts bad fortune. Alternatively, should there be an entrance in the sector of *ushitora*, the conjunction of ox and tiger (north–east), then sickness may enter the house since this is traditionally known as the 'gateway of sickness' (*byōmon*).

The rules of *kasō* are one thing, but its implementation may be quite another. Thus, although few families are prepared to tempt fate by ignoring the *kami* altogether, most of them are unwilling to sacrifice desirable projects for diffuse spirits. The result is usually a compromise between the dignity of divination and the demands of design. In 1975 in the Isagozawa, for example, an old *magariya* farmhouse was to be replaced with a fine new building following the same plan. The addition of an ornamental pond in the L-shaped courtyard of the house, however, was deemed by the *ogamiyasan* to be inauspicious. Disappointed, but not deterred, the family sought a 'second opinion'. The new diviner agreed to the idea but insisted that a member of the family should take part in the work in order to pacify the spirits. This condition was satisfied early one morning when the mother of the household dug a small pit in the pond area before leaving for work. In this way the requirements of *kasō* were fulfilled, the spirits were pacified, and the family was content. Easy and trivial though this example seems, the family were convinced of the necessity of some gesture of this kind since a neighbour who had paid little heed to *kasō* had recently expired in the lavatory!

It is possible to find many examples of the ways in which divination has been responsible for the alteration of details in the planning of houses in *Tōno*. These range from changing the location of the principal entrance to the house to alterations in the basic room plan to ensure that guest rooms should be furthest from unhealthy or inauspicious influences. In a detached view many of the rules of *kasō* seem to be expressions of common sense. The kitchen, for example, should not face the directions of the strongest summer sunlight; houses should not be built below the level of proximate roads, and so on. But these explanations, sound though they may be in practical terms, require the weight of *kasō* approval to ease the uncertainties of a people whose lives still recognise the influence of a powerful and fickle world of natural deities.

In divination the *ogamiyasan* may be either Shinto or Buddhist. Similarly in the ceremony of ground-breaking (*jichinsai*), no one religion has exclusive rights, and elements of both can normally be observed in the ceremonial objects employed. The essence of *jichinsai* is to create a sacred area in the centre of the building site, aligned with the general plan of the building. The act of purification which this involves takes place at an altar from which the priest intercedes on behalf of the client, the builder, and the workmen, with the *kami* of the natural world.

Jichinsai ceremonies are usually held on days of good fortune defined according to the six-day Buddhist cycle. This means that *daian* ('great safety') and *sengachi* ('early victory') are especially popular. In Tōno the *jichinsai* is often the province of the Shinto priest of the local shrine called Hachiman. The ceremony centres on a portable arrangement of symbolic objects enclosed within a square (*kekkai*) which can be aligned to the directions of major walls. The sides of the square are marked with rice-straw rope (*shimenawa*) and with the white cut-papers (*heisoku*) which are common to Shinto ceremonial. The arrangement also contains a small tree, decked with *heisoku*, with a mirror to symbolise the sun, and with lengths of hemp (Fig. 8). The particular design of the portable *kekkai* employed in Tōno differs in fine detail from the more substantial structures recommended for the use of Shinto priests (*Jinja yūshoku kojitsu*, 1982). The *sakaki* wood in the recommended version is not available in the local area

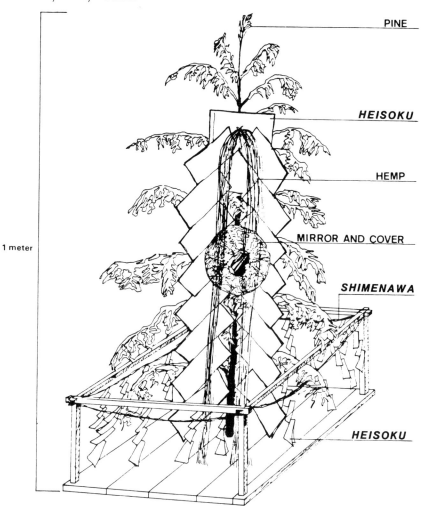

PINE

HEISOKU

HEMP

MIRROR AND COVER

SHIMENAWA

HEISOKU

1 meter

8 Shinto *jichinsai* used by the Hachiman shrine

and is replaced by pine, and in Tōno the addition of a mirror contributes to a generally more elaborate, though smaller, arrangement.

Where a Buddhist priest conducts the ceremony, the *kekkai* is usually marked out with sprigs of pine, but *shimenawa* and *heisoku* are still employed, as is the *rissa*, a popular Shinto symbol consisting of a cone of sand (Fig. 9). It is important to the detail in both the Shinto and Buddhist *kekkai* that the *shimenawa* rope, which is used to mark any sacred area or

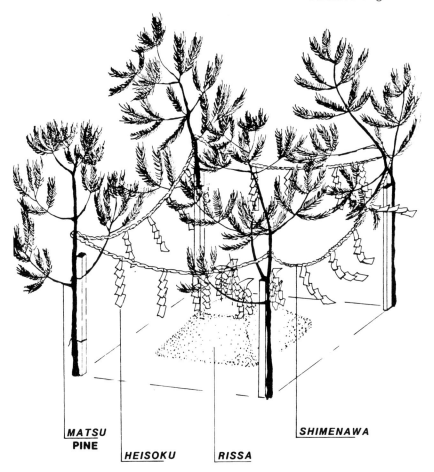

MATSU PINE

HEISOKU

RISSA

SHIMENAWA

9 Buddhist *jichinsai*

object in Shinto belief, is plaited to the left rather than to the right. This is the opposite of the direction employed for everyday use, but it signifies the closing of a *kimono* with the right hand covering the right-hand side of the body first. The opposite action, which would take the left hand towards the body in the act of plaiting, mirrors the *kimono* arrangement employed for a corpse. The connection between action and idea which this signifies draws together the symbolism of *fuku*, which means both 'clothing' and 'wealth', and which obliquely refers to anticipated prosperity in the new home.

Into this scrupulous arrangement of the *kekkai* the priest will summon the *kami* deities. The ceremony itself consists of a series of acts, offerings, and incantations which, though specific in themselves, do not have immediately specific spiritual or symbolic referents, beyond a general obeisance to the spirit world and a defence of the 'demon gate' (north-east) of potential evil. This recalls Sansom's (1977) observation that the idea of the *kami* remains diffuse despite the specific ritual of object and ceremony. Writing of early Japan he says, 'We find lavish creations of deities but their characters are confused and shadowy, their powers ill-defined, and their habitation either unknown or indistinguishable from that of ordinary beings'. For the Japanese of Tōno in this ceremony, as in others, it seems enough that the action is performed in keeping with tradition and expectation, anchored in nebulous associations but expressed with physical precision.

Despite the interlacing of Buddhist and Shinto symbols in the *kekkai* construction there are differences in the treatment of materials, in the offerings employed, and in the prayers delivered. According to the conventions of *kasō* the association of colours and compass directions which might be employed in the *kekkai* are white in the north-east and north-west, green in the south-east, black in the south-west and yellow in the centre. Buddhist *jichinsai* in Tōno, however, employ a different arrangement in which the corners of the *kekkai* are marked in the following way by coloured *heisoku*: north-east, black; north-west, blue; south-east, red; south-west, white; central, yellow.

There seems to be no obvious reason for this arrangement of colours which is internal to the *jichinsai* ceremony. It may be significant, however, that it mirrors the association of colours, compass directions and seasons which are found in the later *tatemae* ceremony. The associations reflect Buddhist funeral practices and have special significance in Tōno, where the *tatemae* ceremony is linked to a particularly tragic folktale. In contrast to the colourful Buddhist display, Shinto *heisoku* are invariably white. This symbolises the deep-seated concern of the Shinto way with the idea of purity.

In the Buddhist *jichinsai* the priest faces north and lays a series of offerings on the south side of the *kekkai*. Those offerings include one *shō* of *sake* wrapped in red and white paper, a selection of seasonal fruits and vegetables, rice, wheat, *azuki* beans, *awa* and *kibi* (glutinous and Chinese millet), some salt, and a tray of *mochi* rice cakes covered with thin *hanshi* rice paper. A pair of short candles completes the display. The client, the builder and the workers kneel on a rug behind the priest who delivers a short incantation pleading for good fortune and safety in building the house. One by one the people attending the *jichinsai* are then invited to come forward, to bow, and to clap once. Sometimes, they are also invited to take a sip of *sake*. After the ceremony the priest removes the offerings and the party adjourns to the client's house for a small celebration.

In the Shinto *jichinsai*, as in the Buddhist ceremony, the priest stands between the audience and the *kekkai* interceding in the direction of perceived evil. Unlike Buddhist ceremonial, however, the Shinto way lays great emphasis on the character and the ordering of the offerings that are to be made. They consist of seven separate groups of foodstuffs which must be arranged, facing north, in a very precise manner. In the centre the first offering consists of washed rice. To the right of the washed rice the priest places rice wine called *omiki*, two-tiered *mochi* rice cake, and fruit which is taken to represent trees. To the left of the washed rice the remaining three offerings are placed. These consist of two fish, which are often sea-bream, and which are placed closest to the rice, then odourless vegetables to symbolise the earth, and on the extreme left a small white dish of salt and a white porcelain bowl of water.

The Shinto ceremony proceeds in a series of twelve prescribed stages. To begin with the guests are seated, and the ceremony is officially opened. This is followed by a symbolic cleaning or clearing of the building area before the important act of *koshin* which summonses the *kami* to the site. In the presence of the *kami* the seven groups of foodstuffs are offered in an act called *kesen*. The priest then delivers an incantation to the spirits, asking their permission for the building of the house. Each compass quarter is then purified by a wave of the priest's staff in the order south, north, west, east. Once the spirits have been appeased in this way the first physical act of construction occurs as the priest breaks the ground with a mattock or clears away some of the grass on the site. In the Shinto ceremony the priest then offers to the guests sprigs of *sakaki*, which are replaced by pine in Tōno, in an act called *tamagushi*. Each of the offerings is then displayed in order before being purified. The final act in the *jichinsai* is completed when each guest partakes of the offerings through a symbolic sip of *sake*. Again, the orderliness of the ceremony requires that the client should drink first, the builder second, and finally the workmen.

Despite the differences in the details in the Buddhist and Shinto *jichinsai*, both of them are built upon the same *kasō* conventions, both of them emphasise house-building as a transitory phase in the continuity of the *ie*, and for a moment at least both of them make the vague and mysterious world of the *kami* specific and concrete. This is achieved by defining it in the world of human interests, in the earth or the fruit of trees, in the directions of the compass and in the abstraction of a space which becomes momentarily sacred.

Once the roof of the new house is in place a decorated pole is raised on the ridge in the ceremony called *tatemae*. In essence this ceremony marks the completion of the main structure of the house (literally its skeleton, *honegumi*), with the roof forming a complete covering and the floors giving the appearance of a platform suspended under the eaves. The objects employed to decorate the ridge-pole are rich in symbolism. The head of the pole is topped with the white *heisoku* papers of purity, with pine tied with hemp, and with a round fan depicting storks. Below this is a box called *yashiro*, (literally 'Shinto Shrine'), which contains a variety of symbolic objects and which bears a crude drawing of the *tama* or seed of life. Amongst the objects contained in this box are a pair of wooden bobbin-like dolls called *metobina* which are made in the traditional *kokeshi* form. From the centre of the pole male and female *obi* kimono sashes are hung, and a horizontal crossbar is festooned with five long streamers. Finally, two crossed arrows with large, square heads are attached to the main ridge-pole (Fig. 10).

The arrows are particularly ornate (Fig. 11). Traditionally they were painted by the carpenter himself, and building manuals still begin with instructions for their preparation. In practice, however, they are now usually purchased at local hardware shops for around £80 a pair. The heads of the arrows may carry a variety of depictions including the dragon (*ryū*), the tiger (*tora*), the hawk (*taka*), and the Chinese lion (*tang kara shishi*). The most usual combination, though, is of the stork (*tsuru*) and the turtle (*umigami*). Both of them serve as symbols of longevity. The stork carries a painted scroll with the characters *fukujū jōtō* which signifies 'prosperity and long life' and also 'ridge-pole raising'. The turtle frequently has long hair to signify its age and the 'feathers' of the turtle arrow carry paired groups of markings in arrangements of three, five, and seven. As in other Japanese ceremonies, odd numbers are regarded as extremely auspicious, signifying the ideas of imbalance, interdependence, and movement, and thence the idea of life. The 'quill' of the stork arrow depicts *shōchiku-bai*, the celebratory combination of pine, bamboo, and plum.

Much of the symbolism of *tatemae* in Tōno seems to owe its existence to an influential local legend. As Horiuchi *san* recounted it, the story concerns a carpenter commissioned to build an important temple. Unfortunately, the carpenter cut his pillars too short and in desperation explained to his family both his problem and his impending shame. The daughter of the household suggested that he should build up a capital on the pillars with an ornate crosswork structure which proved in the event to be both effective and highly decorative, and which is now widely repeated in the temples of Tōno (Fig. 12).

The carpenter, however, was incensed by the admiring reception of his daughter's idea and in a fit of jealous rage he killed her. The dedication of the new temple, therefore, also became a memorial service for the daugh-

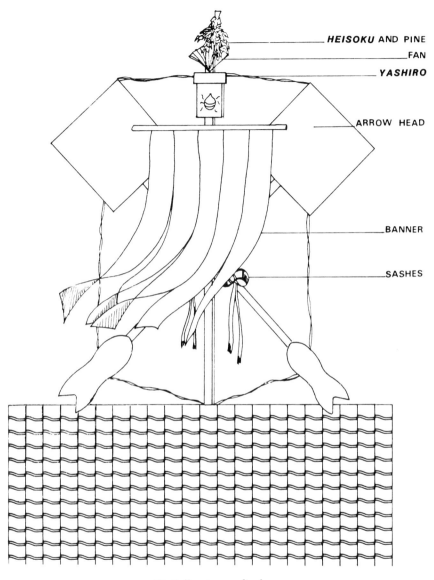

HEISOKU AND PINE

FAN

YASHIRO

ARROW HEAD

BANNER

SASHES

10 Full *tatemae* display

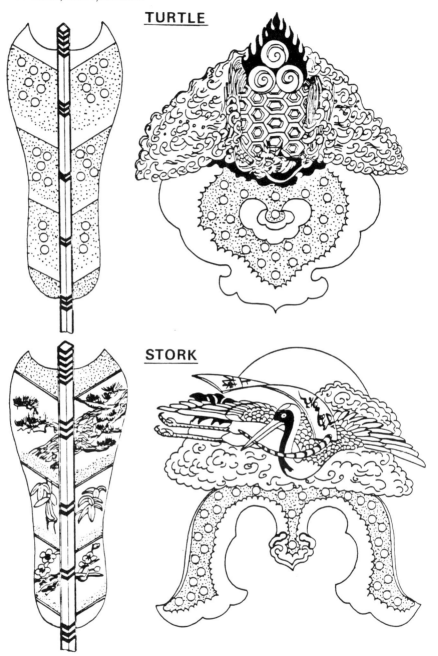

TURTLE

STORK

11 Tatemae arrowhead display (source: Arasei, 1959)

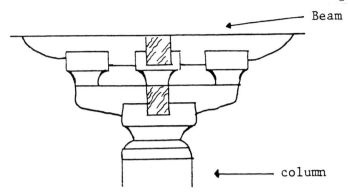

Beam

column

12 Crosswork capital

ter, and in recognition of the tragic act the *tatemae* continued to incorporate much of the symbolism of death. The streamers that hang from the horizontal crossbar, for example, have colours that match the streamers carried at a Buddhist funeral: black, which is associated with north; white with west; yellow with the earth; red with the south; and blue with the east. Similarly, it is common for the smaller objects contained in the *yashiro* box to be wrapped in envelopes which carry the black and silver thread of burial ceremony.

As in *jichinsai* there are other details in ridge-pole ornamentation which have important symbolic connotations. Perhaps the most interesting of these are the ways in which the *obi* sashes are tied in knots called *ōtatami musubi*. The sash on the left denotes the male knot, called *ishitatami*, a name which reflects the arrangement of stones in an ornamental path. More directly the female sash which is called *enmusubi*, recalls the symbolism of *en*, of destiny or fate, and which literally means 'bound'. The two knots are tied as in Fig. 13.

Of all the house-building ceremonials *tatemae* is the most elaborate. The ceremony focuses on a small board called the *mune fuda* which contains the names of the builder and the head carpenter, and which also records the date of the ceremony as the formal start of house construction (Fig. 14). The preparation of the *mune fuda* board echoes some of the symbolism previously discussed in connection with *jichinsai*. The right side of the board top is cut at an angle facing forwards, while the left side is cut at an angle facing away. Once again, the intention is to suggest the action of putting on a kimono and to recall the phonetic symbolism of *fuku* which can mean both clothing and wealth. On occasion, this symbolism is also repeated on the ridge-pole by the addition of red and white cord,

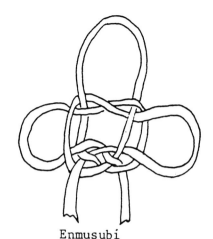

Ishitatami   Enmusubi

13 *Otatami musubi*

twisted to the right, which serves the dual purpose of reiterating the theme of *hidarimae* and sumultaneously bracing the ridge-pole display.

In addition to names and a date, the facing side of the *mune fuda* also contains a summons to the *kami* in the form of a revolving three-winged symbol called a *tomoe maru*. In form this recalls the yin–yang symbol, but its purpose is to represent the wailing cry by which the priest summons the *kami*. The remaining inscriptions record in the centre 'ridge-pole raising ceremony' and ask for the protection of the *kami* over the house and the family who will live there. This central prayer is flanked on the left by the dragon which symbolises the male *kami* and which represents the head of the *ie*, and on the right by the female equivalent, *myōshin* (or *megami* or *joshin*) representing the mother.

The *mune fuda* plaque is fastened to one of the upright posts which support the roof timbers. In Tōno the post which is usually selected is the principal symbolic post of the house, the *daikoku bashira*. In a two-storey house it is usually positioned on the first floor, and even in the older single-storey farmhouses the *mune fuda* is positioned close to the roof in an attic area. Because the buildings are incomplete, and because ceilings and second floors are rarely in place, the ceremony takes place on a loose collection of boards precariously strung across the timber frame. For this reason only the more intrepid and mature female members of the family take part in the ceremony of *tatemae*.

Tatemae in Tōno are usually, but not exclusively, the province of Shinto priests and, as in *jichinsai*, great care is taken in preparing offerings and

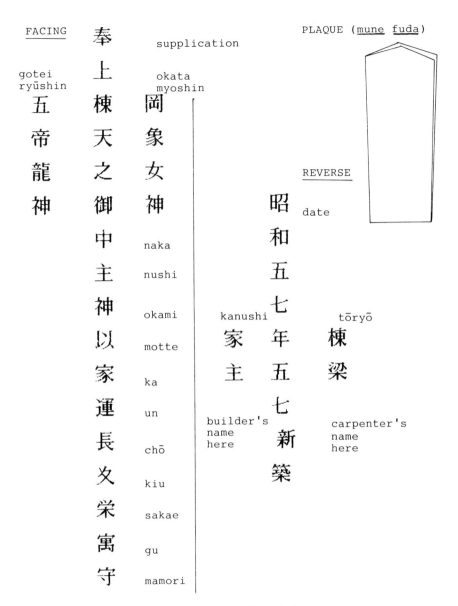

FACING

gotei
ryūshin

五帝龍神

奉上棟天之御中主神以家運長久栄寓守

岡象女神

supplication

okata
myoshin

naka

nushi

okami

motte

ka

un

chō

kiu

sakae

gu

mamori

PLAQUE (<u>mune</u> <u>fuda</u>)

REVERSE

date

昭和五七年五七新築

kanushi

家主

builder's
name
here

tōryō

棟梁

carpenter's
name
here

14 *Tatemae* plaque and inscriptions

conducting ritual. The arrangement of offerings and the seating of guests is shown in Fig. 15. Because of the precision which seems to attend *tatemae* in Tōno, it is worthwhile listing these offerings in some detail.

1 An elaborate *heisoku* paper bound with hemp (*asa no himo*).

2 A wide tray (*sanbo*) containing rice cakes called *sonae mochi* on a clean sheet of rice paper. Within the township of Tōno two layers of *mochi* were usual, whilst in the countryside people preferred three.

3 The working plan used by carpenters. This shows the arrangement of posts as simple dots in a grid which follows an 'alphabet' of characters horizontally, and numbers vertically. The first point is called *ichi-i*, and is synonymous with anything which is 'first rate'. The same alphabet can also be read as a poem which recalls the Buddhist yearning for peace and freedom from the illusions of reality:

> colours are fragrant,
> but they fade away.
> In this world of ours
> nothing lasts forever.
> Today, cross the high mountain
> of life's illusions,
> and there will be no more shallow
> dreaming, no more drunkenness. (after Nelson, 1962)

4 Three shallow *sake* cups. If there has recently been a wedding in the *ie*, the *san-san-ku-do* cups are used. Alternatively, even a single glass is acceptable.

5 Two large sea-bream, following the *omedetai* analogy.

6 Small red and white rice cakes called *maki mochi*. Some contain a five *yen* coin, reflecting the *go-en* symbolism which re-introduces *en*, or karmic destiny.

7 Two bottles of *sake* wine, the *o-miki*, wrapped in red and white.

8 Three carrots with leaves.

9 Two or three burdock roots.

10 Two *daikon* giant radish, with leaves.

11 Oranges or apples.

12 Soya beans or red beans (*daizu*).

13 Dried sardines called *ni-boshi*.

14 A piece of *konbu* or dried kelp.

15 Some salt in a white dish, which is a symbol of purity.

16 A glass of water.

17 Some walnuts (*kurumi*).

18 Washed rice.

19 Twelve cakes of *mochi* called *yama no mochi* ('mountain *mochi*'),

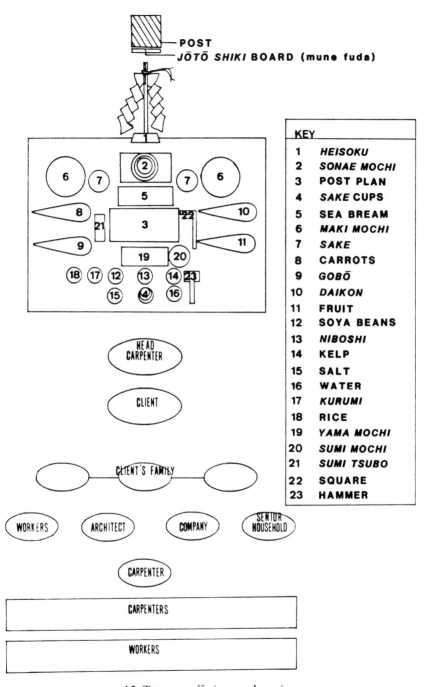

POST
JŌTŌ SHIKI BOARD (mune fuda)

KEY
1 HEISOKU
2 SONAE MOCHI
3 POST PLAN
4 SAKE CUPS
5 SEA BREAM
6 MAKI MOCHI
7 SAKE
8 CARROTS
9 GOBŌ
10 DAIKON
11 FRUIT
12 SOYA BEANS
13 NIBOSHI
14 KELP
15 SALT
16 WATER
17 KURUMI
18 RICE
19 YAMA MOCHI
20 SUMI MOCHI
21 SUMI TSUBO
22 SQUARE
23 HAMMER

HEAD CARPENTER

CLIENT

CLIENT'S FAMILY

WORKERS   ARCHITECT   COMPANY   SENIOR HOUSEHOLD

CARPENTER

CARPENTERS

WORKERS

15 *Tatemae* offerings and seating

an offering to mountain *kami* and to the spirit of the woodlands, *mokuzai* or *kodama* (meaning 'echo').

20 Four rice cakes called *sumi mochi* ('corner *mochi*').

21–3 The carpenter's hammer, inkpot, and square, called *mawari kane*.

The ceremony itself begins with introductory remarks preparatory to reciting the *norito* incantation. Because of the importance of carpenters in the construction of the house the *norito* makes special reference to them and to their implements. The modern name for carpenters' tools is *kōgu*, simply construction implements. But because of the traditional closeness of the carpenter's 'art' to the other 'ways' or arts such as the way of tea (*sadō*) and the various martial disciplines, the *norito* incantation retains the traditional word *dōgu*, which emphasises the significance with which these objects are invested.

The priest also calls for the co-operation of the *kami* in the process of construction and refers to the site as *ōmiya*. This is a name usually reserved for temple precincts and its use in the *tatemae* indicates the momentarily sacred nature of the house-space. The primacy of the carpenter's role is recognised by calling upon the spirit of the *kami* to pay particular attention to the joints between posts, rafters, beams, and roof supports, and even to fixing bolts, the *kugi*, and clamps (*kasugai*).

Once the *norito* is over the priest steps aside. At one time this provided an opportunity for the head carpenter to respond. Even in Tōno, however, it seems that this part of the ceremony has been abandoned. Instead, the head carpenter approaches the altar, bows and claps twice followed by the two oldest apprentices (*odeshi*). Each of the *odeshi* takes up a bottle of *sake* and, flanking the master, pour *sake* three times, starting at his right hand. In turn the carpenter offers *sake* to the *kami* by pouring a little over the twelve cakes of *mochi* on the altar. Replacing the *sake* bottles, the *odeshi* then stand silently before the display. The carpenter's role is not yet finished. He takes up the *sumitsubo* inkpot and draws out its cord to the right with outstretched arms. Bowing once, he then sets this down, and exhibits the measuring square, first with the shorter side to the left and then to the right, showing both surfaces. Finally, he strikes the base of the post three times with a hammer, beginning on the left-hand side.

Once the carpenter's role is complete the client steps forward, bows, claps twice, and is also served with *sake* by the *odeshi*. He is followed, in order of seniority, by the members of his family, each of them receiving this *omiki*, or drink of purified *sake*. Next come the head of the construction firm, the designer, and possibly a senior representative of a related *ie* or *honke*. The labourers are called last of all, and where more than one is present the *omiki* is given only to the senior member.

When the ritual drinking of *sake* is complete a representative of the working carpenters, called *wake tōryo*, recovers the four rice cakes called *sumi mochi* (corner *mochi*) from the altar. Together with three other carpenters the cakes are taken to the four corners of the roof. They are then thrown diagonally across the centre of the house in an action which draws together the alignment of the building and the men who are principally responsible for its erection. The same carpenters also bring the *maki mochi* from the altar and distribute them amongst the participants who leave the building to throw the red and white rice cakes across the roof. This is usually the signal for an indiscriminate scramble as children try to catch the cakes and the good fortune of the five-*yen* coin which they contain. The final act of *tatemae* requires that the ridge-pole arrows and the *yashiro* box are packed under the highest point in the roof where they will remain for the lifetime of the house. The front of the *yashiro* is surreptitiously broken by one of the carpenters in order to give the impression that the *metobina* dolls have been stolen. In fact they are removed and given as gifts to friends of the *ie*. The *yashiro* and usually the arrows face south under the roof in order to avoid the malevolent influences of the demon gate.

The *tatemae*, therefore, ends informally and drifts easily into a general celebration. Because of the numbers of people involved this can present a catering problem on a scale comparable to a small wedding, except that the guests are given no gifts and the atmosphere inside the half-constructed building is wholly relaxed and informal. There is, however, a general hierarchy of status which is reflected in seating arrangements, but this bears no specific relation to the incomplete structure which houses it. Like other ceremonial events, the joviality of *tatemae* is easily extended as small groups of friends prolong the celebration with a night on the town.

The dedication of a new construction, particularly in the *tatemae*, is a communal event. In the rural areas in particular both the demolition of an old farmhouse and its replacement were once a shared labour, and each year saw arrangements to build perhaps three houses in one valley. These arrangements were made at the New Year or else in the atmosphere of preparation for the summer festival of the local shrine. This was certainly true of the Isagozawa ('Silver Sand Ravine'). Reconstruction has now become a contract between client and builder, although some local experts may be employed to select timber from the surrounding hills. The communal element, once a necessity where roofing, for example, required the labour of cutting large quantities of reed thatching, has now largely disappeared. Paradoxically, one of the few remaining large-scale communal events involves not the construction of a new house but the demolition of an old one (Plate XXV). In Tōno these older houses are of the traditional thatched *magariya* type and represent the source of many of the day-to-day influences on house plans and house building in the area.

Early houses: the *magariya*

The architectural tradition of Tōno is epitomised in the L-shaped thatched farmhouse called *magariya*, literally a house which 'turns a corner' (Plate XXVI). The name identifies its most salient feature but it does not locate the style within an overall classification of vernacular Japanese houses. As Noguchi (1981) says, it is possible to create a list of such house types but 'these names, whilst identifying regional styles, do not really classify the body of Japanese *minka*' (folk-houses). Relatively few traditional *magariya* now remain. They were associated with an economy of rice growing which was complemented by sericulture and horse breeding, but with the steady decline of the latter elements the peculiar structure of the *magariya* has declined also. This structure is distinguished by the way in which the house was designed to provide both living quarters and stabling under the same massive roof. The intimacy of *magariya* life, therefore, provided the setting for many of the legends and folktales of man and horse which were documented for Tōno by Yanagita in 1910.

Even today the remaining old houses blend easily into the countryside and weather to the same shades as the surrounding mountain forest. Fed by the expanse of mouldering thatch, mosses and reeds and small rooted saplings sprout from the roof in the mild weather of spring, and in winter snow the *magariya* merge imperceptibly into the surrounding white hillsides. The *magariya* are notably sturdy structures. Their strength seems to derive from the enormous weight of thatch pressing on similarly massive beams. In contrast, the supporting framework consists of relatively slender upright posts, set at regular intervals, and distinguished by the total absence of diagonal cross-members. This framework is tied at the base by the *dodai*, or foundation beams, which are not set in the earth but which are laid free on top of rounded stones to provide some flexibility against the frequent earth tremors of the region. The floor of the house is then laid as a platform suspended between the roof and the *dodai*, and originally open under the eaves. In building the traditional *magariya*, therefore, the *tatemae* ceremony marked the effective completion of the basic structure of the house. Walls, as such, did not exist. In their place were movable outer screens which were packed aside on summer days to open out the house and to encourage the circulation of air. The prevailing view in Tōno is that, despite the long and cold winter, the principal purpose of the thick thatch and drooping eaves of the *magariya* was to provide shade and protection from the heat and humidity of summer.

The *magariya* also possesses a verandah. It is called *engawa*, and the name indicates something of its role as an intermediate space between the house and the outdoors. The *en* component, meaning 'to join', is a familiar part of *ie* symbolism, whilst *gawa* means 'side'. Rather than marking the limits of the house, therefore, the space of the *engawa* connects both dwelling place and outdoors. This is not to suggest that the *engawa* is in any sense a self-consciously created symbolic structure: its role is essentially practical in complementing the low thatched eaves which deflect the strongest heat of the sun. In winter, though, it may be shuttered along its entire length on the outside, and divided from the living areas on the inside by translucent screens called *shōji*. Little light can filter into the house on these occasions and the air is soon filled with the smoke of charcoal hearths. The atmosphere of the winter *magariya* recalls the world of the *komori*, a studious shutting out of nature and a specific delineation of an outdoors which is alive with mountain spirits (Isozaki, 1981). In this closed and private space the folktales were born and recounted, the New Year festivals were held, singular household deities were worshipped, and the hearth became the focus of communal winter talk.

The plan of a typical large *magariya* is illustrated in Fig. 16. This particular house has now been replaced by a new one (Fig. 17) which follows a plan similar to the *magariya* and which certainly obeys the same site and *kasō* orientation as the original. The floor plan of any Japanese house is called the *madori*, literally 'a space' or 'interval' (*ma*) which has been 'taken' (*tori*) from a larger whole. This recalls the work of *jichinsai* as a form of asking permission to build. The *madori* of the *magariya* encloses an inner courtyard called the *tsubomae* which gives access to the *engawa*, to the house, and to the stables. The house itself usually encloses the *tsubomae* on the north and eastern sides, symbolically the direction of potential evil, but also the principal direction of wind and rain. The stabling areas, built into the narrower of the *magariya*'s two limbs, are called *ōmaya* and *komaya*, the large and small 'rooms for horses'. Despite the fact that the horse has now largely disappeared in Tōno, these rooms retain the original names and echo the influence of an earlier way of life. The stable area itself has a floor of packed earth extending into a working area called the *niwa* where hot mash was once prepared in an earthen steamer called the *kamma*, and where most of the dirtier household chores were performed.

Entry into the *magariya* is always through the courtyard. As in most Japanese houses, the entrance area (*genkan*) is lower than the living

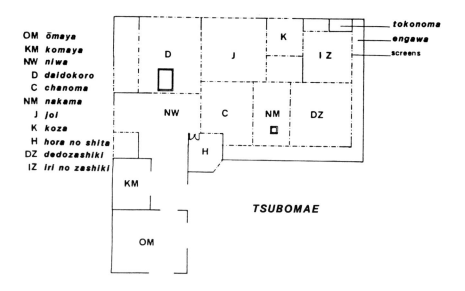

OM *ōmaya*
KM *komaya*
NW *niwa*
 D *daidokoro*
 C *chanoma*
NM *nakama*
 J *joi*
 K *koza*
 H *hora no shita*
DZ *dedozashiki*
IZ *iri no zashiki*

tokonoma
engawa
screens

TSUBOMAE

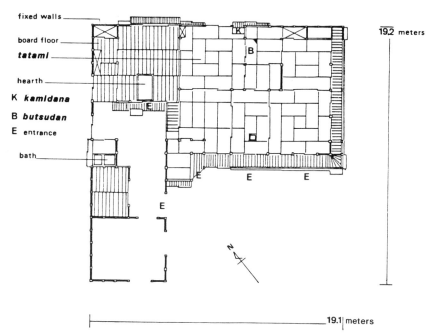

fixed walls
board floor
tatami
hearth
K *kamidana*
B *butsudan*
E entrance
bath

19.2 meters

19.1 meters

16 The *magariya* of Matsuma Yoshitsugi (source:
Local Education Committee Survey, 1977)

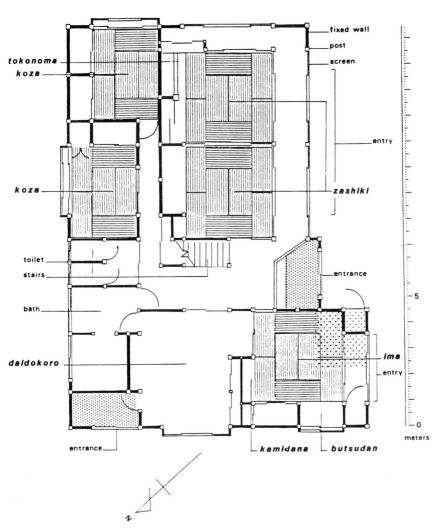

tatami

niwa

murō

Second storey plan : four six mat rooms

tokonoma
koza

koza

toilet

stairs

bath

daidokoro

entrance

fixed wall

post

screen

entry

zashiki

entrance

ima

entry

kamidana   butsudan

5

0

meters

17 Matsuma Yoshitsugi house

platform, and is the place where indoor slippers are kept. In the traditional *magariya* the *genkan* always gives access to the earth-floored kitchen (*daidokoro*). This is a dark, airless room with open rafters shrouded by skeins of soot hanging from its beams, and open to the flies which invaded the house from the stables (Plate XXVII). Not surprisingly, special charms were conjured for the *daidokoro* to protect it against the risk of fire from cooking flames and the risk of disease from the ubiquitous flies. As the domain of women, however, the *daidokoro* was low in the hierarchy of rooms.

The principal living areas of the *magariya* are located in the broader of the two limbs and marked by a general lateral division between guest rooms, at the far gable end, and the family living spaces. The principal living room may be the *chanoma* ('tea room') or the *ima* ('living room'). These are located on the inner side of the house. They can, therefore, be entered directly from the *tsubomae* via the verandah. Traditionally these rooms contained a sunken hearth called *robatta*, but in recent years these have been largely replaced by the electric *kotatsu* table (Plate XXVIII). The *robatta* was not only a source of heat but also a place to cook immediate snacks of small fish and the like, and to heat *sake*. The basic fuel was charcoal laid on a bed of *kuntan*, the ashes left from the burning of rice stubble. In the humid weather of summer, smoking green branches were banked on the hearth to drive insects up into the rafters before the family went to sleep.

Both the *chanoma* and *ima* (which is sometimes also called *nakama* or 'central room') are small and frequently cluttered with everyday paraphernalia. Behind them, on the outer wall of the *magariya*, are two other rooms called the *joi* and the *koza*. The *joi* was traditionally the heart of the *magariya*, the focus for the family's winter retreat, and the setting for the telling of tales and the planning of festivals. Today its role has changed: it may be simply a storage space, but often it is set aside as a *butsuma* to house the *butsudan* shrine. The *koza* are smaller interstitial rooms, originally unspecific sleeping areas, but now often serving to give children some privacy as 'bedrooms'.

The largest rooms in the *magariya* were the *zashiki* or guest rooms which often contained the socially-elevated *tokonoma* ('picture recess'). Even in modern houses in Tōno the same kind of emphasis and consideration can be observed. It is significant, however, that in the *magariya* these large rooms were developed for two very practical reasons. First they were large in order to accommodate the many guests who would attend a wedding or a funeral. Though these are only occasional events, they are inevitably recurrent for an *ie* which may trace a lineage of five generations. But in addition the *zashiki* in the *magariya* were also used for sericulture.

152

They were sealed with tape and heated with fires, even in summer, to increase the ambient temperature for the silkworms on their wickerwork nests (*tokka*). It is likely that the first ceilings fitted in the *magariya* were designed to further increase the temperature in these rooms and to prevent soot from falling out of the rafters and on to the silkworms.

The disappearance of sericulture has allowed the *zashiki* to assume another role. They are now the focus of the *ie*'s expression of wealth and status: their size and ornate splendour makes them a fitting place for events like the *yuinō* betrothal or important family gatherings. In particular, the *tokonoma* recess has been exploited to develop an ornate area for the display of craftsmen's skill. In surviving *magariya* the *zashiki* now have their own divisions of status. Furthest from the *tokonoma* is the outer *dedozashiki* and closest to it is the inner *okuzashiki* or *iri-no-zashiki*.

Many characteristics of modern house design can be traced to the lingering influence of *magariya* life, but the original was singularly vernacular, a house developed by local people, not by architects, and not even by carpenters. It was principally the setting for a difficult agricultural life and in consequence its architectural details signify most clearly the practical requirements of living. This living was primitive. Only a generation ago the people of the Isagozawa packed their sleeping rooms with rice straw as a protection against the cold of winter. For the horse breeder the day began by cutting up to six large bundles of grass for the horses before the man himself could breakfast. Green tea which is now so much a part of everyday life was a luxury that farmers could seldom afford, and the one comfort in the exhausting daily round was the rough and illegal home-made *sake* called *dobroku*.

In the old farmhouse both lavatory and bath were located outside in their own sheds (Plate XXIX). The lavatories consisted of a deep pit framed with narrow boards, and leading sometimes to a collecting urn for the night-soil. Bathing tubs consisted of wooden barrels. They were originally heated by inserting hot charcoal into metal pipes leading directly into the water. These early baths were called *teppō buro* ('rifle-barrel baths') and the bather could expect to emerge liberally coated with ash from the pipe, as dirty as before, but at least warmer.

Many of the rigours of rural life still remain in valleys like the Isagozawa (Plate XXX). To some extent they have been eased by the availability of modern technology and by the changing emphasis of the rural economy. The practicalities which governed *magariya* design are no longer necessary, but the genealogical associations which are so important to *ie* dignity ensure the continuance of *magariya* influence if not *magariya* form. This can be seen most clearly in the changes that have been made as old *magariya* have been demolished and new houses erected on the same site.

153

The deliberate efforts that have been made to preserve elements of the internal plan and appearance of the *magariya* indicate the importance in *ie* life of the principle of continuity. In the village of Nakazawa for example a *magariya* was recast in 1982. The stable section was removed and the distinctive 'L-shape' was lost. A fine tiled roof in the *hirōya* style replaced the dense mat of thatch on the original house (Fig. 18). Superficially, the new building seems very different from the old, but in fact the restyling was achieved almost wholly within the traditional framework of the *magariya* form. The internal beamwork remained untouched, except for cleaning; floor coverings were replaced, *shōji* panels were renovated and the *engawa* was glazed. In place of the old *daidokoro* a large Western-style kitchen was installed and the *joi* was fitted with an impressive stereo. Beyond the demolition of the shorter *magariya* limb, however, the plan of the house remained unchanged.

Rebuilding in this essentially cosmetic way is quite common, but sometimes the changes that are made are more extensive. In another house in Nakazawa a traditional *magariya* was rebuilt in the ornate and impressive *sengai tsukuri* style (Fig. 19). This has involved complete structural replacement, stairs have been added, storage areas have been constructed under the eaves and a wallpapered first-floor Western-style room (*yōma*) has been created. The mixture of styles which is apparent in the house might be called *wa-yō-se'chu* or 'kitsch'. But despite the aesthetic tensions that this produces, even this house has retained some of the traditional features of the older life. The bathroom and toilet areas remain separated from the main living quarters, and in the coldest area of the house a concrete-lined cellar (*murō*) has been constructed to serve as a cold store for vegetables during the winter. Furthermore, the two *zashiki* in the house conform to the *magariya* tradition in terms of their size and status.

Houses like this in the lower Isagozawa, in Yokouchi, Hijiri, and parts of Nakazawa, are large, often new and usually in good condition. At the head of the Isagozawa, however, in the Yūbatta, is a post-war *kaitaku* ('frontier') of settlement. There is little lowland, rice-fields are terraced, soils are poor, and crop yields are low. Many of the residents of the upper valley are first- or second-generation *ie* who still live in simple boarded constructions, roofed with inexpensive unglazed tiles or tin and characterised by the open rafters and earth floored kitchen that formerly typified the *magariya*. These houses are usually small and, although they sometimes incorporate modern features like the private bedroom, their evolution and appearance indicates the same kind of practical response to an arduous rural existence that led originally to *magariya* development. The *daidokoro*, for example, is basic, dark and uninviting; family life is centred on the *ima*, and precedence is again given to *zashiki* which by the standards of the Yūbatta are relatively ornate and luxurious.

18 The *hiroya*

Whether the house is a fine *sengai tsukuri* type or a simple frontier farm there seem to be similarities in the treatment of important features like the *butsudan* or *kamidana* shrines. In general the Isagozawa *magariya* had a *butsudan* in the *joi*. Several factors probably contributed to its location there. In a sense, this was the heart of the *magariya*, its deepest recess, and in addition it is likely that *kasō* influences sought protection for the vulnerable northern side of the building. In modern houses both *butsudan* and *kamidana* are commonly found in the *ima* or *nakama* living areas. But in recast *magariya* a small room (*koza*) might be set aside as a *butsuma* and general storage area while the *kamidana* may be located in a variety of places including the *daidokoro*, the *joi*, the *zashiki*, or even in a hallway.

The drift of *ie* practices in the Tōno area displays an outward tension that seems to derive from the pressures of the modern economy. Many *ie* now appear in competition with each other and the necessity for co-

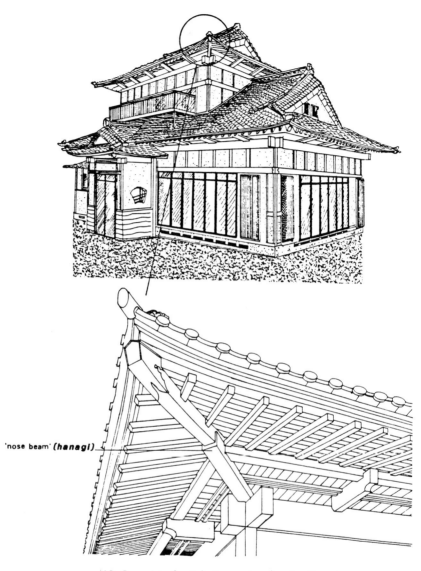

'nose beam' *(hanagi)*

19 *Sengai tsukuri* design and eaves detail

operation, which marked earlier lifestyles is disappearing. *Ie* discriminate status, not only in terms of honour, genealogy, and a powerful association with place, but also in overt material ways, in the purchase of new tractors or seeding machines, and most emphatically of all in the construction of a new house. Underlying these outward trappings of *mie* ('show'), however, there remain complex congeries of religious and spiritual influences. These mingle with the personal histories of individual *ie* in ways which ensure an infinite variety of expression which is made concrete in the organisation and practices of each separate household.

Housebuilding

All modern house designs must now include plans drawn up in the metric scale. In Tōno, however, carpenters still employ the traditional system of measurement. This is associated with the division of one *ken* and with the dimensions of the *tatami* mat. Using these dimensions there are at least five widespread *tatami* combinations which can be employed to fix the plan of a house and the arrangement of structural posts, and even by tradition to

Table 5: Principal types and dimensions of tatami mat

Name	Popular terms		length	width	Post spacing
metric *ma* メートル間	*honkyō ma* *honma ma* *gosun ma*	本京 本間 五寸	191 6, 3	95.5 3, 1.5	E
—	*san sun ma*	三寸	185 6, 1	91 3	E
naka ma 中間	*chūkyō ma*	中京	182 6	91 3	E
inaka ma 田舎間	Edo *ma* Kantō *ma*	江戸 関京	176 5, 8	88 2, 9	C
—	*danchi ma*	団地	170 5, 6	85 2, 8	—

The *ken* measurements establish post spacing and mats are then fitted to take account of fine variations. The *danchi ma* is a recent innovation created specifically for apartment blocks (popularly known as *danchi*), and this has no need of post spacing because of concrete construction.
(sources: *Tatami geijitsu daizukan*, 1978 ('Compendium of the art of the tatami'), *Tatami Makers' Newspaper*). Dimensions in cm, *shaku/sun*; post spacing: E inner post edge to post edge; C post centre to post centre

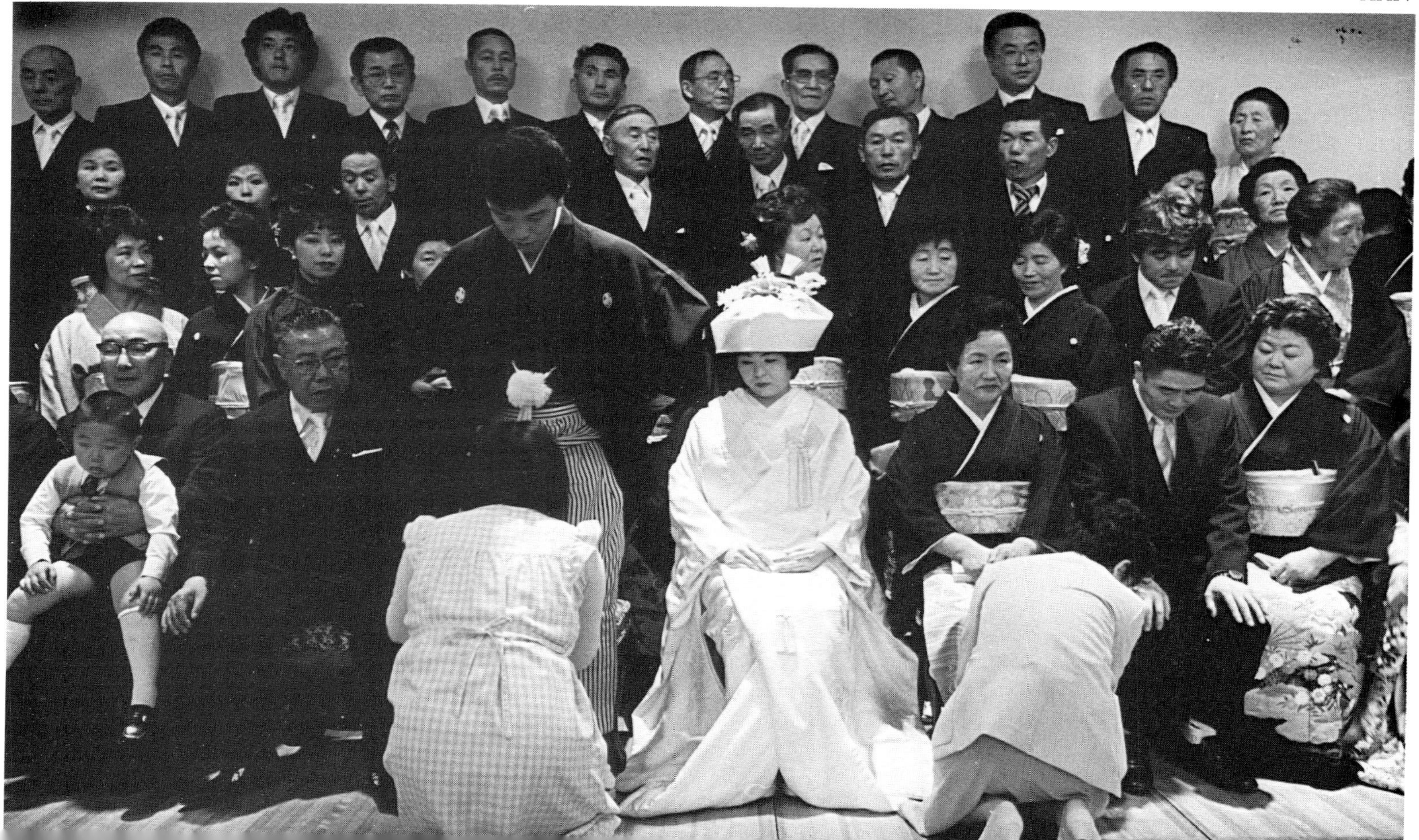

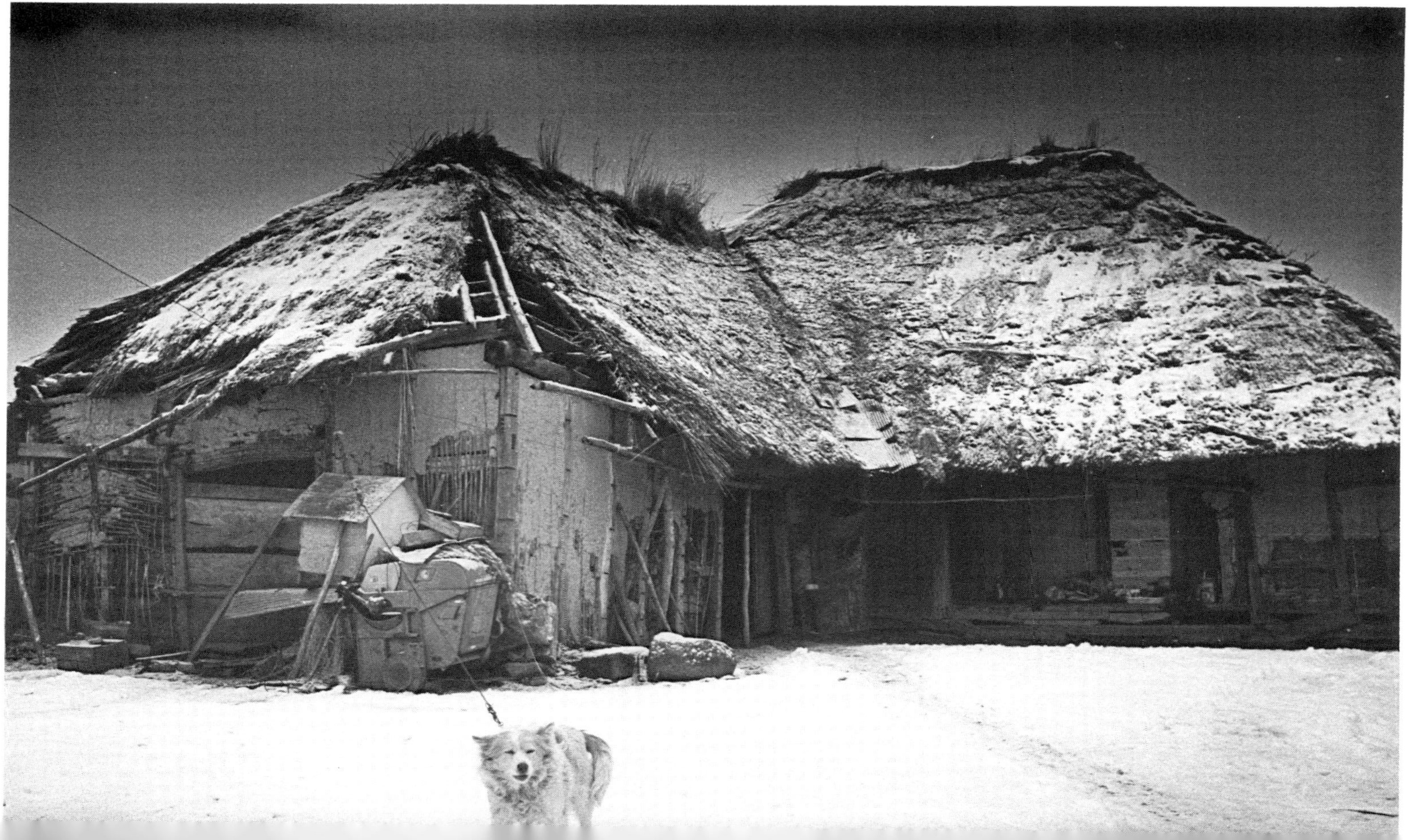

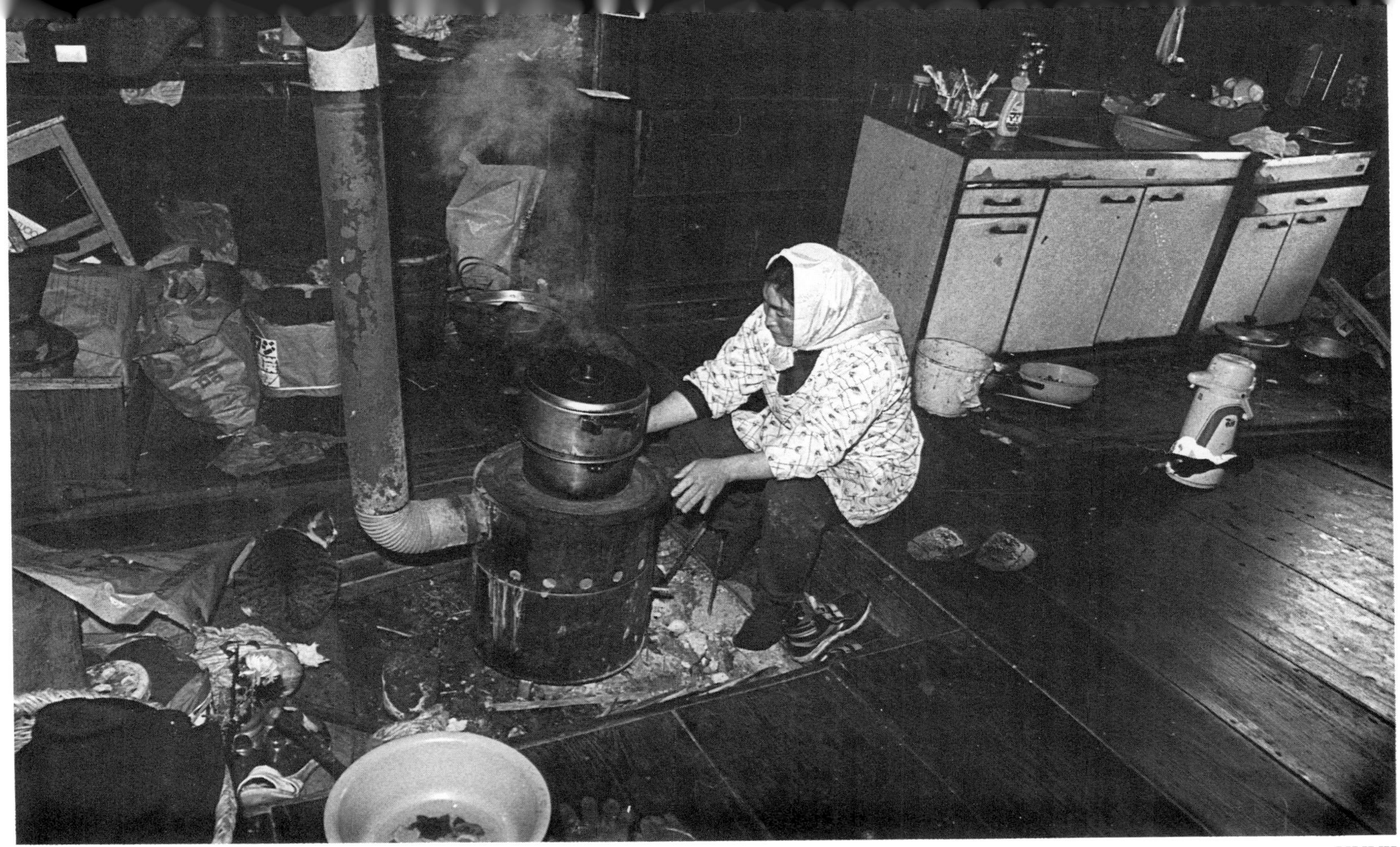

XXVII

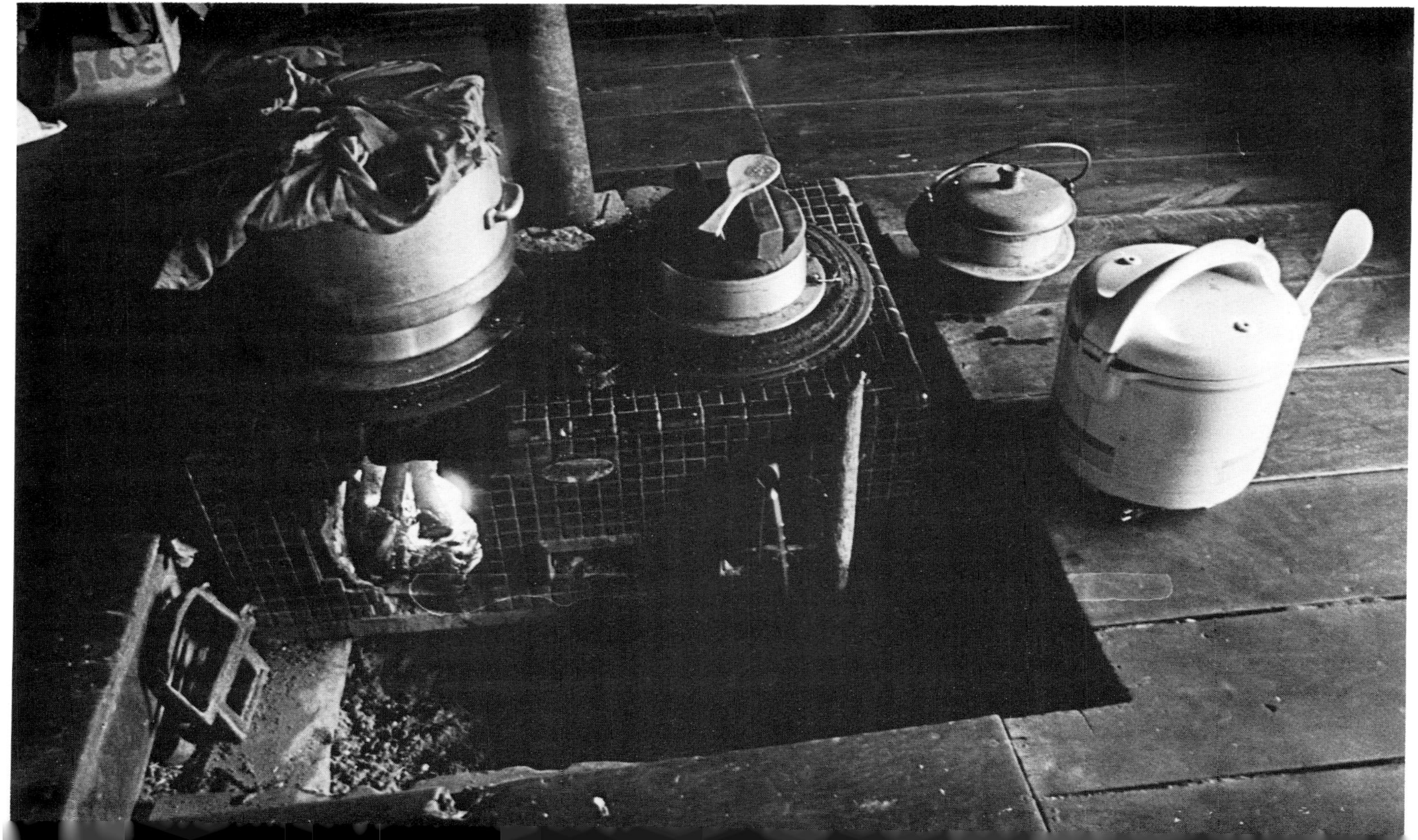

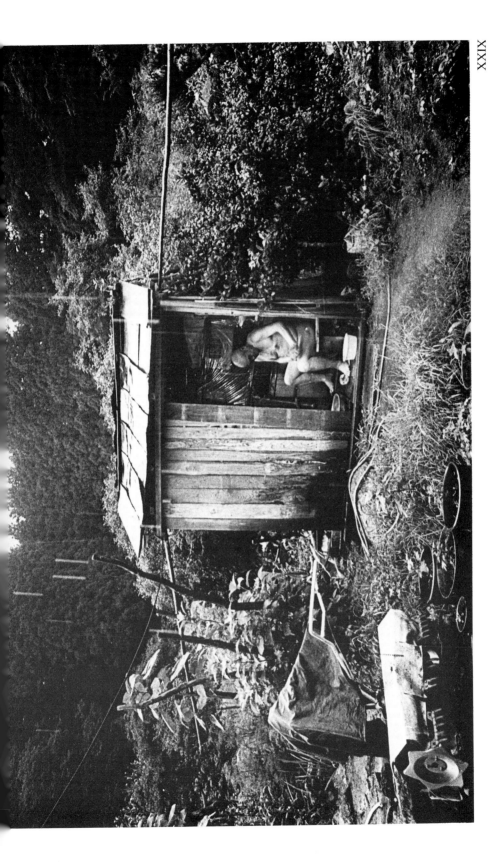

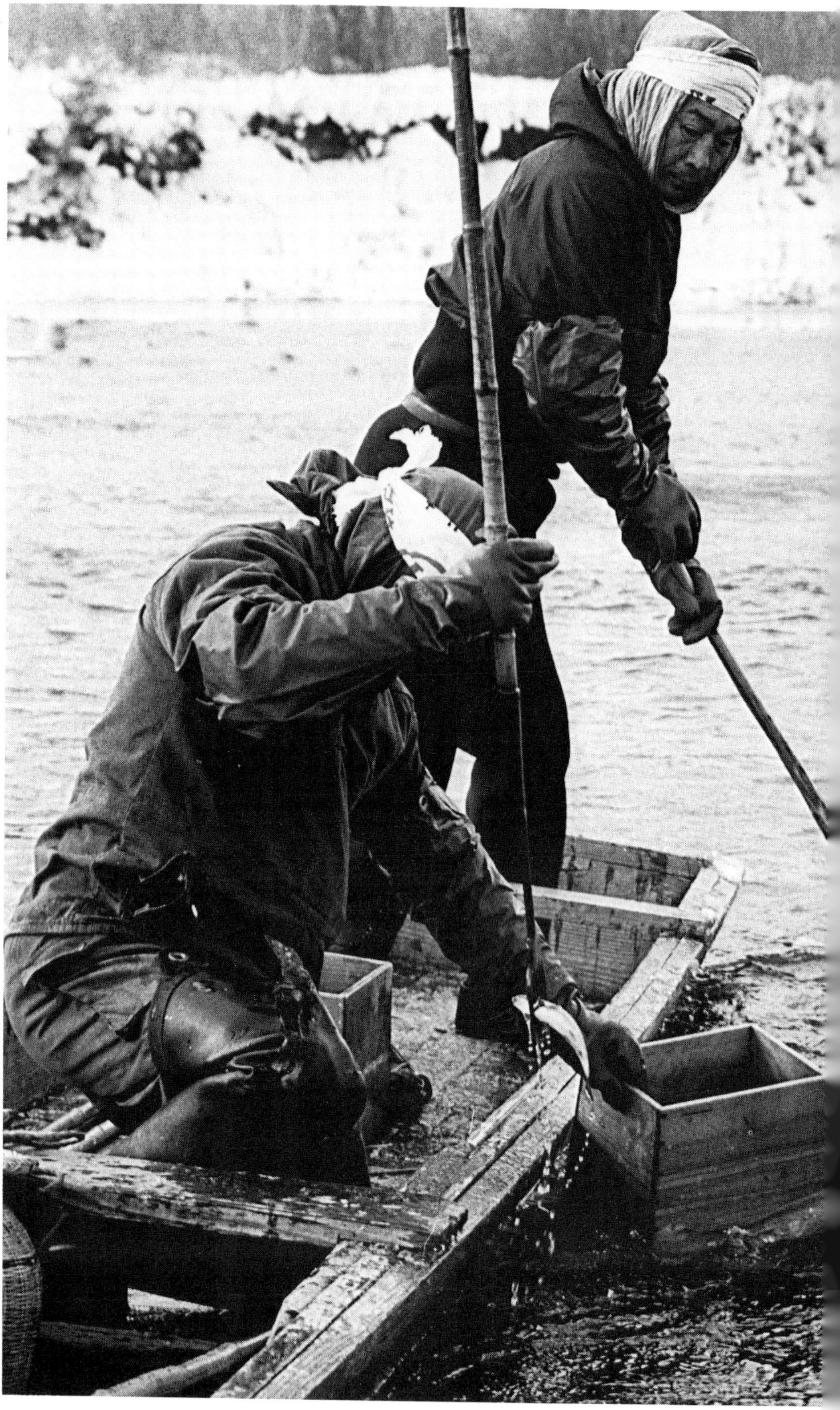

determine the height of ceilings in relation to the area of 'rooms' (Table 4). The unitary consistency of the *ken* system and the predetermined combination of measures to which it gives rise has led to its description as a comprehensive method of 'modular design' (Engel, 1964). Given the influence of the *tatami* mat on the dimensions of construction, it is easy to see how this description has arisen. The mat has two features which introduce both this modular theme and also the popular, but mistaken, idea that space in the Japanese house is in some way 'flexible'. First, mats are never cut in the manner of a carpet, but are made in whole or half *ken* units; within these units they are indivisible and hence conceivably 'modular'. Second they are not, in the European sense, a 'floor covering'. They provide seating, they require that shoes be removed, they induce their own etiquette and even, in the tea ceremony, they act as a means of precisely positioning utensils.

The idea that the relationship between *tatami* and the house structure is merely one of modular measurement, however, reduces a complex and ambiguous accommodation between the skills of the craftsman and the properties of traditional, everyday, objects to a level of mathematical

preceding pages

XXIV The bride is called *hana yome* or 'flower bride'.

XXV Paradoxically one of the few remaining large-scale communal events involves not the construction of a new house but the demolition of an old one.

XXVI The architectural tradition of Tōno is epitomised in the L-shaped thatched farmhouse called *magariya*.

XXVII The kitchen is a dark, airless room.

XXVIII Traditionally these rooms contained a sunken hearth called *robatta*.

XXIX In the old farmhouse both lavatory and bath were located outside in their own sheds.

XXX Many of the rigours of rural life still remain in valleys like the Isagozawa.

objectivity that the craftsman himself would have difficulty recognising. It is, perhaps, more faithful to the traditions of Japanese architecture to see in the relationship between house structure and the *tatami* unit a symbiotic evolution which has its origins not in theory but in practical convenience. Moreover, the traditional dimensions evolving out of the employment of *tatami* in the design of the rural Japanese house have come to acquire their own particular aestheticism which ensures the continuation of the system through the concept of the 'rightness' of these ways of doing things.

People describe the size and layout of rooms in terms of numbers of mats, giving a readily-appreciable feeling of dimensions, and manuals even provide instructions on the proper arrangement of mats for each season and for special events (Fig. 20). Festive events, for example, require that mats have an 'uneven' arrangement, in a manner redolent of the symbolism of odd numbers. For a funeral the *tatami* would be arranged in parallel, geometric ('even') patterns. This is difficult to achieve, however, since each individual mat is invariably made to fit a particular place in a specific room. Since these rooms seldom have true right angles, much of the skilled work of the *tatami*-maker involves the exact construction of unequal angles. They are not, therefore, identical and interchangeable. Each one is a unique element in a crafted structure and in this sense the *tatami* seems very far from a deterministic modular unit.

It is also clear that the *ken* measurement is a unit which has been inserted into an established decimal system originating in China (Table 5). The standard unit most widely used in this system is the *shaku*, which is now roughly equivalent to the English foot. As Engel (1964) notes, it can be traced to the Chinese T'ang period (618 to *c*. A.D. 907), but its absolute size has varied historically as the *shū-shaku*, *shinzen-shaku* and *kōrai-shaku* (Seike, 1977). The *ken* was originally recorded as seven *shaku* (2.12 metres), and seems only recently to have become the present six-*shaku*, or 1.8 metre version (Seike, 1977). The one-*ken tatami* is believed to have been developed as a portable mat which was used principally by the aristocracy. As the *Tatami geijutsu daizukan* (1978) notes, it is mentioned in the earliest Japanese writings, the *Kojiki* ('Record of ancient things') in 712, and was available only to the wealthy until the Ashikage period (1392–1573) when there is the first evidence of a wide-spread *tatami*-maker's craft.

As a unit of measurement involved in construction, the *ken* system appears to have been developed by families of temple carpenters like the Abe family (twelfth to fourteenth centuries), and the Heinouchis in the seventeenth century (Seike, 1977). In laying out the design of a house, carpenters employ formulae known as *kiwari* to determine the relationships between post width and post separation in units derived from the

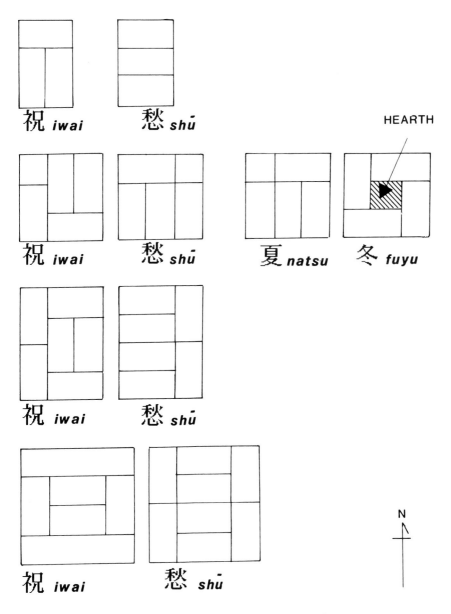

HEARTH

祝 iwai   愁 shū

祝 iwai   愁 shū   夏 natsu   冬 fuyu

祝 iwai   愁 shū

祝 iwai   愁 shū

N

祝 CELEBRATORY   夏 SUMMER

愁 MOURNING   冬 WINTER

20 Suggested arrangements of *tatami* mats

Table 6: The traditional Japanese measurement system

Japanese unit		English units	Metric units
1	rin 厘	0.012 inches	0.303 mm.
10 rin = 1 bu 分		0.12 inches	3.03 mm.
10 bu = 1 sun 寸		1.2 inches	3.03 cm.
10 sun = 1 shaku 尺		0.994 feet	30.3 cm.
6 shaku = 1 ken		1.99 yards	1.82 m.
10 shaku = 1 jo 丈		3.31 yards	3.03 m.
60 ken = 1 chō 町		119 yards	109 m.
36 chō = 1 ri 里		2.44 miles	3.93 km.

Source: Nelson (1962)

tatami. Once again, whether this is viewed as a classical 'modular' arrangement which possesses 'no visual-aesthetical considerations' (Engel, 1964), or whether it is viewed as only one element in a complete practical and aesthetic blend is a matter of opinion. In the Japanese house, however, texture and detail are inseparable from structure and from the unitary tatami elements out of which this structure evolves. Its character is created from the careful choice of materials, from the deliberate revelation of its skeletal structure and from the conscious decoration of features like windows and the recessed tokonoma. In such interdependent features, to deny the existence of an overall aestheticism is to ignore an essential aspect of the indivisibility of the Japanese treatment of concept and materials.

The building or rebuilding of a family house in Tōno is a joint venture between the family and the carpenter who is usually responsible for the design. As Seike (1977) notes, the Japanese name for 'carpenter', daiku (san), means literally 'great artificer'. He draws a parallel between this and 'architect' in English, which is derived from the Greek archos (chief) and tekton (carpenter). The Japanese daiku san traditionally held high status as a craftsman and as the tōryo ('master') mentioned in the tatemae ceremony. In a rural area like Tōno carpenters are still important figures. They design houses and often employ their own draughtsmen and teams of regular contract workers. These contractors will deal with the major areas of construction: carpentry, plastering, screen-making, window and door panelling and labouring. In addition it is not unusual for master carpenters to teach woodworking skills in the local apprentice schools.

The carpenter's tools still reflect some of the traditional significance of the trade, bound up as it originally was with temple construction. It is said that a carpenter needs only two devices to make all the measurements required in the jointing and framing of a house. The first of these is a simple L-shaped square, called *mawari-kane* or *sashi-kane*, and second is a pot of ink called the *sumitsubo*. The *mawari-kane* is graduated in *sun* units on its outer edge (ten *sun* equal one *shaku*) and its inner edge has a scale which enables the carpenter to measure the largest squared section which may be taken from a rounded log. The *mawari-kane* also has some symbolism built into its divisions, with characters inserted at the specified points.

1 *sun*, 9 *bu*	財	*zai*, money, wealth
2 *sun*, 1 *bu*	病	*byō*, illness
3 *sun*, 5 *bu*	離	*ri*, isolation
5 *sun*, 1 *bu*	義	*gi*, justice, morality
6 *sun*, 6 *bu*	官	*kan*, government
8 *sun*, 1 *bu*	却	*kyaku*, contrary
9 *sun*, 5 *bu*	害	*gai*, harm
11 *sun*, 1 *bu*	吉	*kichi*, good fortune

With the *mawari-kane* the carpenter decides the width of posts (usually four *sun*). The length is determined using a lath on to which the relevant divisions of *sun* and *shaku* have been marked with the *mawari-kane*. Where long lines of more than one *shaku* need to be marked on the wood the ink pot is used. A length of cord wound on a wheel is drawn through the inked lambswool that is contained in the pot. A small pin fixes the end of the cord which is tightened gently on to the wood, and a deft flick transfers the straight line on to its surface.

The skills of the carpenter are most apparent in the construction of joints between different sections of wood which reflect the structural needs of the house. The framework of houses in Japan must be light and flexible in order to allow for the cumulative effects of small earth tremors, but at the same time it must be strong enough to support a roof which will be heavy with tiles. Even in Tōno many recent buildings employ modern materials such as weatherboard, lath and tin. But it is still possible to find examples of new houses which are constructed of traditional materials in the old ways of the country. The house illustrated in Fig. 21, 22, and 23 and built by Horiuchi *san*, is an example.

SOUTH ELEVATION

zashiki

NORTH ELEVATION

genkan

21 Horiuchi house: elevations

As in the regional *magariya*, this modern house rests on relatively shallow foundations. They are formed of projecting concrete footings rather than rounded stones, but their role is still to provide a rigid base for the flexible structure which they are to carry. It is essential that the floor of a *tatami* room is raised from the ground in order to allow the circulation of air and to avoid the pervasive damp of the summer climate. Intervening supports for these floors, which traditionally consisted of stones, have

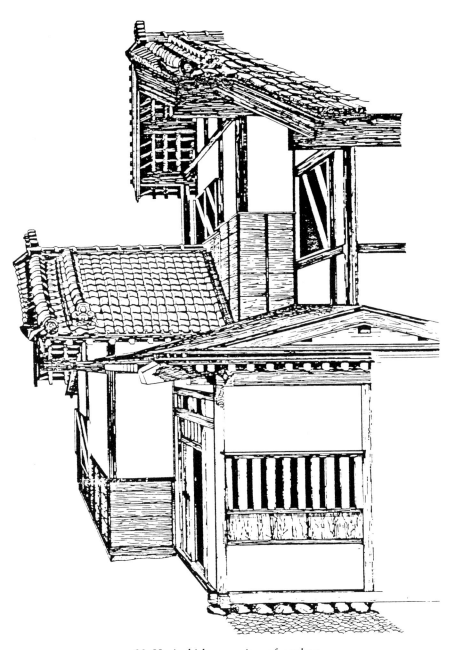

22 Horiuchi house: view of *genkan*

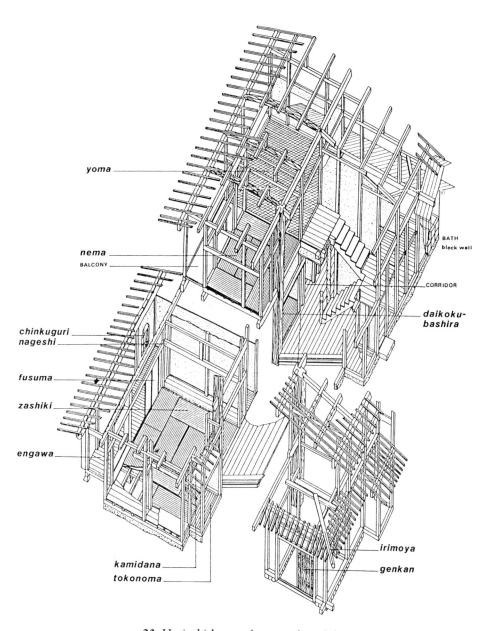

yoma

nema

BALCONY

BATH
block wall

CORRIDOR

daikoku-
bashira

chinkuguri
nageshi

fusuma

zashiki

engawa

kamidana
tokonoma

irimoya

genkan

23 Horiuchi house: framework and features

again been replaced by small concrete pillars. The foundation of the wooden structure of the house is the encircling *dodai*, literally 'earth plinth' which is now anchored to the footings by bolts. The joints of the *dodai* must be particularly well knit in order to retain coherence against the lateral forces of earth tremors.

It is usual for families to accord special symbolic significance to one of the upright posts in the house structure. Sometimes this post is the first post on the carpenter's plan, and often it is a part of the *genkan* entrance. The post then becomes the site of special charms acquired from the Shinto shrine and designed to secure the house against the ingress of evil influence. Some carpenters, however, have created of this symbolic post a central design feature for the house as a whole. This is the case in the house illustrated in Fig. 23. These posts, usually carved from a single trunk, are called *daikoku bashira*. The name refers to the Shinto god of 'Five Cereals' Daikoku who is the source of good fortune and wealth. Within the *ie* the name Daikoku is sometimes given to the head of the household who is immediately responsible for the *ie* fortunes. Thus within the house itself these connections find symbolic expression in the identification of a part of the structure with the aspirations of the *ie* as a whole.

The traditional method of constructing outer walls employs a framework of hand-split bamboo woven with rice-straw and plastered with local clay. It is a slow process due to the length of time required to allow the clay to dry thoroughly. The final layers, however, are applied with great speed. They are sealed with a rough blue mortar and finished, while still wet, with a skimming of pure white dolomite plaster (Fig. 24). Where internal walls are employed, in addition to the opaque *fusuma* screens, they are plastered with a pale green, sandy, or even sparkling metallic, mix which will probably remain untouched and unpainted for the life of the building. The texture of plasterwork, like the grain of wood employed on exposed posts, is therefore an important part of the overall 'finish' of the house.

In many modern houses, as in older ones, the height of ceilings varies from room to room. Small rooms have higher ceilings and large rooms have lower ones relative to the floor area. This arrangement is an essential part of the aestheticism of house design. Ceiling height is determined by the number of *tatami* mats which comprise the floor area of the room. A freize rail (*nageshi*) is fixed six *shaku* above the floor and the distance between this rail and the ceiling is given by multiplying the number of mats by 0.3 *shaku*. The ceiling is then suspended at the required height and boarded with laths which reflect the pattern of *tatami* mats employed in the room.

Apart from the aesthetics of proportion that are embodied in traditional

173

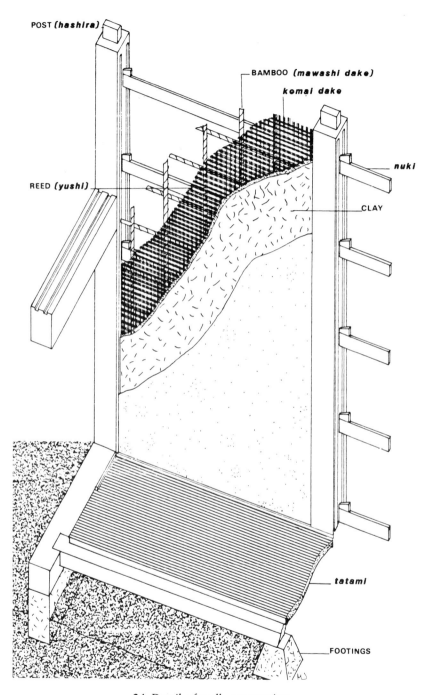

POST (*hashira*)

BAMBOO (*mawashi dake*)

komai dake

nuki

REED (*yushi*)

CLAY

tatami

FOOTINGS

24 Detail of wall construction

building methods, considerable importance is also afforded to features of the house which are decorative as well as symbolic or practical. This is clearly the case, for example, with the modern version of the *tokonoma* and its associated *chigaidana* shelving. The original purpose of the *tokonoma* was to serve as an elevated seat for the *tono sama* or local feudal lord. Over the years they have become a desirable element in the design of most houses. They are used as a display area in which the family's most prized possessions are exhibited and on which the yearly round may be recorded by the display of seasonal objects (Fig. 25).

Care and initiative mark the construction of the *tokonoma*. Though many of the fittings are standard, their arrangement differs from house to house and reflects the imaginative exercise of the carpenter's skills. The central post of the *tokonoma/chigaidana* is called the *tokobashira*. The tree from which the post is to be cut is often selected well in advance and may even be bound with plastic lenses to enhance the natural texture of the trunk whilst still growing. In exceptional cases, in very large houses for example, a whole bough or trunk may be employed and this is usually polished with ochre or rust to emphasise its textural qualities.

The *chigaidana* may appear on the surface to be nothing more than an area of shelving and cupboard space. In fact, however, it is created with great care and with great respect for the proportions which are involved. There is invariably an upper and lower cabinet space and two split-level shelves which suggest the recurring symbolism of anything that is uneven, unequal, and therefore life-giving. Small details, like the *fude gaeshi*, take on a form which reflects other arts. The purpose of the *fude gaeshi* is very practical; it prevents objects from falling off the upper shelf. Its form, however, is an attempt to represent, in the carving of the wood, the small return stroke which marks a paper as the calligrapher's brush leaves it. The *chigaidana* and *tokonoma* may be joined by windows let into the plaster between them (*chinkuguri*) and constructed to 'reveal' the split-bamboo framing underneath. They echo a distant and more primitive past when window spaces were simply punched through the wall of a rural cottage or barn. These *chinkuguri* are a frequent decoration in the houses of Tōno, particularly in porches or near entrances and they indicate the aesthetic preferences for asymmetry and natural materials which are so often to be found in the area. The reverence which is shown towards the use of wood in structures like the *tokonoma* is called by the Japanese *wabi-sabi*. It is an attitude which is difficult to interpret and which some people think is beyond the comprehension of foreigners, but *wabi-sabi* implies the slightly melancholy, tranquil quality which comes to wood as it ages and changes.

Almost invariably, the *tokonoma* is found in the *zashiki* and contributes

175

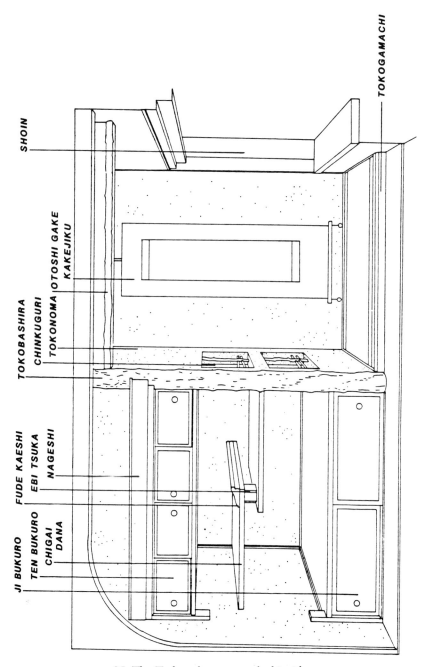

SHOIN

TOKOGAMACHI

TOKOBASHIRA
CHINKUGURI
TOKONOMA | OTOSHI GAKE
KAKEJIKU

FUDE KAESHI
EBI TSUKA
NAGESHI

JI BUKURO
TEN BUKURO
CHIGAI
DANA

25 The Tada *tokonoma* and *chigaidana*

largely to the relative ornateness of the guest room. In modern houses it is also common to find in the *zashiki* a study recess called the *shoin* (Fig. 26). It is a stylised rather than a practical feature, though it is possible to treat the broad shelf as a desk-top by kneeling or sitting cross-legged on the *tatami* mat laid in front of it. The *shoin* is illuminated by a window covered with paper *shōji*, but these screens tend to be more ornate than those found elsewhere in the house. Again, they provide an opportunity for wood carving in the *ramma* or clerestory window. *Shōji* screens are exceptionally delicate and finely balanced. They are designed to slide under the pressure of a single finger and in older houses their runners were constructed of greasy balsa wood. It is now more usual to find runners made of nylon. In the poorer areas of the Isagozawa, or in the work rooms of rural houses, broken paper screens are often replaced by sheets of newspaper. In more important rooms, however, the paper lights of the *shōji* are replaced by soaking and peeling off the old sheets, glueing new ones in place, and spraying them with water so that they will shrink and tighten as they dry in the sun.

The concern with decorative effect allied to symbolic significance can also be seen in the roof design and tilework of modern houses, especially in the larger *sengai-tsukuri* or *hiroya* designs. The distinctive roof style employed in these houses is shown in (Fig. 27). It is known as *irimoya* ('hipped gable'), and it consists of an exposed and projecting upward-curving corner beam (*sumigi*) surmounted by a variety of tiles. The ridge tiles are known as *kazekiri* ('wind cutters'). They end in an elaborate facing tile called the *onigawara* ('demon tile'), or in a still more elaborate *shachihoko* or 'tiger fish'. According to legend these are the fish which inhabit the sacred Ise Sea near the most important of the Shinto shrines. Both these tiles have a dual purpose. In practical terms they secure the ridge tiles, but in addition they also provide symbolic protection for the weak gable corners of the roof. The *shachihoko* are manufactured locally in Tōno and may stand up to 1.2 metres high. Anchored with wires, they face inwards along the roof ridge and are said to provide mystical protection against fire.

The *irimoya* represents the most severe test of skill for any carpenter. Its principal corner joint is the *sanjū hozo*. The most important feature of this pegged joint, and the reason it must be exact, is that its strength depends on a correct balance and proportion of all its parts. The wood must be made to co-operate' as one carpenter put it. Fig. 28 illustrates some examples of the classic shapes that can be achieved in *irimoya* construction. Finally, it is possible to extend the corner beamwork with a *hanagi* or 'nosebeam' which adds to the depth of the eaves but which also adds considerably to the cost of the roof as a whole.

177

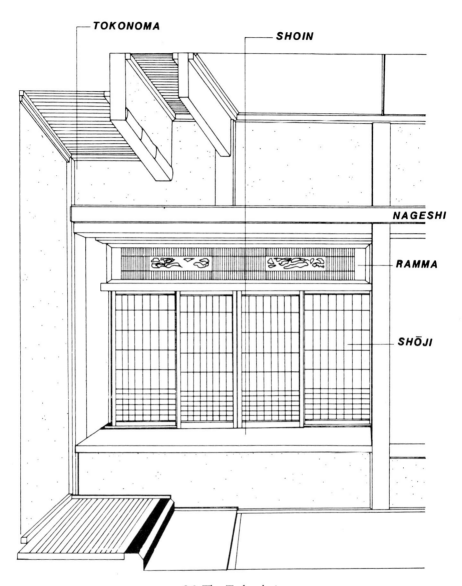

TOKONOMA

SHOIN

NAGESHI

RAMMA

SHŌJI

26 The Tada *shoin*

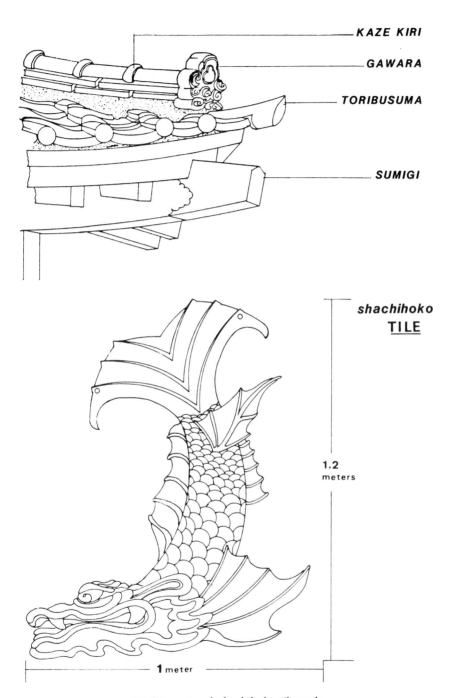

KAZE KIRI

GAWARA

TORIBUSUMA

SUMIGI

shachihoko
TILE

1.2
meters

1 meter

27 *Kimoya* and *shachihoko* tilework

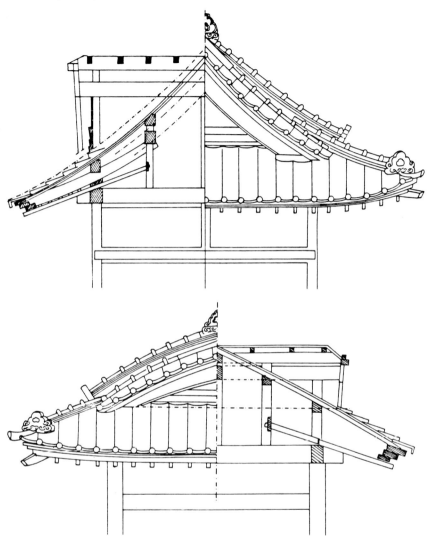

28 Examples of *irimoya* construction (source: Arasei, 1959)

A minor but significant aspect of roof construction is that each small fringing tile bears the imprint of the *tomoe-maru* (Fig. 29). These are hand-pressed and trimmed at Tōno's tile factory. They follow the same design as the *tomoe-maru* which appears on the *mune-fuda* board in the *tatemae* ceremony and again they symbolise the trailing note by which the

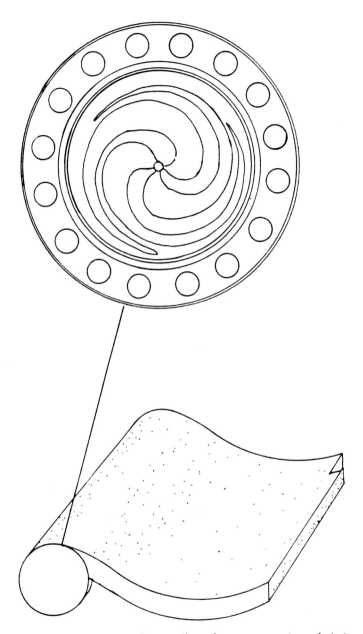

29 Detail of eaves tile and *tomoe-maru* (actual size)

kami is summoned and resemble rotating halves of the yin–yang polarity. The retention of small, barely visible symbols of this kind illustrates the lingering significance of the spiritual element in Japanese house construction.

Conclusions

Day-to-day life in the houses of Tōno presents something of a paradox to a stranger. Modern houses now have fitted kitchens like their European counterparts and bathrooms are usually tiled throughout, with sunken baths and a large boiler or heater which circulates water in the tub. The paraphernalia of technology is everywhere apparent in ubiquitous television sets and the like. The familiar clutter of living seems sometimes to clash with the scrupulous care with which the materials of the house are selected and crafted. The details of hue, grain, and smell in the woodwork of the house seem to sit uneasily with the proliferation of wiring and electronic gadgetry. But the paradox, though seeming apparent, is not real. The Japanese house does not stand apart from or outside of the Japanese *ie*. The *ie* itself sees no separation between the practical, the aesthetic and the spiritual. None of them has precedence because none of them exists apart from the others. The blend of tradition and modernity which the houses of Tōno display is merely a contemporary expression of the same influences which found form in the *magariya*.

We began this chapter by indicating the importance that is attached to the rebuilding of a house in a place like Tōno. The influences of economics and of status within the community are now expressed in the size and the elaboration of dwelling places. Superficially this is a trend which is shared as much by the country people of the Isagozawa as it is by their more 'sophisticated' cousins in Tōkyō. Underlying these outward manifestations of materialism, however, there are important senses in which the people of these rural areas continue to live with an indissoluble tradition. It is a tradition that stems from a deep-seated acceptance of the relationships between men and between a world that is at once natural and supernatural. For them the core of their existence is the *ie*, its historical ties to a particular place, and the demands which its continuation imposes on each individual member. In the act of house-building, therefore, the *ie* reaffirms its own integrity and redefines its relationship with the wider world of which it is a part.

6

Reflections

The details of life that we have recorded grow out of, or tie into, the ordinary processes of memory and recall. In places they depend heavily on *aides mémoire*, on notes, sketches, photographs and the like. But they hinge critically on a level of involvement that is too personal to be usefully revealed, except in the context of a very different kind of book. From this standpoint of proximity, then, we have tried to step a few paces back, to impose a shape which the experiences themselves never possessed and to provide a context which would be largely unfamiliar and irrelevant to the people whose lives we shared. This is not to say that the things written down are in any sense 'false', but simply to recognise that knowledge gained in closeness is sometimes best shared through distance. In these closing pages, though, we want to reflect on this closeness as it affected the 'method' of inquiry and the subject matter with which we have been concerned.

The basis of the venture was the familiar human faculty of curiosity. In this case it was curiosity concerning the *ie*, its meaning for the Japanese, and the expression which it finds in their lives. The intention was not to dissemble it but to share in it, and so it was not a curiosity disciplined into the constraints of academic method. On the contrary, it had its origins in rather shapeless notions, it unfolded in a serendipitous way, and it coalesced only in the acts of reflection and recording. For these reasons we stake no claim to the generality of the observations we have made, though it is comforting to know that they touch, here and there, the more scholarly and systematised accounts of Japanese life and character on which we have relied so heavily in our own search for perspective. At the same time we should admit that many of these connections were made retrospectively, standing the normal chronology of academic research on its head. The point of working this way was to avoid taking preconceptions into the field, to avoid the seduction of hypotheses, and as far as possible to allow untrammelled intuition to effect the most basic translations between Eastern and Western ways.

This meant that the time spent in Tōno was not a period of structured 'search' in the usual sense. Rather, it was a period during which we were 'led' into Japanese ways and into the realisations that we have tried to record. It cannot be denied that this approach lacks discipline but in a personal sense at least that is more than compensated by the pleasures and satisfactions that it provided. The process of learning was largely a matter of allowing circumstances to take their course: cycling up the Silver Sand Ravine, day after day, in the searing heat of summer; eating lunch by the same concrete sluice gate; and hoping that inquisitiveness would overcome reserve and open opportunities for casual talk. And, of course, it did.

Within the home itself, the cultivation of the same unforced learning allowed the intrusive aspects of our presence to be minimised and family life to continue in a more or less normal way. We were there, as it were, simply to learn about living, not to probe, or dissect, or analyse. Thus we had no need to *seek* explanation for the things that were going on around us: it was *offered* naturally and in the wake of events as it might be to a growing child. With the development of our language skills and the general growth of our awareness, so it was possible to be told more as time and circumstance required. As our relations with the Tadas matured and our appreciation of family life widened, we were able to assume a share of domestic responsibility. So, for example, on the day of *oniisan*'s wedding, it fell to Igirisu no Maiku san ('Mike from England') to welcome and amuse the male guests with beer and stories. Later, at the *hirōen* reception, we were both called upon to play our part in the provision of 'spontaneous' entertainment. More than a little nervously we sang the popular local song *Monomi yama kara* ('When I look out from Mount Monomi'). Then, in the quiet of the late evening, when all the guests were gone, it seemed natural to sit with the parents around the *kotatsu* and to share final thoughts on the events of a momentous day.

The measure of good-will, help and lasting affection that we found could not have been pre-planned and probably would not have survived a deliberate and systematic reduction of family and social relationships. Indeed, it is out of respect for the intimacy which we were allowed to share that we have chosen not to reveal it in fine detail in this book. In closing, however, we want to draw attention to the most deep-seated residual impressions which our life with the Tadas conveyed. First, we are convinced of the value and significance of the Japanese concept of *ma* in which the dimensions of space, time and social relativity can be so succinctly imagined. We are convinced that these realms are intuitively grasped, if not intellectually defined, from a relational perspective which *ma* embodies. A good example, perhaps, is the symbolic absorption of *Daikoku* into the ethos of the *ie*. The Tadas themselves, of course, do not ponder the interdependence of spiritual, social and physical principles. Yet the head of the house, *otōsan*, was accorded identity with its guardian diety Daikoku *sama*, and the house's central pillar, *daikoku bashira*, re-echoed the symbolic theme of support and strength. Almost unwittingly, so it seems, the essential relationships through which *ie* grows find an appropriate name, daikoku, and through it an objective focus for survival. Viewed in terms of *ma*, daikoku embodies and preserves all three definitive aspects of *ie* and acceptance of the symbol confirms the unity of the things it represents.

Following on from this, we were profoundly impressed by the apparent need to realise beliefs, values and sentiments in concrete terms, in action directed to objects. This, to us, seemed to be the real significance of the *butsudan* and the god-shelf. The meanings which are attached to these 'holy' or special things appear to reside in their real physical presence. Through their being, existence, imagination and memory is given a tangible material expression, over-riding the need for reflection and condensing in a physical thing the abstract structure of *ie*. That is to say, the *butsudan* and the god-shelf are not so much symbols of things as material residues of the things themselves.

Our final point continues in the same vein, for now we wish to dispense with the terms 'ceremony' and 'symbolism'. The point of using them in the first place was to facilitate the identification and description of events and relationships which were initially unfamiliar. Rejecting them now, we believe is one means of moving closer to the experience of people like the Tadas. The circumstances and behaviours that we have called 'ceremonial' are, for them, integral parts of a daily and annual routine, pleasant and meaningful to be sure, but no more so than the other pleasant and meaningful acts which fill the family days. In a similar way, the 'special' status of people, language and things that we have called 'symbolic' have about them a quality of immanence that shifts them into the realm of the ordinary. In conventional Western terms, we may want to think of them as 'reflecting' underlying ideas and meanings. For the Japanese family, though, they *are* the meanings, they must be tended and re-affirmed, but they are a tangible picture of *ie* there for all to see. Lao Tsu wrote:

What is firmly established cannot be uprooted.
What is firmly grasped cannot slip away.
It will be honoured from generation to generation. . . .
Therefore look at the body as body;
Look at the family as family;
Look at the village as village;
Look at the nation as nation;
Look at the universe as universe.

How do I know the universe is like this?
By looking!

(*Tao te Ching*, trans. by Gia-fu Feng
and Jane English. Wildwood, London, 1972.)

Bibliography

Abbeglen, J. C. and Stalk, G. Jr. 1985 *Kaisha: the Japanese Corporation*. New York: Basic Books.

Ariga, K. 1943 *Nihon Kazoku Seide to Kosaku Seido*. Tokyo: Kawade Shobo.

Befu, H. 1962 'Corporate emphasis and patterns of descent in the Japanese family.' *In* Smith, R. J. and Beardsley, R. K. (eds.), *Japanese Culture: its Development and Characteristics*. Viking Fund Publications in Anthropology No. 34. New York: Wenner Gren Foundation.

Befu, H. 1963 'Patrilineal descent and personal kindred in Japan.' *American Anthropologist*, 65:1328–41.

Befu, H. 1971 *Japan: an Anthropological Introduction*. Tokyo: Chandler Publishing Ltd.

Befu, H. 1986 'The social and cultural background of child development in Japan and the United States.' *In* Stevenson, H., Azuma, H. and Hakuta, K. (eds.), *Child Development and Education in Japan*. New York: W. H. Freeman and Company.

Blacker, C. 1975 *The Catalpa Bow: a Study of Shamanistic Practices in Japan*. London: George Allen and Unwin Ltd.

Bennett, J. W. 1967 'Japanese economic growth: background for social change.' *In* Dore, R. P. (ed.), *Aspects of Social Change in Modern Japan*. Princeton, New Jersey: Princeton University Press.

Brown, K. 1966 'Dōzoku and the ideology of descent in rural Japan.' *American Anthropologist* 68, 1129–51.

Brown, K. 1968 'The content of dōzoku relationships in Japan.' *Ethnology* 7, 113–38.

Cornell, J. B. 1955 'Matsunagi: a Japanese mountain community.' *In* Cornell, J. B. and Smith, R. J. (eds.), *Two Japanese Villages*. New York: Greenwood Press.

de Garis, F. 1934 *We Japanese*. Hakone: Miyanoshita.

DeVos, G. A. 1973 *Socialization for Achievement: Essays on the Cultural Psychology of the Japanese*. Berkeley: University of California Press.

Doi, T. 1973 *The Anatomy of Dependence*. Tokyo: Kodansha International.

Dore, R. P. 1958 *City Life in Japan*. Berkeley and Los Angeles: University of California Press.

Dore, R. P. 1959 *Land Reform in Japan*. London: Oxford University Press.

Engel, H. 1964 *The Japanese House: Unity in Diversity*. Tokyo and Vermont: C. E. Tuhle.

Fukutake, T. 1972 *Japanese Rural Society* (trans. R. P. Dore). Ithaca and London: Cornell University Press.

Fukutake, T. 1980 *Rural Society in Japan*. Tokyo: University of Tokyo Press.

Fung, Yu–lan 1937 *A History of Chinese Philosophy*, Vol. 1 (trans. Bodde, D.). Peiping: H. Vetch.

Hall, J. W. and Beardsley, R. K. 1959 *Twelve Doors to Japan*. New York: McGraw Hill.

Hamaguchi, H. 1980 *Nihon No Aidagaru* Genzai no esprit, No. 178. Tokyo.

Hendry, J. 1981 *Marriage in Changing Japan*. London: Croom Helm.

Hendry, J. 1986 *Becoming Japanese: the World of the Pre-School Child*. Manchester: Manchester University Press.

Hess, R. *et al.* 1986 'Family influences on school readiness and achievement in Japan and the United States: an overview of a longitudinal study.' *In* Stevenson, H., Azuma, H. and Hakuta, K. (eds.), *Child Development and Education in Japan*. New York: W. H. Freeman and Company.

Hori, I. 1968 *Folk Religion in Japan: Continuity and Change*, ed. Kitagawa, J. M. and Miller, A. L. London and Chicago: University of Chicago Press.

Hori, I. and Ooms, H. 1970 'Yanagita Kunio and "About our ancestors".' *In* Yanagita, K. (ed.), *About our Ancestors: the Japanese Family System* (trans. Mayer, F. H. and Yasugo, I.). Tokyo: Japanese Society for the Promotion of Science.

Isozaki, A. 1981 'Ma: Japanese time-space.' *Kenchiku Bunka*, 36, December, 105–164.

Jeremy, D. M. H. 1984 *Ceremony and Symbolism in Japanese Family Life*. Ph.D. thesis, Department of Geography, University of Manchester.

Kitano, S. 1951 'Dozuku soshiki to hoken isei.' *In Hoken Isei*, ed. Nihon Jimbun Kaggakai. Tokyo: Yuhikaku.

Kitano, S. 1962 'Dozuku and ie in Japan.' *In* Smith, R. J. and Beardsley, R. K. (eds.), *Japanese Culture: its Development and Characteristics*. Viking Fund Publications in Anthropology No. 34. New York: Wenner Gren Foundation.

Lanham, B. B. 1966 'The psychological orientation of the mother–child relationship.' *Monumenta Nipponica*, 21 (3–4): 322–33.

Lebra, T. S. 1976 *Japanese Patterns of Behaviour*. Honolulu, Hawaii: University of Hawaii Press.

Merleau-Ponty, M. 1964 *The Primacy of Perception* (trans. Edie, J. M.). Evanston, Ill.: Northwestern University Press.

Miyaki, K., Campos, J., Bradshaw, D. L. and Kagan, J. 1986 'Issues in socioemotional development.' *In Stevenson*, H., Azuma, H. and Hakura, K. (eds.), *Child Development and Education in Japan*. New York: W. H. Freeman and Company.

Morioka, K. 1986 'Privatisation of family life in Japan.' *In* Stevenson, H., Azuma, H. and Hakura, K. (eds.), *Child Development and Education in Japan*. New York: W. H. Freeman and Company.

Morse, R. E. 1975 *The Legends of Tono*. Tokyo: Japan Foundation and UNESCO Commission for Japan.

Nakane, C. 1967 *Kinship and Economic Organisation in Rural Japan*. Athlone: University of London Press.

Natanson, M. 1973 *Edmund Husserl: Philosopher of Infinite Tasks*. Evanston, Ill.: Northwestern University Press.

Noguchi, M. 1981 'Regional styles of farmhouse in northeast Japan.' *Process Architecture*, No. 25. January: 65–82.

Sansom, G. B. 1977 *Japan: a Short Cultural History*. Tokyo and Vermont: C. E. Tuttle.

Saunders, E. D. 1964 *Buddhism in Japan: with an Outline of its Origins in India*. Philadelphia: University of Pennsylvania Press.

Scott Morton, W. 1974 *Japan: its History and Culture*. Newton Abbot: David and Charles.

Seike, K. 1977 *The Art of Japanese Joinery* (trans. Yuboko, Y. and Davis, R. M.). Tokyo: Weatherill.

Seike, K. 1981 'Today's house divination and examples of traditional planning practice.' *Sumai no sekkeu*. Tokyo: Sankei.

Smith, R. J. 1955 'Kurusu.' *In* Cornell, J. B. and Smith, R. J. (eds.), *Two Japanese Villages*. New York: Greenwood Press.

Smith, R. J. 1974 *Ancestor Worship in Contemporary Japan*. Stanford: Stanford University Press.

Smith, R. J. and Beardsley, R. K. 1962 (eds.) *Japanese Culture: its Development and Characteristics*. Viking Fund Publications in Anthropology No. 34. New York: Wenner Gren Foundation.

Stevenson, H., Azuma, H. and Hakuta, K. 1986 *Child Development and Education in Japan*. New York: W. H. Freeman and Company.

Takeuchi, K. 1959 ' "Yoshi" (Adoption).' *In Social and Ethnographic Dictionary of Japan*, 4, Japanese Society of Ethnology. Tokyo: Seibundo Shinkosha.

Uemichi, I. 1984 'Japanese plant lore: a brief survey.' *The Folklore Society: Mistletoe Series*, 18:148–61.

Vogel, E. F. 1967 'Kinship structure, migration to the city, and modernization.' *In* Dore, R. P. (ed.), *Aspects of Social Change in Modern Japan*. Princeton, New Jersey: Princeton University Press.

Vogel E, and Vogel, S. H. 1961 'Family security, personal immaturity, and emotional health in a Japanese sample.' *Marriage and Family Living*, 23: 161–6.

Watsuji, T. 1961 *Fudo; Climate: a Philosophical Study* (trans. Bownas, G.). Tokyo: Japanese National Commission for UNESCO, and Iwanami Shoten.

White, M. I. and Levine, R. A. 1986 'What is an *Ii Ko* (Good child)?' *In* Stevenson, H., Azuma, H. and Hakuta, K. (eds.), *Child Development and Education in Japan*. New York: W. H. Freeman and Company.

Yanagita, K. 1910 *Tono Monogatari* ('Folk Tales of Tono'). Tokyo: Daiwa.

Yanagita, K. 1970 *About our Ancestors: the Japanese Family System* (trans. Mayer, F. H. and Yasuyo, I.). Tokyo: Japanese Society for the Promotion of Science.

188

Glossary and Index of Principal Japanese terms

Reading	Character	Meaning	Page
aidagara	間柄	mutuality	43
aijō	愛情	love	42
amae	甘え	indulgence	4
amaeru	甘える	indulge	43
baishakunin	媒酌人	go-between	44
Benten/Benzaiten	弁天	Sarasvati, god of fortune	70
Bishamonten	毘沙門天	Vaisravans, god of treasure	70
bon odori	盆　踊り	obon dance	63
bōnenkai	忘年会	year-end party	84
bonno	煩脳	desires	76
bunke	分家	branch family	34
bunkintakashimada	文金高島田	wedding wig	116
buraku	部落	village	83
butsudan	仏壇	family Buddhist altar	60
butsuma	仏間	room for the *butsudan* altar	60
dai-an	大案	'great safety'	109
daikoku bashira	大黒柱	symbolic central post of the house	39
Daikoku sama	大黒　様	God of Five Cereals, Mahakala	39
dekasegi	出稼ぎ	work away from home	19
dodai	土台	foundation beam	148
dōgu	道具	implement/tool	146
dōkyūsei	同級生	classmate	41
dōzoku	同族	same family	34
Ebisu sama	恵比須様	god of wealth	68
engawa	縁側	verandah	149
engumi	縁組	marriage	109
enmusubi	縁結び	marriage	109
fude gaeshi	筆返	return stroke of the brush (calligraphy)	175
fuku	服	clothing	135
fuku	副	wealth	135
Fukurokuju	福禄寿	god of wealth and longevity	70
gaijin	外人	foreigner	2
ganchomairi	元朝参	temple visit on New Year's morning	76
go en	五円	five yen	63

189

go-en	御縁	good fortune	63
hachijūhachiya	八十八	88	88
hana	鼻	nose	40
hanamuke	餞	parting gifts	115
hatsubon	初盆	first *obon*	64
hatsuyume	初夢	first dream of the New Year	78
hi	火	fire	129
hinamatsuri	雛祭	dolls' festival	87
hirōen	拾う縁	wedding feast	118
hito-gami	人神	tutelary shrine gods	68
hitsuji	未	sheep	129
honke	本家	head family	34
Hotei	布袋	pot-belly god	70
i no shishi	亥	boar	72
ie	家	house, household	13
ihai	位牌	mortuary tablet	61
ii-ire	言入れ	betrothal	110
in, an, on	陰	yin, female, negative	127
inu	戌	dog	72
ittai-ka	一体化	oneness, union	4
iwai	祝い	celebration	50
jichinsai	地金真祭	ground-breaking	125
jikkan	十干	10 calendar signs	129
jōbutsu	成仏	attained Buddhahood	64
jōtōshiki	上棟式	ridge-pole raising	125
jūni-shi	十二支	twelve horary signs	129
Jurōjin	寿老人	God of Longevity	70
ka	金	metal	129
kadomatsu	門松	New Year's decorative pines	70
kage	蔭/陰	shade	127
kagura	神楽	Shinto dance	81
kaiyōshi	買い養子	buyer, adoptive son	33
kakā	婦	wife	40
kakizome	書き初	first writing of the New Year	77
kami	神	gods	11
kamidana	神棚	Shinto shelf or shrine	67
kanai	家内/妻	family/my wife	38
kangeiko	寒稽古	midwinter training	86
kāsan nogyo	母さん	farming by the mother	19
kasō	家相	house divination	125
kasugai	鎹	clamp, pin	146
kazoku	家族	family	31
kekkon	結婚	marriage	109
ki	木	wood	129
kichiji	吉事	auspicious event	109
kimono	着物	kimono	66
kodama	木霊	spirit of a tree	146
kōgu	工具	implement/tool	146
kōkei-sha	後継者	inheritor	3

kome	米	rice	88
komoru	籠	to seclude	129
konbu	昆布	dried kelp	112
konbu	子生婦	fertile woman	112
koshōgatsu	小正月	lunar new year	68
koshu	戸主	household head	39
kyūreki	舊暦	old lunar calendar	68
ma	間	room; social relations generally	184
madori	間取り	house floor-plan	149
magariya	曲がりや	L-shaped farmhouse	19
mi	巳	snake	129
miai	見合い	arranged marriage	33
miokuri	見送り	*obon* departure	67
mizu	水	water	82
mokuroku	茂久緑	luxurient greenery	111
mokuroku	目録	record/index	111
mon	紋	family crest	109
mukaebi	迎火	obon fire	64
muko yōshi	婿　養子	adoptive son-in-law	32
mune fuda	棟札	ridge-pole plaque	141
muneage	棟上	ridge-pole raising	125
mushin	無心	detachment	64
nakōdo	仲人	go-between	44
ne	子	rat	129
norito	祝詞	Shinto prayer	74
noshi	熨	sea-ear	111
obāsan	お祖母さん	grandmother	38
obon	お盆	*Obon* festival	60
ogamiyasan	拝み屋さん	Buddhist or Shinto diviner, skilled in geomancy	126
okage	お蔭	by the grace of, thanks to	59 59
okāsan	お母さん	mother	38
oku	奥	inner part	40
okusan	奥さん	wife (polite)	40
omote-ura	表裏	both sides	35
on	恩	obligation	42
onigawara	鬼瓦	ridge-end tile	177
oniisan	お兄さん	eldest brother	30
onna	女	woman	40
onna-no-taiyaku	女大厄	bad luck year for women	86
osechiryōri	お節料理	New Year's food	76
ren' ai	恋愛	love	33
rikuzen	六月喜	*obon* tray	61
risshun	立春	first day of spring	86
roku	六	six	66
sadō	茶道	'way' of tea	51
saiken	再建	reconstruction	33
saimon	祭文	sacred recitation	79

sakaki	榊	sakaki tree	133
sake	酒	Japanese rice wine	66
saketate	酒立	betrothal meeting	108
saru	申	monkey	129
segaki	施餓鬼	'feeding the hungry ghosts'	66
seijinshiki	成人式	coming of age ceremony	78
sempai/kōhai	先輩/後輩	senior/junior	41
sengachi	先勝	early victory	133
setai	世帯	household	31
setai nushi	世帯主	household head	39
shachihoko	鯱	tiger-fish ridge tile	177
shaden	社殿	Shinto shrine main hall	68
shimenawa	注連縄	Shinto rope festoon	87
shimeru	締める	tie up/seal	109
shinpu	新婦	bride	120
shinrō	新郎	groom	120
shinseki	親戚	groom's family	120
shintō	神道	Shinto	9
shōbu	菖蒲	Japanese iris	88
shōbu	尚武	militarism	88
shōgatsu	正月	New Year	68
shujin	主人	household head	38
Sōdōshu	曹洞宗	Sodo sect	60
sunao	素直	gentle/obedient	6
surume	鯣	dried cuttlefish	112
surume	寿留女	female longevity	112
taisho	大将	leader	39
takarabune	宝船	treasure ship	78
tamashii	魂	soul	60
tan	檀	hardwood	60
tatami	畳	woven-rush matting	48
tatemae	建前	ridge-pole raising	125
tatsu	辰	dragon	129
tauc	田植え	rice planting	83
tengu	天狗	genie, long-nosed goblin	90
tokonoma	床の間	alcove	113
tomoshiraga	友白髪	cord or hair	112
tora	寅	tiger	129
tori	酉	cock	129
toshiiwai	年祝い	age-related	85
toshikoshi	年越し	New Year's Eve	75
tsuchi	土	earth	129
tsuki	月	month	66
tsuno-kakushi	角隠し	bride's hood	116
tsuru-kame	鶴亀	crane and tortoise	109
u	卯	hare	129
uchi	内	inside	35
uchi-soto	内外	inside-outside	35
ujigami	氏神	tutelary deity	11
uma	午	horse	129

Index

age, celebrations 78, 85–6, 88
agriculture 17, 47, 63, 154; crop types
  19–20; decline of 20; employment in
  19; religious festivals 67, 70, 83, 91,
  92
ancestors in household 36, 58, 65, 68;
  influence of 11–13; veneration of xi,
  11–13, 63–7; see also Buddhism;
  butsudan; Obon
architecture in Tōno xii, xiv; see also
  housebuilding; magariya

bathing 4, 48–9, 56, 89, 153
behaviour, qualities of xi; see also
  children
birthdays 58; see also age
Buddhism 9–13, 49, 58, 62, 133; see
  also ancestors; butsudan; Obon;
  religion
butsudan 33, 37, 43, 48, 49, 51, 58–67,
  155; 185; contents of 61–3; cost of
  60–1; replacement of 60–1; see also
  ancestors; Buddhism; Obon

carpenter 168, 173, 177; tools of 169;
  see also housebuilding
children, behaviour of 4–7, 106;
  celebrations for 86–8; importance of
  43; relations between 40–1; see also
  ie; mother; socialisation; women
clothing, celebratory 67, 86, 109, 116–
  17; Western influence on 18, 66, 76

dekasegi 19
dolls, daruma 72–3; festival of 87;
  metobina 138, 147; straw (wara
  ningyo) 87; see also tatemae

earthquakes 18

employment, seasonal 17; see also
  dekasegi

family, authority within 8, 107; concept
  of 14; influence on society 8;
  organisation of xi; relations within
  42–3, 45–7; see also household; ie
father, and children 5, 106; see also
  family; household; ie
food, family preferences 48; for New
  Year 74–6; local tastes in 20;
  mealtimes 48–50; preparation of 49;
  seating arrangements for 49, 75
fox, reputation of 70

geomancy xiv, 12, 125–33; see also
  housebuilding; jichinsai
gifts 49; and marriage 108–13;
  symbolism of 110–13; see also
  marriage
grandparents, and children 5; see also
  family; household; ie

horses, 19, 148, 149, 153
household xi; coalitions within 5, 106;
  decline in numbers 19; deities 30;
  responsibilities in 46–8; see also
  family; ie
housebuilding xiv, 30, 125–82;
  carpenters 168, 173, 177; ceiling
  heights 173–4; floors and
  foundations 170, 173; geomancy
  125–33; ground-breaking (jichinsai)
  133–7; magariya influence 153–4;
  measurement and planning 157, 165,
  166; ridge-pole raising (tatemae)
  137–47; roof styles 177, 180; Shinto
  offerings 137; Shoin 177, 178; tatami
  units 154, 165–8; tokonoma and

194

DATE DUE